materializing new media

INTERFACES: Studies in Visual Culture
Editors Mark J. Williams and Adrian W. B. Randolph, Dartmouth College

This series, sponsored by Dartmouth College Press, develops and promotes the study of visual culture from a variety of critical and methodological perspectives. Its impetus derives from the increasing importance of visual signs in everyday life, and from the rapid expansion of what are termed "new media." The broad cultural and social dynamics attendant to these developments present new challenges and opportunities across and within the disciplines. These have resulted in a trans-disciplinary fascination with all things visual, from "high" to "low," and from esoteric to popular. This series brings together approaches to visual culture—broadly conceived—that assess these dynamics critically and that break new ground in understanding their effects and implications.

Recent books in this series

Anna Munster, *Materializing New Media: Embodiment in Information Aesthetics*

Luc Pauwels, ed., *Visual Cultures of Science: Rethinking Representational Practices in Knowledge Building and Science Communication*

Lisa Saltzman and Eric Rosenberg, eds., *Trauma and Visuality in Modernity*

For the complete list of books in this series, please visit www.upne.com and www.upne.com/series/IVSS.html

materializing new media
embodiment in information aesthetics

ANNA MUNSTER

DARTMOUTH COLLEGE PRESS
HANOVER, NEW HAMPSHIRE

PUBLISHED BY UNIVERSITY PRESS OF NEW ENGLAND
HANOVER AND LONDON

Dartmouth College Press
Published by University Press of New England,
One Court Street, Lebanon, NH 03766
www.upne.com
© 2006 by Anna Munster
Printed in the United States of America
5 4 3 2

Library of Congress Cataloging-in-Publication Data
Munster, Anna.
Materializing new media : embodiment in information aesthetics / Anna Munster.—1st ed.
    p.   cm.—(Interfaces, studies in visual culture)
Includes bibliographical references and index.
ISBN–13: 978–1–58465–557–2 (cloth : alk. paper)
ISBN–10: 1–58465–557–7 (cloth : alk. paper)
ISBN–13: 978–1–58465–558–9 (pbk. : alk paper)
ISBN–10: 1–58465–558–5 (pbk. : alk. paper)
1. Computers and civilization.   I. Title.   II. Series.
QA76.9.C66M86 2006
303.48'33—dc22   2005031080

For Michele

CONTENTS

List of Illustrations   ix
Acknowledgments   xi

Introduction: The Body in the Machine   1

1 Sampling and Folding: The Digital and the Baroque   25

2 Natural History and Digital History   55

3 Virtuality: Actualizing Bodies, Abstracting Selves   86

4 Interfaciality: From the Friendly Face of Computing to the
Alien Terrain of Informatic Bodies   117

5 Digitality: An Ethico-Aesthetic Paradigm for Information   150

Postscript: Emerging Tendencies in Embodied Information Aesthetics   178

Notes   187
Bibliography   211
Index   225

ILLUSTRATIONS

FIGURE 1
Frontispiece to Ferrante Imperato, *Historia Naturalae* (Venice, 1672).   12

FIGURE 2
Stelarc, *Ear on Arm* (2003).   20

FIGURE 3
Juan de Valdés Leal, *The Assumption of the Virgin* (1659), oil on canvas.   46

FIGURE 4
An example of a "patch" written using the MAX/MSP
programming environment.   49

FIGURE 5
Pockets Full of Memories visual map (2005) by George Legrady.   59

FIGURE 6
Attributes screen of *Pockets Full of Memories* Questionnaire
(2001) by George Legrady.   59

FIGURE 7
Frontispiece to Olaus Worm, *Museum Wormianum Seu Historia
Rerum Rarariorum* (1655).   74

FIGURE 8
Table xlv in James Petiver, *Opera Historiam Naturalem Spectantia
or Gazophylacium*, vol. 1 (1764).   75

FIGURE 9
Screenshot of the "petri" interface from *1:1* by Lisa Jevbratt
and c5 (1999).   83

FIGURE 10
Screenshot of the "every" interface from *1:1* by Lisa Jevbratt and c5
(2001 and ongoing).   84

FIGURE 11
Installation shot of *The Virtual Body* by Catherine Richards (1993).   87

FIGURE 12
Screenshots of *BorderXing Guide* by Heath Bunting (2001).   105

FIGURE 13
A participant interacts with Anatomically Lifelike Interactive
Biological Interface (ALIBI) from "The Madhouses: 2001–2004.
Pandaemonium," by Alan Dunning and Paul Woodrow.   107

FIGURE 14
Virtual Environment Workstation Project at NASA-Ames
Research Center.   110

FIGURE 15
David Rokeby in *Very Nervous System* (1986–90). The interface
is installed in a street in Potsdam.   119

FIGURE 16
Screenshot of *Memory Flesh 2.0: A Micro Media Record* (2004)
by Diane Ludin.   121

FIGURE 17
Stelarc, *Skin for Prosthetic Head* (2002).   131

FIGURE 18
Installation shot of *RAPT II* (2005) by Justine Cooper.   144

FIGURE 19
"Hogarth, My Mum 1700–2000" from the website *Uncomfortable Proximity* by Graham Harwood (2000).   158

FIGURE 20
Screenshot from *In My Gash* CD-ROM (1999) by Linda Dement.   161

FIGURE 21
Installation shot of *location 'n'* (2002) by raqs media collective.   165

FIGURE 22
Screenshot of *sentiment-express* (2001) by Shilpa Gupta.   171

ACKNOWLEDGMENTS

The writing of this book was undertaken while I held a "Discovery Project" grant from the Australian Research Council from 2003 to 2005. A section of chapter 4 was originally published in German as "Returns of the Diminishing Body" in *Future Bodies. Visualisierung von Körper in Science und Fiction*, edited by MarieLuise Angerer, Kathrin Peters and Zoe Sofoulis (Vienna: Springer Verlag, 2002), and a section of chapter 5 was originally published in *Life in the Wires: The CTheory Reader*, edited by Arthur and Marie-Louise Kroker (Victoria, Canada: New World Perspectives/CTheory Books, 2004).

A great many friends and colleagues have contributed to and supported the work that has gone into this book. I would especially like to thank Moira Gatens and Paul Patton for many years of intellectual generosity, comment and humor; Jill Bennett and David McNeill in the Center for Contemporary Art and Politics at the College of Fine Arts, University of New South Wales, for their ongoing collegiality and for understanding that new media aesthetics should be considered in a global and political context; Andrew Murphie for the leading example that his work is to new media aesthetics, and for the intellectual support he has given me; and Geert Lovink for the invigorating mix of politics, pragmatism and theory that he has brought to the field and to our online and offline engagements.

I have been inspired and encouraged by my collaborative work with a number of people and networks over the past few years. Intellectual and artistic networks provide the underacknowledged basis of a great deal of new media theory and artwork. For me, these include the online network *fibreculture* and particularly my discussions with Danny Butt, Chris Chesher and Ned Rossiter, and the editorial team of the *fibreculture journal*, especially Lisa Gye, Esther Milne and Gillian Fuller, who set such high and meticulous standards in their own work. In the project of editing a special edition of the online journal *Culture Machine* during 2004, Melinda Cooper was a marvellous colleague as well.

A number of artists contributed directly and indirectly to making this book an exercise in taking seriously the conceptual work done by artists in producing information culture. I would like to thank Justine Cooper, Linda Dement, Diane Ludin and Trebor Scholz for their time and hospitality over the last few years. Finally, I would not have been able to write this book without the support of Michele Barker and the inspiration that her artistic work gives me. Her own sense of the aesthetic possibilities for new media is finely honed and her faith and encouragement have been the basis on which this project has been sustained. There are others—students, colleagues, friends and supporters—who are numerous and to whom I can only say thank you here.

I would also like to thank those who have assisted with the preparation of this manuscript. Uros Cvoro has been an enthusiastic and efficient research assistant. The readers of this manuscript provided helpful commentary, and I would especially like to thank Ursula Frohne for her encouragement. The editorial team at University Press of New England has been extremely professional; in particular I would like to thank my editor, John Landrigan, for being so quick and efficient and for always being at the other end of an email.

materializing new media

The computer as a medium is strongly biased. And so my impulse while using the computer was to work solidly against these biases. Because the computer is purely logical, the language of interaction should strive to be intuitive. Because the computer removes you from your body, the body should be strongly engaged. Because the computer's activity takes place on the tiny playing fields of integrated circuits, the encounter with the computer should take place in human-scaled physical space. Because the computer is objective and disinterested, the experience should be intimate.   — DAVID ROKEBY[1]

Our world is governed not only by nonlinear dynamics, which makes detailed prediction and control impossible, but also by nonlinear combinatorics, which implies that the number of possible mixtures of meshwork and hierarchy, of command and market, of centralisation and decentralisation, are immense and that we simply cannot predict what the emergent properties of these combinations will be.   — MANUEL DE LANDA[2]

introduction
the body in the machine

In 1995 I attended the 22nd annual American Computer Machinery Conference on Computer Graphics and Interactive Technologies, known in the digital graphics world by the acronym SIGGRAPH. Having endured four days of technical papers on issues such as "spline modeling," "polygonization of non-manifold implicit surfaces" and "cellular automata," all in the heat of Los Angeles in early August, I was lured as an artist and a thinker toward a particular panel session near the end of the conference. Titled "Grids, Guys and Gals: Are You Oppressed by the Cartesian Coordinate System?" the panel promised to tackle a controversial statement made by artist Joan Staveley at SIGGRAPH '93.[3] In keeping with a then-emerging critique of information culture, Staveley had declared that the aesthetic effects of the dominance of the Cartesian coordinate system in computing were oppressive. Here was a bold statement about a relatively new technology that linked its technical and epistemological premises to four hundred years of Western culture in which the mind had been privileged over the body.

The premise for the 1995 session rested upon the concern raised by increasing numbers of cultural theorists and new media artists during the 1990s that digital spaces were subtended by a strong desire for control over the messiness of bodies and the unruliness of the physical world. Yet the session's critical tenor was offset by a series of glib, crowd-pleasing arguments that glided rather sweepingly across the last few centuries of Western visual history. Cartesian optics was characterized as facilitating and seamlessly merging with the nineteenth-century production of the disciplined body ruled by the panopticon and analyzed in the work of Michel Foucault.[4] However, the session that materialized on an oppressively humid Friday morning at the Los Angeles Convention Center was a testament to the disorder and contingencies of embodied life. A group of staunch neo-Cartesians filled the front rows of the audience and—bringing the seventeenth century into an odd alliance with late-twentieth-century computer geekdom—sported logos emblazoned across their mass-printed t-shirts declaring "I ♥ Descartes." In a style that surely would have obscured René Descartes's self-professed love of serenity and clarity, these lovers and champions of information culture and its mechanistic antecedents heckled the panel. For them, the session represented an assault on the epistemological foundations of present-day computing technologies. Unfortunately, the invited panelist best suited to analyzing the trajectory of rationalist desire in computing culture and subcultures, Alluquere Rosanne Stone, failed to materialize during the session at all. The irony of Stone's absence was not lost on many in the audience; in a session devoted to issues of embodiment in technology, the literal absence of this key speaker confirmed the haunting of debates on contemporary machines by the old dualities of the mind/body split.

I was struck by the extent to which a philosopher like Descartes, who was embedded in sciences and practices far removed from contemporary computer visualization and new media technologies, nevertheless galvanized and polarized the responses of two modern subcultures. What I witnessed were the critical humanities academician and the culturally informed artist aligned with the subjugated body on the one hand, and the computer boffin championing the powers of mind on the other. Yet from both sides of the Cartesian battle line an unquestioning faith held sway in the foundational place of classical rationalism and visual perspectivalism as the genesis of digital culture. If one "loved" the computer—its power, its speed, its ability to deliver high-resolution graphics, its promise of immersion, interactivity, convergence or whatever else was on offer on the information superhighway—then one had to love Descartes. After all, he had produced the entire coordinate system that formed the mathematical basis for the development of three-dimensional computer graphics.

But familiarity with the legacy of Cartesian ontology and post-Cartesian rationalism within the knowledge systems that have informed the rise of computation reveals that there is little place for the body within computational spaces. Likewise, pragmatic and everyday engagements with computing interfaces have seemed to confirm that interacting with digital technologies is kinaesthetically and proprioceptively limited. If these experiences and understandings are highlighted—as a number of practioners and new media theorists began to do during the 1990s—then it is not difficult to reach the conclusion that the Cartesian schema pervading information culture are oppressive. Terminal identity, so aptly described by Scott Bukatman, with its isolated, individualized and dematerialized consciousness, sometimes disengaged from and other times merging with the machine, does seem to echo the subjective terrain of the ideal rational cogito.[5] As the spectacle of the SIGGRAPH session progressed amid the contraction of centuries of visual culture, practice and technologies, on the one hand, and the impassioned raucousness of neo-Cartesian nerds arrogantly self-assured of their corporeal existence, on the other, the germinal concepts of this book began to grow from the ensuing chaos.

I am here concerned, then, with what I believe were the inextricably entwined problems of that panel: the question of the genealogy of digital culture and the insolvent place of the body in relation to new media technologies and the culture they help to shape. We need to radically question the birth of digital culture as one that has been shaped largely via a binary logic. This outdated cartography has previously forced us to either celebrate or denigrate the Cartesian mind, the disembodied gaze and the transcendence of dematerialized information as salient features of digital aesthetics. What if we were to produce instead a different genealogy for digital engagements with the machine, one that gave us the room to take body, sensation, movement and conditions such as place and duration into account?

While the debate for and against disembodiment in new media aesthetics and culture raged throughout the 1980s and 1990s, a number of artists were already experimenting with the different kinds of embodied experience afforded by digital speeds and spaces. Works such as David Rokeby's *Very Nervous System* (1986–90) and Ulrike Gabriel's *Breath* asked their participants to conjure digital environments by turning their bodies into performing instruments or by harnessing bodily functions that would draw attention to the sensory aspects of the interaction. Yet these new media artworks do not represent a simple reassertion of the body's brute presence in the face of a technology intent on dematerializing it. In both Rokeby and Gabriel's pieces the participant's body does not operate as the point of origin through which digital images, sound and environment are summoned. Instead, embodiment is produced through the relations between the participants' bodily capacities and the operations and limitations of the particular information technologies. *Very Nervous System*, for a variety of conceptual, aesthetic and design reasons, was a piece well ahead of its time. It preempted the development of responsive media environments, in which the participant's body and the computer system together learn, adapt and change in relationships facilitated by information feedback. I will give detailed attention to Rokeby's installation when I examine issues concerned with embodiment and computational interfaces in chapter 4.

In Gabriel's *Breath*, the participant wears a sensor harness around his or her waist that monitors and collects data on the rate of breathing. The values from this data are then entered into the installation's image database and in turn change the way in which the blue polygonal edges of the projected, moving image unfold across the screen. The blue polygons and their faceted edges stretch, distort and fold into and out of each other as if taking on a breathing rhythm of their own. Importantly, neither image nor sequence simply repeat or directly react to the breath of the participant. Instead, they are influenced slowly by the new information. When a participant comes to the installation, it is usually already affected and has changed according to data from a previous user, the traces of someone else's interactions are already animating the moving footage. Gabriel notes that there is a sense of slow confluence between the installation and the user: "It's a kind of interaction which is not direct, like one-to-one interaction, [where] you push a button and immediately something happens . . . you influence it slowly by putting energy in it through your breathing . . . this again you then perceive by watching it, which influences your breathing so you are somehow connected to outside by this circuit."[6]

Any counterhistory that emerges from foregrounding these kinds of artistic practices and aesthetic experiences cannot be based upon the promise of a new founding origin for digital culture. Rather than construct yet another prehistory for the digital, I will be arguing for both a broadening and a complication of the generative base of information aesthetics by conceiving of the digital as part of a "baroque" event. Information aesthetics, popular uses of new media technologies and emerging ideas about post-human identity constitute a particular twist of this baroque event. Here we need to think about events as time-based, rather than locked into only a particular period of history. Here an analysis of time-based electronic art will demonstrate how it provides audio and visual access to flows of discrete instances at a perceptual level and therefore expands our conceptual understanding and aesthetic experience of different kinds of time.[7] A baroque event in a similar way summons specific aspects of the culture and thought of the European early modern period and allows them to produce flow-on effects in the contemporary moment, expanding our limited preconceptions about the aesthetics of digital culture.

The digital, conceived as part of a baroque flow, now unfolds genealogically out of the baroque articulation of the *differential* relations between embodiment and technics. This differential logic places body and machine, sensation and concept, nature and artifice in ongoing relations of discordance and concordance with each other. The baroque, here defined as an event responsible for generating this differential logic, produces a pulsing field of aesthetic forces. In this "force-field" the binary pairs that have populated our understanding of digital culture and new media technologies—physicality and virtuality, analog and discrete states, real and hyperreal—can be seen to impinge upon each other rather than be mutually exclusive. The effect of these areas' convergence and divergence is to produce ever-new and consistently mutating outcomes.

Baroque modes and devices of visual display, such as curiosity cabinets, the extravagant scenes of *trompe l'oeil*, and the appearance of scientific specimen alongside mythical beast in early modern science illustration, have been connected with the navigational meandering and frequent juxtapositions that comprise online experience and contemporary multimedia museal display.[8] I was first drawn to these relations between styles of baroque and digital visual display by Barbara Maria Stafford's argument for a visual trajectory reaching from early modern medicine and natural history to the postmodern image space of assemblage and bricolage.[9] Stafford has suggested, through analysis and comparative visual illustrations, that the baroque *Wunderkammer* present us with a kind of underbelly of Western aesthetics that subtends the dominance of classical optical space and its emphasis on precision, order and clarity of form. But here a schism opens up for contemporary aesthetics: a baroque counterlineage asserts itself on one side and a more orthodox classical heredity, supported by Cartesian space and then Enlightenment visual culture, faces us on the other. My focus on the baroque and its love of the curious seeks to circumvent these kinds of grand rupture. Although the information aesthetics I discuss often echoes the teeming chaos and emergent order of visual display in the baroque cabinets of wonder, it is the relation of spaces of matter, knowledge, memory and technics to each other—as it is revealed in baroque visual display—that is my particular concern.

Both baroque and digital spaces engage the viewer visually, seductively and affectively. They operate by creating clusters of objects, images, sounds and concepts that belong together in variation and in dissonance. These clusters are not formed through arbitrary associations but emerge as the outcomes of differential connections. In baroque display, in natural history inventories, in the early encyclopædia and compendia of the seventeenth and eighteenth centuries, these differentials were concerned with the organic matter of objects and the artifice contrived upon this; the scientific discovery of a specimen and the anecdote and narratives accompanying it; and the representative status of a specimen in relation to its oddity (which would have guaranteed its place within the collection). This balancing act of moderating the natural and the artificial, the real and the mythical, the scientific and the aesthetic, was designed to lure the viewer into an affective experience of baroque space. Digital spaces, ranging from the space of virtualized online travel to entirely immersive environments, likewise operate to induce participation through sets of unfolding differential relays. Today the object clusters of baroque display have transmuted into entire nodes of experiencing spaces. These include but are not limited to being both aware of and losing one's proprioceptive sense of space; the goal-seeking and purposeful behavior of information searches (and the meandering stroll through avenues of meaningless yet intriguing data-based information); and the actual here and now of a user's body manipulating interfaces and a virtual environment in which time seems to stretch out forever. All of these nodes cohere and divide within a single digital experience.

What qualitatively distinguishes this baroque-digital connection from a straightforward narrative of art historical influence is the key role played by this notion of the differential. In the world of information, in which everyone is increasingly urged to become "connected," this baroque legacy, reverberating with differential relations, produces unassimilable, if infinitesimal, differences that slip away from the rhetoric of connectivity. Gaps and remainders sit alongside the interconnections, mitigating against, and testifying to the failure of, a fully technologically connected and serially standardized world. A difference always remains, and it operates to produce a gap, a leftover that is a heterogeneous element amid these forces of bland connectivity.

My aim, then, in both aesthetic and conceptual terms, is first to rethink the baroque within its own time. Phenomena such as the *Wunderkammer,* and their place within the arts, sciences and philosophies of the early modern period, produced a qualitatively different space from the classical space of disembodied optics and cogito. The baroque is not the underside of classicism but instead an entirely different project, one functioning through its own logic. Its particular differential spaces and logic are reproduced, albeit in radically different ways, through aesthetic experience in digital times. These spaces permeated and produced by an ongoing production of differences can help us rethink contemporary questions of subjectivity and the body. Posing the Cartesian subject as a good or an ugly underpinning of digital culture fails to account for the material and affective forces that contribute to this culture's continuing production and renewal. Within this framework, the baroque cannot be considered the historical genesis or origin of new media technologies. Instead, I will position digital aesthetic experience as a reverberation that enfolds and is enfolded by baroque inflections of the relations between bodies and technics.

In order to consider the baroque in its own time and then connect it to digital spaces, I will mobilize the conceptual and aesthetic notion of the fold, which was first elaborated by Gilles Deleuze.[10] Deleuze uses the work of the baroque philosopher and mathematician Gottfried Wilhelm Leibniz (1646–1716) to grasp the notion and process of folding in its conceptual and aesthetic dimensions. Deleuze's notion of folding is understood as simultaneously form and process. This doubled movement-structure is the mode in which, he suggests, baroque thought understood matter to be organized. Folded in its structure and form, matter cannot be divided into atomistic units—parts that add up to a whole—but instead is both continuous *and* differentiated in and between its parts. It is also the mode in which baroque matter dynamically contracts (enfolds) and extends (unfolds) as it grows and decays. We can think about this idea visually, Deleuze suggests, by imagining the way a fold rearranges a piece of paper.[11] It changes the surface, direction and volume of the paper; it marks points of inflection; it distinguishes areas of the surface from each other; and it connects one side of an inflected area to another.

Folds abound in baroque painting and sculpture and become points of interest in all thought of the period, including the emerging sciences.[12] But Deleuze is also engaged in the ways Leibniz's radical concatenation of continuity and difference, gathered up in the concept and process of folding, reverberates through arts and sciences today. In particular, he looks at the way in which certain branches of the life sciences, such as developmental embryology and genetics, have also deployed the fold as a formal organizing principle of matter.[13] The development of the embryonic organism from cell division to differentiated organ and tissue embodies principles of both continuity and difference that are suggested to us by the processes of folding and unfolding. So, too, the tightly wound structure of the chromosome as it unravels and begins the process of producing copies of itself at the level of life's molecular reproduction suggests a folded architecture.[14]

My interest in the fold as an aesthetic and historiographic device lies with both its preponderance through the baroque and its reverberation through information aesthetics. My project here is to produce a *critical* genetic relation between the digital and its various histories, especially the extent to which certain important ideas in digital culture, such as the differential, unfold in early modern European art and science. Folding this historical period into the present becomes a way of producing a creative genealogy for the digital that deliberately disturbs the idea that there is one history or one set of values embedded in its technologies, spaces or aesthetic manifestations.[15] By extending this concept of folding into contemporary information aesthetics, I have been able to explore the embodied experiences and ideas that occur through—rather than are excluded from—aesthetic engagement with new media technologies. These range from the design of human-machine interfaces to virtual reality and experimental online artwork. My fashioning of a creative genealogy for the digital proceeds via neither linear trajectory nor archaeological prehistory but via a folding of baroque spaces and preoccupations into digital ones.

The device of the fold provides us with two interrelated ways for thinking about this genealogy. First, it produces a dynamic manifold that circumscribes the space between past and present and connects a series of early modern singularities to the events that comprise what we might call information aesthetics. Second, the fold, while allowing historically and conceptually different times to touch each other by following their lines of connection and development, also produces discontinuity. These "synapses" between the folds or reverberations demand conceptual and sensory crossings. More than just a device for writing different kinds of histories of the digital, the fold simultaneously describes the experience of living the discontinuities and connections of digital sensory experience. These experiences of crossing thresholds between here and there, continuous and differentiated, corporeal and incorporeal, are common facets of engaging with virtual and telepresent technologies and environments. Thought about the body and actual sensory participation and engagement must be re-engaged in our analysis of digital culture in order to assist with this kind of threshold existence. The nuanced baroque idea of series of sensations and aesthetic experiences unfolding according to differentials of degree, speed and intensity gives us a way to think about relationships between embodiment and information.

In chapter 1, I will outline the contours of a new topography for the digital by examining its conceptual relation to the baroque production of aesthetic and affective spaces. In order to think productively beyond the closed space of the Cartesian *cogito* and the reductive cyberfantasy of flesh-machine fusion, we need a way to conceive of the relay of connections and disjunctions that is set off between the sensate and code in engagements with digital technologies. I have turned to the fold as a conceptual and aesthetic device in relating the digital to the baroque. In this first chapter, I will review the making of digital histories that have limited the present and future possibilities for bodies in culture. My enfolding of digital and baroque aesthetics concomitantly marks a new space for understanding the relations of connection and difference between bodies, other materialities, affect, and the inhuman spaces of code and its flows. I look for how this idea of folding plays out within contemporary information aesthetics and experience and find it proliferating through the work of digital architects and designers. Work by architect Greg Lynn, the architectural firms Foreign Office and Asymptote, and designer Bernard Cache provides us with contemporary examples of digital folding. Both Lynn and Cache overtly explore the topology of the fold and hence provide us with detailed new media case studies.

In order to think through what the experience of having a body means in information culture, which contrarily is undergoing processes of dematerialization, I have found it necessary to review and develop different directions for our understanding of technology itself. The question of what constitutes a digital machine correlates to the issue of what bodies have, and what they might become. My project for producing critical genealogies of information aesthetics intersects with the need for providing a more productive epistemological space for the effects of new media technologies, a space relatively unburdened by the entropy that accompanies the hype surrounding the information age. Much of the criticism about the disappearance of "the body" in the virtual world rests upon the assumption that modern technology reaches its apotheosis in the digital.[16] Thus the deconstruction of hypostases such as "the information age" or "the digital revolution" has been a necessary theoretical gesture. But this has also lead to a conceptual and tactical impasse for thinking and living through the ubiquity of new media technologies. As the debate at the SIGGRAPH panel bore witness, either one is positioned on the side of technohype or, from a lonelier outpost, one earnestly criticizes the political implications of naïvely accepting and deploying these technologies. An effect, unintended or otherwise, of taking up with either side is the conceiving of technology as the transcendental subject of "history," which thereby governs its flows and directions, rather than as immanent to history. This is not simply a point of academic contestation: everyday interactions and aesthetic explorations of digital technologies have often been governed by the idea that "technology" determines, and hence stands above and beyond, contemporary culture. As I will suggest, new media technologies are held to be responsible for privileging consciousness over embodiment in virtual environments or for favoring the machine over the human in the design of computer interfaces.

There has, of course, been a privileging of consciousness and information over bodies and the everyday world within cyberculture. In literature and research as diverse as Kevin Kelly's *Out of Control: The New Biology of Machines,* geneticist Lee Silver's *Remaking Eden: Cloning and Beyond in a Brave New World* or the cybernetic antics of Kevin "I am Cyborg" Warwick, a notion of the machine as a means of reconfiguring human biology to be purely informatic holds sway.[17] Warwick, a professor of cybernetics at Reading University in England, has devoted considerable research funds toward manufacturing his image as the ultimate twenty-first-century cyborg. In his view, the organic part of the human is limited, and hence cybernetic components need to be added in, as they are infinitely upgradeable. Unfortunately, Warwick's cyborg transformation has been limited to two projects of chip implantation that have interfaced with nerves in his arm to send and receive information signals.[18] In the first of these, Warwick essentially used his arm as a remote control device for opening and closing doors and various amenities in his research laboratory. In his more recent endeavors, the implanted chip interfaces with and stimulates internal nerves and sensory impulses in Warwick and also interacts with a simpler chip implanted in his wife. Rather than exploring the feedback between the organic and information systems, Warwick opts for the posthuman public relations machine that hypes his relatively simple robotic circuits as replacements for the human body. An engagement with information technologies under these circumstances places matter under the aegis of a grander and more overarching design: "technology." The posthumanism espoused in these scenarios is dedicated to articulating nothing more than a vacant buzz around the latest versions of new media technologies and to an antimatter proclivity thinly disguised as antihumanism. These post-evolutionary and postbiological celebrations of the machine give technology a utopian or transcendental place in cultural development, situating it spatially or temporally beyond embodiment.

Certain metaphors drawn from, and popular narrative constructions of, natural history have provided a platform for a conception of a new digital biology as the next evolutionary stage, one that will surpass organic human biology. In chapter 2 I will take an alternative approach to natural history, elaborating instead upon the wandering "incipience" that characterized the early practices of its visual display and narrative description. These practices afforded equal attention to artifice and nature. By looking in detail at baroque natural history collection, display and commentary and using them to inflect contemporary issues concerning materiality in digital times, I will seek to complicate the smooth genesis of digital culture in information and dematerialization. The specimens populating the European *Wunderkammer*, which later became the basis for Western museum culture, best demonstrate the multiple aesthetic, philosophical and scientific crossovers then permitted between the organic world and artisanship. I look to the *Wunderkammer* as evidence of natural history practices that operated by combining anecdote, humor, oddity and visual amplitude and relied upon affective relations to "science." Here we encounter an alternative to the perspective of the development of science through a linear progression away from the natural and toward the technological. In order to understand an epistemology that did not operate via binary divisions between nature and technics, we can look to the relation between the passions and knowledge in seventeenth-century thought. The discussion of this relationship permeated philosophical and scientific work then, including the writings of both Descartes and Leibniz. I will argue that the baroque passions were configured as a sphere through which body and thought might be understood to moderate each other.

Similarly, early scientific visual display, especially the objects and arrangements of the *Wunderkammer*, demanded that both thought and passion be activated in the viewer. Furthermore, the concentration on wonder and curiosity in the *Wunderkammer* that was present in the way artificial and natural objects were placed relative to each other indicated to their collectors and the viewing public an embodied relation of viewing and conceiving of the natural sciences (figure 1). It is the *Wunderkammer's* proximity of materiality, science, narrative memory and affectivity that resonates

FIGURE 1. Frontispiece to Ferrante Imperato, *Historia Naturalae* (Venice, 1672). Courtesy of the Wellcome Library, London.

in digital spaces as well. In this second chapter, I will explore the revival of the *Wunderkammer* as a structuring device in contemporary virtual displays within museum and experimental artistic spaces. Here a notion of wonder that recalls both the baroque passions and cabinets of curiosity plays an important aesthetic role. In the design and visualization of these spaces, aesthetic objects, textual fragments and the digital presence of others are differentially proximate to the engaged viewer or user. They provide the means to both navigate and stray through information, inflecting any time spent there with feelings of surprise, curiosity, irritation or even vertigo.

If our current engagements with technologies do not require us to surpass the human, what are we to make of the changes wrought upon our understanding of the human and induced by the suprahuman flows of information, particularly as we reconsider our understanding of humans as agents who control both the natural and artificial worlds? As Manuel de

Landa puts it, "And while these views do indeed invoke the 'death of man,' it is only the death of the 'man' of the old 'manifest destinies,' not the death of humanity and its potential for destratification."[19] Perhaps we require a conception of the digital that neither capitulates to a transcendental idea about "technology" nor disposes so lightly of the human. We need to situate the digital within a broader field of approaches to machines and technologies rather than view it as simply a kind of technology that improves upon other technologies (such as the analog or even the "technology" of human biology). Instead, we need to treat the matter of humans and the materiality of technologies as open-ended propositions that are continually in the process of being made and unmade. Following upon a conception of the "machinic" that was initially elucidated in the work of Gilles Deleuze and Felix Guattari and subsequently elaborated upon by writers such as de Landa and Keith Ansell Pearson, I conceive of the digital as a machinic movement.[20] The digital is a flow of information, technologies, cultural and social deployments, potentialities, delimitations and regulations. It possesses intensive and extensive properties and circumscriptions, such as its range of speeds and its poles, that provide a kind of directionality for its flow. When considering the machinic abstractly as *any* kind of material flow, these poles are less causes of this movement than oscillatory horizons toward and out of which any material flow whatsoever will tend.

At one limit or pole, we find the potential directions in which a flow of matter moves or can be organized. Here, a set of exchanges is laid out that describes all of the possible relations a flow might enter into: what capacities and functions allow the movement of this flow into a specific or more localized material formation, such as a particular technical machine. This pole organizes the limits around which a specific technical machine, like the desktop computer, is capable of functioning. In the case of the digital, at this abstract limit pole we would find the capacity of silicon to conduct electrons at particular speeds; its resistance to degrees of deterioration; its ability to change its composition and properties according to temperature; the possibility of its combination (or not) with other material flows, such as particular organic molecules; and the functions, such as superconductivity at high speeds, that all of these capacities enable and that specifically characterize the operation of computers. These qualitative traits, potentialities and delimitations of matter flows comprise the *virtual abstract* pole of machinic movement.

At the other limit or pole, we discover the concrete and situated forms that these capacity-function relations are capable of assuming at a given time. These forms are actualized through assemblages of social, technical and material elements that can be quite specific, such as the human hand/keyboard/monitor assemblage. This latter arrangement dominates our most common interactions with computers. It also privileges certain sensory faculties over others; for example, sight over the haptic, kinaesthetic and proprioceptive senses. Hence this form of organization also invokes epistemological and ontological dimensions. The elements an assemblage deploys will depend upon a tussle between existing and emerging sociocultural relations. Alternatively, these forms may be actualized as larger formations by mobilizing rhetoric and narratives of technology, such as "the information society." In this case, the "actual" pole of machinic movement will have been captured and constrained by given social, technical and political conditions. These conditions position new media technologies as determinants of contemporary culture and life. Effectively, the virtuality—or abstract pole—of the machinic movement of the digital has been blocked during the movement of its actualization. Although the virtuality of the digital is not unlimited—it has very real material parameters—it is also not yet exhausted by these current forms of actualization.

This oscillating horizon, which I have described as the directional field for machinic movement, always combines the flows of technics with the work of a social machine, which captures and drives their development in specific ways. The technical element is always in a relation with elements outside itself; its form is therefore indeterminate and virtual. It cannot be known ahead of the actualization that occurs as a result of these combinatory relations. As Felix Guattari argues, it is not possible to understand a technology without locating it within its social ensemble of relations.[21] Although the machinic can be seen as the potential for movement of technical, material, social and aesthetic elements between limit poles, any actual formation of a machine (whether technical or social) cuts across and separates itself from the flux of all of these constituents. This provides us with a starting point for a new way of conceiving of machines as movement-capture formations: they arise out of heterogenous flows yet sever the flows' movements in myriad directions. As Deleuze and Guattari state, "We define the machine as any system that cuts the fluxes."[22]

We are now in a better position to situate the terms and tensions of the debate at the SIGGRAPH panel I attended. The assumption—which is built into the subtitle of the session, "Are You Oppressed by the Cartesian Coordinate System?"—is that the scientific or mathematical underpinnings of technologically produced spaces and practices exert a regime of power upon the *representational level* at which technologies operate. The argument proceeds thus: new digital technologies can be shown to be the heirs of old epistemologies and ontologies. These knowledge systems and conceptions of the disembodied self remain embedded in machines; concomitantly, machines act as conduits for the perpetuation of these systems and ideas of the self in culture. We have a model in which technologies provide the "wiring" through which ideas and representations run. The danger here is that technologies can be considered either "hard-wired" and immoveable or neutral, that is, circuits that have no impact upon the social and cultural spheres. But as Ansell Pearson argues, "One is not 'oppressed' by a technical machine but by a social machine, which governs at any given moment what is the usage, extension, and comprehension of technical elements."[23] Conceiving of technology instead under the umbrella of machinism facilitates an analysis of the technical from the viewpoint of its potential movements (its capacities to be more or different than it actually is) *and* its regulation, management and maintenance by concrete entanglements with social, political and economic relations. In order to understand something about the subjective effects of the Cartesian coordinate system, we need to understand this as *more* than just the technical specifications used to map out the space of three-dimensional computer graphics but *less* than a regime responsible for deploying power over subjective life.

We need to understand the system of disembodied optics that the Cartesian system advocates machinically, in terms of its recombinant technical, discursive, aesthetic and social elements. The Cartesian coordinate system brings with it a set of unresolved ideas about identity and the body inherited from early modern European thought and culture. It has a long nonlinear history that stretches back into its complicated place within Descartes's own work. Indeed, the dualism of mind over matter he is accused of supplying to the social machine of contemporary computing culture could be considered a contemporary cut into the seventeenth-century flux of his projects, for Descartes also addressed the affective relation of thought to the body. It is therefore far from certain that his idea of the self, taken in its breadth across his work, necessarily instantiated a regime of disembodiment. In order to understand the Cartesian ideas about the relations of body to thought and the many contradictions that they entail, we need to situate them within the broader production of baroque aesthetic, social and technoscientific machines. By reexamining Descartes as part of the event of baroque culture, we will complicate our present conceptions of Cartesianism as a system that perpetuates a disembodied and mechanistic view of the self.

The relations immanent to the digital, understood as an abstract machinic movement, with regard to its capacities to produce its matter-flows in particular ways are not exhausted by how the digital has been produced within specific sociocultural assemblages, or influenced by regimes of thought such as Cartesianism. One of the effects, then, of situating the digital within this broader notion of machinism is that new media technologies no longer appear solely geared toward the realization of specific social outcomes such as "the information society." The digital, in fact, may materially, socially and aesthetically combine in ways other than closed systems such as dematerialized, entropic conceptions of information culture or of the disembodied posthuman.

Moreover, it is not as if the abstract limit designating the direction of the machinic movement's capacities and functions will remain constant; they may expand into or be regulated by other capacities and delimitations within an assemblage. Hence the actual feeds back into and changes the virtual. So, for example, current scientific limits to successfully splitting the electron (which would lead to increasing the speed of electroconductivity in silicon) mean that the capacities of digital technologies to work infinitely faster are limited. In the race for absolute speed, material constraints upon the current technosocial ensemble we might call "infomanic" are encountered at the virtual limit pole of the digital. Consequently, we are forced to rethink our fantasy that new media technologies can provide unlimited speed for information flows. Indeed, we may need to modulate our entire understanding of digital culture as infinitely fast.

Considering the digital as machinic, then, means that we think about technology as part of an ensemble that differentially combines the capacities and functions of its matter-flows in relation to the other elements in that assemblage. Thus we cannot know ahead of time the actual nature of technological forms or technologically inflected formations. The machinic is not a model for producing a global morphogenesis of technologies.[24] But given that one limit of the machinic pulls specific elements such as the digital toward a dynamic manifold of virtualities, we can say confidently that there will always be other ways for conceiving of, manifesting and experiencing digital culture. These other modes include, and indeed foreground, the relatively unexplored terrain of embodied digital experience. This book emerges from an urgent political necessity—our understanding of self, others and social relations in informatic culture—for staking out the areas in which some of these sensory experiences appear.

In traversing the gaps, discontinuities or differentials between bodies and new media, we can begin to situate an emerging digital embodiment.

Although this may appear paradoxical, I will argue in my third chapter that ideas about virtuality that have traversed information aesthetics since the 1980s need to be reexamined. Paring back older notions of the digital as the pathway to the virtual in which we were promised better and more complete access to either the sensorium or hyperreality will leave room to acknowledge the contribution of our corporeal capacities to technological interaction. Embodiment will be explored throughout this chapter as an open and dynamic system capable of oscillating toward the incorporeality of digital code. Much of the hype surrounding the experiences of engaging with virtual reality (VR) technologies has been subtended by a rhetoric of dematerialization, in which actual bodies seem to fade as the virtual sphere beckons. By looking at these technologies as concrete actualizations of the virtual capacities both of the digital and of human bodies, I will show how it is possible to move out of the quagmire of virtual/real, mind/body and informatic/material that characterizes digital thinking about virtuality. This is qualified by an understanding of VR technologies as only one kind of actualization of virtuality. Although VR can provide us with an insight into the ability of our bodies to engage on a material and incorporeal level with new media technologies, there is a danger in assuming that this might be the best or only possible way to access the virtual. Against this assumption, we can propose a different idea of embodiment, one immanently capable of becoming both sensate and virtual.

In the third chapter I will look at both virtual space and virtual time within new media. A study of the popular BBC television series *Walking with Dinosaurs* will allow us to rethink the use of digital animation to tell historical narratives. The relation between digital media and history—its use within museums, computer gaming and fictionalized "documentaries" of past worlds—is often seen to involve a flattening and erasure of time. I argue that we are beginning to encounter modes of nonlinear temporality within these forms of digital entertainment. Virtual spaces have been described as disembodied and lacking a specific location, emptied of the differences that situated bodies and physical geography bring to a sense of place. By revisiting our conception of the virtual as a movement that passes from the abstract incorporeal spaces of information to the concrete actuality of the body, we can rethink the perceptual and aesthetic experiences of VR technologies and of the sense of the virtual that is conveyed through digital media. I will test out these ideas by comparing artistic, entertainment and research applications of virtual and immersive environments ranging from the 1980s NASA-Ames workstations to the artistic experiments of Catherine Richards and Char Davies.

Digital embodiment entails the capacity for us to conceive of and experience bodies as something other than inert, weighty masses distended in space and out of sync with the absolute speed of an unremitting technological tempo. Digital bodies engage *incorporeally* with the informatic universe precisely because digital machines can replicate, amplify and split us from the immediacy of our sensory capacities. New media extend our bodies in the way that Marshall McLuhan suggested that all media are extensions of the body.[25] That is, they extend bodies away from immediate experience and even away from their prior inflections by other forms of media. New media entice bodies to venture toward incorporeal flows of information and combine, in convergent and divergent ways, the capacities and functions of carbon materialities with those of information flows. The doubling and extension of bodily capacities and sensations by digital means differs from the phenomenological experience of bodies in a world populated only by subjects and objects. The interval between incorporeal and corporeal experience opened up by new media sets off the play of relays, deferrals, crossings and recuperations between them.

Walking down the street enclosed by headphones streaming thousands of MP3 files into one's ears initiates a very different kind of movement, gait and navigation than that of even the *flâneur,* whose pace and negotiation of urban space was provoked by the gaze. Immersed instead in a bubble of digital sonic flow, one finds that walking becomes an entry point for the body into what Manuel Castells calls "the space of flows."[26] Here, extensive movement has been transformed into mobility—the capacity to smoothly negotiate the flows of sonic and urban information in concert with each other. Mobility inserts the self, via a new configuration of corporeal movement, into the technological course of information: one becomes a "walk-man" by transforming bodily movement and urban space simultaneously—by gliding over the surface of the physical environment. The walk-man is not an assimilation of the human to informatic space, and hence the loss of embodiment, but rather the transformation of a human capacity through the rearrangement of aspects of aesthetic or sensory life. This transformation takes place through the differential hybridizing of body and technology. The mobile *écouteur* contracts the flows of information that are supposed to keep bodies usefully and efficiently moving around the urban sprawl and that turn them into functions of information flows—the speedy courier, the networking executive on a mobile phone, the scanning eyes of the consumer.

Instead, the *écouteur* amplifies a sensory capacity and splits from the productivity-oriented directions of urban flow, enclosed as she is in a vast and overflowing aural space. The ear becomes an aberrant, almost monstrous zone absorbing flows of information and in the process threatening to out-grow the form of the human body, making the *écouteur* inhuman. This new suprafunctionalism of the ear is already presaged by the images of human audiophiles with elongated alien-like ears in the advertising for the TDK company's "TDK Does Amazing Things to My System" campaign. Like-wise, Apple's iPod digital music player intimates something alien through its very name. In a more provocative way, the artist Stelarc has collaborated with the Tissue Culture and Art Project and attempted to grow a nonfunc-tioning tissue-engineered "Extra Ear" and then have it surgically attached to himself (see figure 2).[27] The "Extra Ear," in Stelarc's view, suggests that the organ has outgrown its former function of absorption and would, as a fully realized future artwork equipped with a tiny sound chip and proximity sen-sor, speak and demand to be heard. Far from disposing of the senses, new media, whether commercially realized or experimentally proposed, point toward the synaesthetic disruptions and reconfigurations of bodily capaci-ties and functions that might be made possible by digital technologies.

Our relations to digital technologies operate across the differential that comprises these negotiations between the continuous and dynamic flux of organic life and the discrete rhythms and inhuman speeds of informatic temporality. Although a surface appraisal of phenomena such as VR or telepresent artworks may tender proof that we are gaining a distance from both the material of our bodies and the ability of art to directly affect the senses, I believe this appraisal rests upon an impoverished view of mate-riality and an unimaginative evaluation of new media art. Instead, I think that the incorporeal vectors of digital information draw out the capacities of our bodies to become other than matter conceived as a mere vessel for consciousness or a substrate for signal. In particular, we might point to the odd kinaesthetic and proprioceptive arrangements for bodies in many in-formation interfaces, where the embodied self is forced into close proxim-ity with itself as *a dematerialized representation* via the cursor, the feedback of virtual and actual gesture in immersive environments or bandwidth, and sensory compression in online interaction. These arrangements of sensation in tandem with information are commonly thought to herald the predominance of the information pattern over the matter it inhabits or hopes to control. Katherine Hayles has termed this entering "the condition of virtuality."[28] But we may also conceive of these experiences as a new ter-ritory made possible by the fact that our bodies are immanently open to these kinds of technically symbiotic transformations.

New media technologies will probably ask for impossible bodily trans-formations at some point. Carbon/silicon, bodies/technologies and analog/

FIGURE 2. Stelarc, *Ear on Arm* (2003). Photograph by Papapetrou.
Courtesy of the artist.

digital are not infinitely adaptable to each other: all are delimited spheres.
But, as I will also argue, the disjunctions, gaps or differentiators here in fact
produce new heterogeneous derivatives—sites in which we can renegotiate
these relations. The total assimilation of flesh to machine or the erasure of
the machine's materiality in its absorption into the anthropomorphism of
humanlike qualities are fantasies of merging. These fantasies conveniently
forget that the embodied zones of connection to the discrete qualities of the
digital form a kind of graft, which is an unequivocal mark of connection
and difference. We can name this engineered mark of alterity "digital embodiment," an arena across which material and incorporeal forces will continue to engender further connection and differentiation.

Following my reworking of the virtual, I will turn to a parallel reassess-
ment of human-computer interaction (HCI). Dominant interface design

within new media has coerced us into face-to-face relations with the computer, either by subsuming the body into a command-control scenario by aligning human and computational "cognitive" processes or by providing the machine with a "human face" to address our own. I call these kind of interactions *interfacial* and, in my fourth chapter, I will analyze the way in which this assemblage forces information to be folded into our corporeality in predetermined ways that leave little room for negotiating other modes of interaction. Here I have recourse to an interrogation of the digital machine via the concept of faciality articulated by Deleuze and Guattari.[29] Faciality is a social, aesthetic and technical machine that organizes corporeal engagement and representation into a relation of subordination to the face. The face, according to Deleuze and Guattari, has become a frozen structure in Western history and culture, perpetuating a cult of "personality" and setting up exclusionary zones between surface "features" and the depth of "mind" that lies behind these. The human has subsequently been evaluated and determined according to this dominant facial system.

It strikes me that this system continues to operate in the design of the inter*face*. My main area of investigation for analyzing the preponderance of this assemblage is the design field of HCI. This takes us into the everyday experience of computing as both entertainment and work, where users primarily interact with information by facing a screen. HCI design has revolved around either making the "face" of computing more visible and friendly or else helping the interface to disappear altogether. But the latter tendency has rarely led to an exploration of new possibilities for embodied interface design; both directions have privileged a model of cognitive interaction with the digital machine.

I will explore possibilities for posthuman-computer interaction through the aesthetic productions of Stelarc and the computer performance artist program named Huge Harry, assessing the extent to which interfaciality works its way into new media art. My argument here is that this facialized assemblage needs to be analyzed and dismantled. Posthumanism gives us some new possibilities for human-computer engagement, but it often continues to subordinate the sensate body to the transcendent technological world that is offered via the interface. I will pose a counter-genealogy of new media experimentation that places human bodies as the key to computational engagement. Detailed case studies follow that demonstrate the concern of new media art with embodied interaction in the work of Myron Krueger, Rafael Lorenzo-Hemmer and Justine Cooper, among others.

It is the strangeness and proximity of bodies to their visualization by new media that lends the particular flavor to what we can call "emerging digital bodies." I will spend my fifth and final chapter exploring the folds of body and information through the proximity and distance that simultaneously mark our relations to others within global information culture. In general, the aesthetic debate concerning new media artwork has concentrated on arguments that seek to locate medium specificity for information aesthetics. Interactivity, virtuality and telepresence have all been offered as defining qualities of new media art. Although there is something specific to new media art, I am not inclined to look for this in the formal qualities of the media or in the technologies themselves. Instead, we need to examine the social and perceptual conditions produced by living "digital" lives. Primarily, these rest upon the emergence of a space and time where relative speeds and differential relations to technologies alter our experience of embodiment. If we are to focus on bodies rather than consciousness as our entré to the world of digital information, we must also think about the heterogeneity of corporeality and materiality with which new media technologies acquaint us. Information aesthetics cannot afford to map out formal or technical standards for evaluating new media art; information flows are characterized by nonstandardization. I will propose instead three vectors that flee from technical and cultural standardization and invent alternative accounts of globalized digital culture. The first, "proximity," sums up the capacity of information to approximate the specifics of corporeal and situated experience. Here I will examine the work of Graham Harwood of the collective Mongrel, and especially his self-conscious deployment of the antinomy "proximity-distance" to explore the social, corporeal and technical relations between online and offline experiences. I am particularly interested in his use of the category of "class" as a marker of embodiment that can nonetheless be catalyzed in information spaces to convey a sense of lived, corporeal difference.

The second vector, "lag," proposes that the temporal delays characterizing new media are a device that disrupts the forces of standardization and homogenization in global information culture. This section will focus upon Indian new media art that demythologizes the notion of a synchronized and perfectly efficient information economy, including the installations and online projects of raqs media collective and the organization Sarai, and Internet/installation artist Shilpa Gupta. The third vector, "distribution," looks at how information aesthetics emerges through the reorganization of data-space as a function of dispersed time. In particular, I examine online animations and websites, as these demonstrate the ways in which artists and designers are operating in the global arena of distributed image production and consumption. These new media forms operate technically by shifting away from data encoded as bit-mapped graphics to data transformed into vectors or nonlinear mathematical equations. The aesthetic implications of this are that the informatic image, for example, no longer communicates or distributes what has been originally encoded and stored—usually a scanned photograph converted to a bitmapped graphic. Instead, it is produced from the outset as pure data and therefore made ready for distribution. Data production and distribution technologies are increasingly synchronized, supposedly enabling seamless production, distribution and reception quality and speeds. This engenders an expectation of immediate temporal exchange and experience in online uploading, transfer and downloading. And yet immediacy is rarely the actual experience of temporality in online engagements; rather lags, corruption and error returns are the order of the day.

Examining the work of new media artists such as Simon Biggs and Mark Amerika, I will show how they turn instead to experimenting with asynchronicity in order to disturb the false expectation of a smoothly flowing world of global information. These three vectors show us that factoring in the differentials of others' experience, place and the material conditions of information culture can lead us from aesthetic to ethical consideration of new media. The issue is no longer one involving just body-computer relations but one involving bodies networked in information culture as its flows disconnect and connect the heterogeneity of embodied lives.

Over the course of writing this book, the question of digital speeds and the relation of new media theory to new media technologies and culture have helped to shape my approach in thinking through information aesthetics. If one is using theory to catch up to the chameleon that is everyday life in relation to new media technologies, inevitably a sense of lag sets in. The connective, disjunctive, linear and nonlinear movements these technologies perform, if taken as a homogeneous "technology," appear to be overwhelmingly rapid. But it is also possible, and important, to understand new media as compositions of relative speeds mediated by relations to, for example, older or other media. To a certain extent, then, understanding new media requires the lens of a media studies perspective. But this should not be one determined by a formulaic notion of media as a mode of communication. A communications-based model remains too dependent on the idea that new media allow the transmission of information at a lower signal-to-noise ratio than other media, such as cinema or television. Accordingly, the function of new media will be to become little more than vectors for the communicational replication of older media practices. The belief in digital media as merely enhanced communicators has led to an enormous investment in research and development into broadband and interactive *television*, digital *cinema*, and so on.

Yet, as Lev Manovich has argued, digital media do not simply translate other media but also redistribute them.[30] This dislocation and redeployment shifts our understanding of the categories we previously used to make sense of older media forms. New media are not simply changing older media forms; they are altering the conceptual taxonomies and paradigms for thinking about them. What's more, there is not just a rearrangement in forms of production, transmission and reception but a reorganization of our epistemologies of media. This shakedown will itself take time and is likely to undergo further changes. Although it is clear that a communications analysis of media is not sufficient, neither can we afford to lose a media studies perspective. The focus must transfer to the mutability of media forms rather than the delineation of form through medium specificity analysis. We must begin to consider both duration and variation in time and speed as material conditions engendered by information technologies and culture and, under these conditions, begin to account for both the continuation and the mutation of old into new media.

I have adopted a course throughout this book of tracking the meanderings and flows of various aspects of new media technologies with the understanding that not all of the connections to older and newer forms to which digital objects lead us can be uncovered or are ultimately relevant for an aesthetically oriented project. Rather than inquire into the overall cultural meaning of the digital, I have specifically looked for the points of intersection that digital flows have with issues of embodiment. Instead of an interdisciplinary study launched from established disciplines such as media and cultural studies, this project proposes and puts into motion the idea of transversal technological studies. The transversal can be configured as a diagram rather than a map or territory: directional lines cross each other, forming intersections, combining their forces, deforming and reforming the entire field in the process. By taking this transversal route as a proposal for traveling the circuits of new media, it is possible to understand digital culture itself as a series of diagrammatic lines. Its intersections trace points and inflections in an undulating curvature of code, silicon, carbon, embodiment, socialities, economies and aesthetics. I land at several of these intersections throughout this book, anticipating that these will provide us with significant directions for understanding the flows of information aesthetics.

No analogy machine exists which will really form the product of two numbers. What it will form is this product, plus a small but unknown quantity which represents the random noise of the mechanism and the physical processes involved. The whole problem is to keep this quantity down.   —JOHN VON NEUMANN[1]

All bodies are in a perpetual flux like rivers, and parts are entering into them and passing out of them continuously.

—GOTTFRIED W. F. LEIBNIZ[2]

1 sampling and folding
the digital and the baroque

The Clone, the Sample and the Differential

In the wake of late-twentieth-century entities such as the "cyborg" or the "posthuman" and with our increasing fascination for the "biotechnological" we have become accustomed to thinking of hybrids as entities that seamlessly graft machines and bodies together. A successful amalgamation of circuitry and flesh would herald our entry into an age of convergence between nature and technics. Accordingly, we no longer appear startled by manifestations of the neomonstrous, such as human hand transplantation or attempts to clone, gestate and release into the wild extinct species of animals. In 1999 the Australian Museum (Australia's largest natural history museum, located in Sydney) embarked on a research project to clone a living Thylacine. This animal—

commonly known as the Tasmanian tiger—is an extinct species of Australian marsupial.[3] The last recorded living Thylacine died in captivity in a zoo in Tasmania in 1936. Using preserved DNA from a pup specimen in the museum's possession, researchers began exploring the possibility of sequencing the Thylacine genome and using cloning techniques to generate a living individual of the species. No doubt the impetus and research for this project followed close on the heels of the publicity surrounding the Human Genome Project (HGP), which reached fever pitch with the announcement of the completion of sequencing in 2001.

The science fantasy surrounding the Thylacine project borrowed from and elaborated upon the rhetoric infusing the HGP. Mike Archer, the museum's director and the initiator of the cloning venture, fueled this alignment with comments directly referencing the HGP metaphors construing DNA as the "book of life": "We can now begin construction of a DNA library that will contain the entire recipe for re-creation." Elsewhere his conflation of genetic and digital code was simply bad science: "The dead DNA extracted from the tissue of a preserved pup has been made to act in the same way as live DNA and millions of copies of the DNA have now been made."[4] The Thylacine project, however, ran out of steam when it was discovered that preserved DNA from the pup and other specimens would only render sequences for four out of a possible thirty thousand genes. In order to initiate the process of cloning, an entire genome (all of the genes of an organism) needs to be mapped. Cloning, as an idea, has proven to be more of a conduit between science and the public's imagination than a smoothly paved road to immediate biotechnical success. The museum's project and its projection into the public sphere captured the public's imagination by seamlessly gliding over a series of complex scientific, cultural and environmental tensions, including the differences between sequencing a limited number of genes from DNA fragments and the mapping of an entire genome; the operations of genetic replication and digital copying; and the ethics of regenerating extinct species and releasing them into ecologically changed habitats versus preserving species that are currently endangered. Building organisms from information is proving to be a haphazard, fraught and rather contingent process.

Yet the optimism that inheres in perceptions of cloning speaks to an ever-increasing perfectionism that accompanies the assimilation of the organic to the technological world. Or have the visible marks of technical operations upon bodies been reduced to such minute proportions, such invisible maneuvers, that they no longer arouse comment? Like the hidden mechanics of baroque automata, which were designed to beguile the spectator in a display of apparently self-propelled motion, clones, the millennial figures of technological wonder, also conceal their artifice. From automata to clone, a host of mutations have featured in the Western cultural imagination at critical junctures in the history of matter's entanglement with technologies. And yet foregrounding some of the most familiar of these—Frankenstein's monster, Fritz Lang's False Maria, the Borg from the *Star Trek/Voyager* television series—we notice the indelible mark left by technology when it confronts matter. The machine, as an animating and disturbing force invading the human organism, has historically featured as an *unnatural and highly differentiated* means of stitching up, reanimating and assimilating flesh.

But the mark of biotechnology, configured as the clone, is its sameness: the promise of endless productions of replicated genotype resulting in armies of identical phenotypes. The cyborg—a visible mark of the amalgamation of body and machine—has frequently been associated with the ascendency of digital technologies and culture, particularly through the work of Donna Haraway.[5] Yet it is the clone that offers us the full promise of what digital code will offer—repetition. The genetic and digital spheres have become aligned by sharing their rhetoric and swapping their metaphors about the properties of code, such as its transferability across platforms or generations, its autonomy from any material substrate, and the guarantee that fluctuation or corruption in subsequent copies/generations will be outweighed by the quality of a high signal-to-noise ratio. These biotechnical conflations deliver us an idea of the clone as a complete integration of techno-organicism. Moreover, as Dolly the sheep attests, the clone no longer looks like a freak, as the cyborg did, but is technology made entirely ordinary. If the properties of replication, reliability and transferability now inhere in our conceptions of digital code, then the clone, produced out of the gesture of "sampling" genetic code, nominally assures us of the smooth exchangeability between technology and biology. It certainly will be smoother than the seventeenth century's automata, which could only awkwardly reproduce organic motion and ultimately were received as spectacles that grotesquely imitated the animate qualities of life.[6]

Yet the figure of the clone belies an important aspect of life riven with the peculiar permutations of digital code. Far from being one of a kind, clones exist as part of a series. Ian Wilmut and Keith Campbell, the scientists responsible for cloning Dolly from the mammary gland cells of an adult ewe, keenly detail the extraordinary serendipity of engineering a living DNA clone out of the series of an initial 277 fusions between donor cells and unfertilized eggs.[7] Similarly, the idea of the clone in the popular imagination is always accompanied by its others—fluctuations and mutations of code that have not quite achieved the status of the perfect replica. In a scene from the 1996 Hollywood comedy *Multiplicity,* starring Michael Keaton as Doug and his three clones, we first encounter the relation between the original and clone as an instance of exact replication. Exhausted by life's frenetic demands on his time, Doug signs up for a cloning program in order to create a replica of himself that can exist in the workplace while he enjoys his home and family life. Lying on the hospital bed, Doug wakes to ask the attendant geneticist how the procedure went, and how his clone has turned out. Startled by the mirror image of another Doug in front of him, he learns that he in fact is the clone, now being examined by both the geneticist and the original Doug. As further copies of Doug appear in the movie to fulfill other demands and functions of modern life, they form a diverging series from the original Doug. The third clone is an effeminate man obsessed with detail and housework, recalling the rather stereotypical image of the invert as a product of hereditary deformity. And the fourth clone turns out to be mentally disabled, explained in the film as the problem that occurs when making a xerox of a xerox: it loses the sharpness of the original. The clone as perfect replica only gains this designation by differentiating itself from the series of failed attempts at sampling the original code.

If the clone is emblematic of a completely integrated body-technology symbiosis, then it can only stand as such by forgetting the genealogy of mutations, fluctuations and failures that constitutes its serial history. No longer displaying the classic cyborgian graft of machine conjoined to bodily being, clones are nevertheless marked by relations of digital repetition and difference. These are the very relations that now bind and separate matter from machines. I want to suggest that the clone does not so much render complete an exultant identification between biology and technology as draw attention to the underacknowledged role of differential relations in arranging, sequencing and replicating the codes of digital culture. In other words, digital and genetic cloning do not simply function as instances of perfect machine-organism duplication but rather raise the specter of their others, the series of differences from which they were born.

Typically, digital code has been conceived of as the operation of abstracted information encoded through a process of reduction to a binary distinction between two states: zero and one.[8] Digitization occurs through two maneuvers: the translation of the material world and its continua into numerical data and the sampling of these continua as discrete sequences by shuffling them through either/or gates. Discussion of the digital encoding of phenomena as diverse as photographs and genetic systems has proceeded as if this capture will herald the coming of an entire cultural and aesthetic regime characterized by dematerialization (abstraction via numerical representation) and the logic of identity (either/or states). In his analysis of the status of the digital "copy" as an exact reproduction of the image, William Mitchell offered a model of a coming digital aesthetics based on the ability of binary code to infinitely replicate itself across any platform without corruption.[9] Precisely because the image was made up of nothing but executable sequences of numbers, the matter in which the image/sequences inhered could no longer be said to impress itself upon representation. Likewise, biologists captivated by technologies of genetic duplication and reproduction have offered similar scenarios for a future world populated by digitally gestated organisms that begin their life as sequences of computer code or even as virtual imaginings on computer screens.[10] Tellingly, the process of differentiating among copies, the attempts and failures that make up the history, context and serial variability of a sequence of code, is superseded or forgotten in both scenarios in the rush to instate the fundamentally binary operation of digitization.

In this chapter I will argue that phenomena of contemporary digital culture such as the clone, the sample of audio that recurs in remixed music and the production of physical urban spaces as replications of computer-modeled or "virtual" space cannot be understood without recourse to series of differences. Invoking the genealogy of mathematical relations to which the digital code must also pay conceptual deference, I will refer to this serial difference as "differentiality." The differential is the variable relation that inheres in a series between its moments of repetition and the gaps or intervals that separate these replicated instances from each other. If the clone, sampled audio and digital image are exemplars of replication, they should also be considered variables that are marked by the series of differences that also facilitated their production. Additionally, they form a differential relation of convergence or divergence with the continua of biology, sound and image, which they promise to reduce through numerical translation. To take the differential into account in an analysis of information culture is to reinsert the value of those intervals of noncapture, malfunction and chance fluctuation immanent to materiality *back* into the series of perfect replicas.

In Natalie Jeremijenko's *OneTree* project, which began in 1999, the exchanges between world and image, abstraction and materiality, artificial and actual are intermeshed, suggesting both a convergence and a divergence between information and the material world.[11] Working with a plant geneticist and using plant tissue-culture techniques, Jeremijenko had one thousand trees cloned from the DNA of a single original Paradox walnut tree and cultivated them to saplings. At the same time she released a CD-ROM with software that produced a representation of a virtual tree growing on the computer into which the disk was inserted. These "e-trees" "grow" using common artificial-life algorithms for simulating self-replicating electronic organisms. They are similar to algorithms used in the SimCity and SimLife computer games and also resemble those deployed by scientists to model replicating systems such as viruses.

But the outcome of Jeremijenko's double-stranded project does not lie in a claim to model the vast processes and systems we call life or to produce a recipe for re-creation. Beginning with the artificial or "cloned" production of the natural world, one hundred of the saplings continue their lives in the soil of various microclimates in San Francisco. The original biological "identity" of the trees will render, through the patterns of each tree's growth and decay, the social and environmental *differences* to which they are exposed over their lifetimes. Their development will record the contingencies of "life" in each public site in which they are planted. The artificial element of Jeremijenko's work slowly diverges from the informatic universe of model and data and stretches outward to the diversity and contingency of material life.

The "e-trees," on the other hand, have to contend with a virtual world for their growth, but not one that is hermetically sealed from contingency or corruption. They are not able to replicate inside the computer without the input of additional data, supplied by readings from a carbon dioxide meter that is distributed along with the CD-ROM and inserted into the back of the computer. Actual CO_2 levels in the immediate environment control the growth rate of the virtual trees. The *OneTree* project is produced by working within the tension between the material and the informatic— the gaps, fluctuations and intervals that mark their relationship. The invisible levels at which code is assumed to operate often allow it to be rendered as a seamless set of operations assimilating the very real differences between the spheres of experience and knowledge. But, as Jeremijenko suggests, information is not simple but entangled and always heterogenous from the outset. Her motivation for staging the many levels and streams of *OneTree* is precisely to empirically show that information and organic life are interwoven but cannot be forced to act in the same ways: "To demonstrate that you cannot *see* or *picture* genes; to demonstrate the irreducible complexity of genetic information; to demonstrate that in the relatively simple form of the tree (compared to such complex social be-

e appears check in at the
will be given the room
interview

hecked in at the Paging
your interview room

to check out with anyone
ew

oms and lockers are located
lding.

door in South Campus Hall

Paging Desk

Job Information Form

-website cecs.uwaterloo.ca

haviours as alcoholism or violent tendencies) there is no simple set of transductions that you can trace through."[12]

The Fold: Convergence and Divergence, Fluctuation and Pleating

Contemporary experiences of embodiment in digital culture are riven with the curious contiguities and collaborations that try to sample the body and other materialities with the computational machine. These non-nuptial engagements trigger processes of relay and referral between categories such as the organic and the technical, the natural and the artificial, or the sensible world and permutations of digital code. The question is how to conceptualize these communications and upheavals set off between sensible bodies and new technologies. Most figurations of the cyborg and theories of posthumanism treat body and code as predefined unities that impinge upon and assimilate one to the other. And yet living with contemporary digital machines produces instead everyday encounters of doubling, splitting and reverberating as new aspects of our bodily experiences. We occupy and produce relations of differentiation and integration between the corporeal and the informatic, such that converging and diverging series of machine-body events begin to map themselves out. At their minima and maxima these series form either slight fluctuations or sharp pleats; their topology is that of the fold.

The fold in a piece of paper or fabric is both confluent and dissonant: it joins sides and marks the difference between them. I suggest that the fold entwines two important issues for information aesthetics: the production of contemporary embodiment—the corporeal experiences of living in and through information culture—and the relation of this to its aesthetic, epistemological and ontological genealogies. From what does the digital unfold? By suggesting that bodies and code in the time of information might be more productively conceived of as differentially related variables, I intend to summon as well a less frequently acknowledged genealogy for digital culture. The differential is initially a concept that comes to us through the history of mathematics, and specifically through the nomenclature of Leibniz's calculus.[13] Leibniz developed an instantaneous value for a rate of change—for example, curvature—as close as possible to the minimum difference between the variables plotted as a series of connected points on an x/y coordinate system. His method, which we now know as calculus, simultaneously heralded the disposability of values that were infinitesimally small in order to assist the calculation of curved areas *and* made indispensable the method of infinite differentiation to calculate these values away. Differentiality denotes both the tendency to discount gaps—seamlessness and continuity—and the ongoing production of intervals or differences that underlies the making of seamless connections. Although I will not pursue Leibniz through the finer details of the calculus, I will invoke his differential thought here, particularly his thought about aesthetic perception as an organizing logic for baroque and then information aesthetics. The baroque can, in its own time, be seen as marking out a topography in which the relations of connection and difference between lived bodies, material objects, *scientia* and the passions formed a mesh of enfolded territories. Increasingly these kinds of relations are also becoming a viable mode for articulating the materiality-information relationships of our contemporary digital habitat. The fold will provide us with a useful concept for inscribing the creases, doublings and separations that characterize the differential relations of bodies and code within information aesthetics.

Further, this topology can be put to work in a temporal mode, mapping a genealogy that produces a vector from the baroque to the digital. The two tendencies in differential calculus, toward the closure of minimum values and toward the infinite, can be expressed nonmathematically through the concepts of convergence and divergence. As I will be suggesting, these are not processes whose outcomes are definitive directions; rather they function as polarities. In digital aesthetics we witness trajectories that move toward or away from one or the other of these polarities. I want to suggest that these movements involve folding: in the case of convergent vectors, the movement is smoother, more of a ripple or fluctuation, whereas in divergent vectors the pleat more sharply describes variable relations of difference. To return to my earlier example, the image of cloning that accompanies and is promoted in the Thylacine project is of a convergence of the variables of genetics and digital technologies. In Natalie Jeremijenko's *OneTree*, the expectation of identity conveyed by the title of the project is blown apart by the divergence and contingencies materialized in the growth of the biological clones. I wish to move primarily in the direction of an elaboration of those aesthetic tendencies belonging to this more sharply pleated topology, rather than toward convergence. Pleated topologies are produced out of relations between bodies/matter and code that productively acknowledge divergence. But convergence and divergence are not mutually exclusive; they offer us poles of attraction within information culture. While concentrating upon divergence it will be necessary to pay some attention to the more culturally dominant counterforce of convergence.

We get a sense of the way polarities might hold together if we think momentarily about the fold in a culinary context. Folding the whites of eggs into the yolks, the cream into the flour, involves an inmixing of separate ingredients so as to maintain something of their singular properties (what each brings to the other) *and* to combine them into a new consistency. The question that folding poses is precisely this: how can differences or singularities hold together to produce something that forms a consistency only via combinatorics? Put specifically in terms of the relation between codes and bodies, how do we claim an enfolded digital sensibility that is not predetermined by the parameters of code or delimited by a fading belief in a humanist triumph over the machine? If our relations to corporeality are made different through our encounters with digital technologies, it is not through a cyborgian assimilation to the machine. Computers offer us multiplications and extensions of our bodily actions: cursors that glide across the screen interface, then stagger abruptly at its edges; three-dimensional *anime*-styled dancing characters that direct us to clumsily mimic their stilted disco moves in the "Dance, Dance Revolution" rides that populate gaming arcades; a gaze that swoops and dives over terrain in simulated game landscapes yet frequently crashes into pixellation as machine processing speeds lag behind gamers' actual movements. These multiplications by no means provide seamless matches between body and code; the mismatch characteristic of divergent series triggers the extension of our corporeality out toward our informatic counterparts. Yet this extension is not of itself corporeal but comprises an intensive capacity for being affected by the diverse speeds, rhythms and flows of information. It is this extensive vector that draws embodiment away from its historical capture within a notion that the body is a bounded interiority.

The Superfold

What can we make of these contemporary pleats, drawing us toward yet markedly differentiating us from the informatic universe; pleats through which our bodies are unbound from a predetermined interiority? As Deleuze asks:

> What would be the forces in play, with which the forces
> of man [*sic*] would then enter into a new relation? It would
> no longer involve raising to infinity or finitude but an unlim-
> ited finity, thereby invoking every situation of force in which
> a finite number of components yields a practically unlimited
> diversity of combinations. It would no longer be the fold or
> the unfold that would constitute the active mechanism,
> but something like the *Superfold*, as born out by the foldings
> proper to the chains of the genetic code, and of the potential

of silicon in third-generation machines, as well as by the contours of a sentence in modern literature, when literature merely turns back upon itself in an endless reflexivity.[14]

What would this relation result in if not the possibility, as suggested recently by the advances in cloning and gene therapy, of an infinite number of productions, combinations and recombinations of a finite component: the human? Or, in digital media technologies, the circulation of multiples of the same file, cropping up as an image stored on a CD-ROM, then a downloadable web picture, then a print image in a magazine?[15] It is the notion that this *superfold* envelops an endless production of folds, or endless combinations produced out of an initial set of constant parameters, that interests me here. Deleuze especially implicates code at the core of this process of twisting.[16]

By understanding digital code as part of this broader movement of superfolding we do not need to assign a position of ontological primacy to information. Nor do we need to draw the conclusion that life is now generated as mere simulation or that our relation to the real and all that this encompasses—bodies, others, politics—has imploded. Digital life and culture are as real as any other kind. The question does not revolve around categories of illusion and reality and their maintenance or collapse. Instead, we can treat informatically mediated conditions for life as actual and ask what we can expect to experience under the influence of forces such as superfolding. Far from according digital code a technodeterminist primacy, we can consider it a genetic element in these conditions for life, if we understand the notion of the genetic here as constitutive. As Daniel Smith has argued, Deleuze's notion of the genetic should not be considered equivalent to its deployment by contemporary geneticism as a set of instructions for programming life.[17] Rather, the genetic quality of digital code lies in its positive contribution toward producing the conditions for real or material experience while simultaneously remaining itself determin*ed*, not determin*ing*. Code is always already recombinant, composed out of its differential histories, in which it has entered into combinations with an ensemble of different elements, such as the social, material, and technical.[18] It does not "self-generate" (as in the notion of self-generative code currently dear to models of artificial life), nor is it governed by a set of transcendental conditions.[19] As a constituent, code joins with other components to produce a cultural and aesthetic arena that comprises the territories of embodied experience. It is the manner in which these combinations form, interact and impact upon each other that results in these experiences, not some determining force embedded in the code itself.

The idea of the superfold leads us to contemplate more than the excessive modulations of code that constitute the encoding, production and reception of the image in contemporary media societies, and the supernumerary unraveling of the sequence of the three billion base pairs comprising the human genome. It opens up for us a twisted topology of code folding back upon itself without determinate start or end points: we now live in a time and space in which body and information are thoroughly imbricated. Yet this need not necessitate a mood of cynical malaise, in which we spiral downward into the prison house of code's self-reflexivity, nor must it lead to the production of utopias erected upon a future supported by an excessive investment in technophilic hankering after "the code to end all codes." But in order to steer a narrow path through this miasma of enveloping folds, we need to keep the digital folding out onto something other than itself via a history that ties the digital's superfolding code to a new genealogy. This genealogy would serve as a useful foil, a differential element, for pursuing a more wayward path than the march toward absolute informationalism. So too might a conception of digital code benefit from situating it within a broader assemblage in which its contribution to digital culture is actualized through social and political relations. We need a lens for perceiving the impact of superfolded digitality without collapsing this perception into one of technological determinism or technophilic futurism.

As I have suggested in my introductory chapter, the notion of the machinic is an expansive concept that draws elements such as the technical (including particular technologies like the digital) or particular social formations into its field to produce both an abstract *diagram* that traces the field of intensive relations between elements and an actual *assemblage*. Machinism is therefore both an abstract and a concrete movement that operates between two limit poles: diagram and concretization.[20] The diagram is not the same thing as a computer program waiting to be executed or some genetic commands waiting to instruct. As Deleuze and Guattari suggest, it plays a "piloting" role in steering the multiplicity of potential relations between elements.[21] Located at the other pole is the assemblage, in which the process of machinism is concretized; its elements are given substance; and its functions are expressed within a particular form. An assemblage, as the term suggests, is a composition of elements—matter, technologies, socialities—whose diagrammatic dimensions have been organized into particular relations. A concretization of the diagram into an assemblage suggests a kind of reification of social, technical or political relations. But it is also the outcome of the differential impact that these elements, brought into relation with each other through attraction, circumstance and accident, produce.

In certain concretizations, such as the social formation of the "information age," the digital conjoins with relations of control and "code" functions as a kind of switching mechanism enabling and disabling access to information and to connectivity: "The digital language of control is made up of codes indicating whether access to some information should be allowed or denied. We're no longer dealing with a duality of mass and individual. Individuals become '*dividuals*' and masses become samples, data, markets, or '*banks*.'"[22] Within an information society, then, digital codes can function as devices for controlling flows of information. Hence, projects for the conversion of material entities, such as human bodies, into digital data are often accompanied by claims of greater control over life itself. James Watson, who headed the public arm of the HGP, made such claims for the control over the material aspects of life that genetic information would provide: "Well, the goal was just to understand life better and when you understand life better you understand disease better. Everyone in their families has particular diseases you'd like to come to grips with. The goal of the Human Genome Project is to understand the genetic instructions for human beings."[23] Increasingly, the language of control that manages and regulates information does not operate through the exclusionary categories of on versus off, access versus denial, material life versus dematerialized information. The shift from digital (encoded, stored, fixed and archival management of data) to networked (distributed, connected and mobile datastreaming) information means that control operates by always being "on." The more connected one is—through mobile phones that are Internet enabled, through wireless technologies accessed via laptops and personal data assistants—the more "access" one has to the world of information, and concomitantly, the more one is profiled, monitored and available to information itself. Hence, control operates less by a strict division between having and not having information than by variations in the degree of access available. The increasing seamlessness—the convergence—of various information spheres such as databanks or mobile and wireless communications folding into each other is now emerging as the concrete formation of a networked information society.[24]

But the potential for other formations of digital culture are not exhausted by this assemblage, and there are indeed ways in which a range of other machinic possibilities for digitality continues to appear despite the kind of stifling conjunctions a "control society" ordains. In certain aesthetic concretizations, digital code is not simply a data translator and manager but a qualifier; its codifying processes may also add something to the mix.

This has especially been the case with experimental digital audio. Many of the audio artists who belong to the online discussion list *.microsound,* founded in 1999, have been involved with producing tracks from the sounds made by the artefact of digital signaling processes.[25] Kim Cascone, an electronic composer who has been working since the late 1970s, became particularly interested in the random corruptions of signal—glitches and "malfunctions" of the "play" command—that are produced as sound is sampled and processed through digital audio technologies. Although Cascone's "aesthetics of failure" can be seen as iterative of various modernist artistic strategies, the difference here is that this corruption of signal is entirely internal to the digital technologies being used. It is the result of noise that interrupts the signal not from an external (nondigital) source but rather from the intensive entropy of digital information. As Cascone states, "it is from the 'failure' of digital technology that this new work has emerged: glitches, bugs, application errors, system crashes, clipping, aliasing, distortion, quantization noise, and even the noise floor of computer sound cards are the raw materials composers seek to incorporate into their music."[26] This additive propensity of digital code comes as something of a surprise if we consider the time of the digital purely as one of informationalism, of the seamless conversion of everything to code. After all, the conventional wisdom accompanying digitization is that it offers to keep down the quantity of noise produced by the "analogy machine," as von Neumann put it in his early distinctions between digital and analog processes.[27]

Interestingly, Cascone's "aesthetics of failure" has mutated into a new form within a networked information environment. Rethinking the ideas of systems theory and possibly a systems aesthetic that permeated information theory and experimental art practice through the 1960s and 1970s, Cascone has parceled out his work from the *Parasites* CD as samples to be reworked and mutated by other members of the *.microsound* list.[28] Other audio users in a networked environment now contribute to the deformation of the "original" audio signals, producing new signals by reprocessing already processed sound through their variations and recombinations of digital processing techniques. Aesthetic failure thus transforms into something immanent to the *networked system* rather than simply internal to digital technologies. Although microsound aesthetics and practices exist at the more experimental edge of digital audio production, there is plenty of evidence to suggest that the use of remixing and processing sound files in networked environments has emerged as a defining trend of contemporary digital sound. Many websites operate at the front end of servers that are store-houses of sampled, remixed, "mashed-up" commercial and noncommercial audio tracks. Sampling audio to remake new audio tracks has a history that stretches back into both 1980s rap and experimental audio groups such as Negativland. But the widespread and distributed processing of digital audio into clashes of music genre and mangled and mutated sound has been the result of an increased network connectivity from the late 1990s onward.

Perhaps, then, there are ways in which the digital can be actualized that neither eliminate the ability of code to add something different to the mix nor reduce code to an operation of erasing the differential intervals that dent it. If we were to rethink contemporary digital culture through a su-perfolded topology, we would need to seek out the spaces in which code ceaselessly gives rise to novel rather than repeated combinations. It will be my argument throughout this book that information aesthetics is capable of offering us both a critical commentary that folds back upon the broader flows of a more reductive information culture *and* a new kind of aesthetics that unfolds into new sensory spaces for lived experience. Before turning to further analysis of information aesthetics, I will prefigure the history of these folded topographies by comparing digital culture to baroque aes-thetics. Part of the process of shifting digital culture away from its regula-tory role as a tool of conversion and erasure involves setting it adrift from the determinist narratives of technological progress that act to constrain its wilder aesthetic tendencies.

Folding the Digital and the Baroque

The fold does not simply raise questions in the present; it is also a mode of gathering present textures up and understanding them in relation to their histories. In his exploration of Leibniz's philosophy and its relation to the sciences and arts of the seventeenth and eighteenth centuries, De-leuze examines the fold as an operation through which baroque style is produced.[29] Folds can be discerned in abundance in the representation of fabrics in painting and sculpture of the early modern period, and they have their conceptual corollaries in the then-common notion of worlds dou-bling worlds within worlds. This understanding of an enveloped and un-folding set of relations organizing the world was detailed in the blossom-ing area of microscopy. In 1676, Anthony van Leeuwenhoek reported to the British Royal Society the microscopic observation of vast numbers of tiny animals within water doused with pepper and left to sit for three weeks.[30] The notion that an entire realm of unobserved activity and being existed in microcosmic form within everyday matter excited the activities of Dutch, British and Italian naturalists from the late seventeenth through the mid-eighteenth centuries and spurred the development of new styles of engraving and scientific illustration that combined the multiple angles made available through the microscope into composite drawings. In the images that graced Robert Hooke's *Micrographia*, these vibrant volumetric illustrations appear to lift the little animals right off the page.[31] Similar imaginings of doubled worlds were also the starting point for Leibniz's metaphysics of substance.

As the philosopher of the monad, Leibniz understood this primary unit of substance to hold and open out onto an infinite universe but to represent this expanse from a particular point of view.[32] He also conceived of a form of differential calculus that provided a method for measuring the degrees of curves that converged upon the infinite decrease of differences between the angles of lines at tangents to the curves. Leibniz was preoccupied with both an ontology and a method that courted, approached and literally unfolded onto the notion of the infinite. This sense of the infinite unfolding of life in Leibniz is best detected through the way in which he doubly treats questions of identity and matter. He was plagued by the dualism lingering between mind and body in post-Cartesian metaphysics, in which rational thought as the lynchpin of human identity had been posited upon the principle of noncontradiction. The thinking being must be extricated from the confusion of his or her opposite: the sensory world. For Leibniz, the problem was not so much how to extract a metaphysical substance like the soul or mind from matter but rather how matters, souls or beings differentiated themselves by degree within what he saw as a serially connected, continuously folding universe.[33] Rather than Descartes's deployment of extension to assign matter a quality distinct from mind, Leibniz saw instead a doubly enfolded and differentiated world: "that there is no part of space which is not full; that there is no part of matter which is not actually divided, and which does not contain organic bodies; that there are also souls everywhere, as there are bodies everywhere; that souls and animals even, always subsist; that organic bodies are never without souls, and that souls are never separated from all organic body."[34]

This thematic of connectivity has become a major concern for working out a notion of embodied life in digital times. From theorizations of the role of global telecommunications as connectors across vast cultural differences, which have steadily gained favor since Marshall McLuhan's "global village," to wilder speculations about underlying species connectionism in the discovery that humans share parts of their genome with other species, the idea that we are increasingly closer to others has become something of a digital mantra. But we should be careful to note that connection can easily become a metaphor and an apology for a sociality lubricated by the overheated promise of technologies of communication. This is an issue I follow in greater detail in the next chapter, when I examine the permeation of digital culture and technologies with the connectionist models spawned by the life sciences.

The fold, with its marks of differentiation ruffling and twisting the surface of the world's infinite continuity, keeps these relations between unity and multiplicity, soul and body, continuation and difference uppermost. And it is the fold, as it conjoins with unfolding in seventeenth-century theories of preformation, in the gratuitous folds of fabric in baroque costume, in the intertwined frames of reference for baroque arts, as painting spills into architecture, architecture into sculpture, that is the operative concept and mode of distribution for these territories. Leibniz's philosophy does not need to be invoked as an architectonic for baroque thought and culture but can be seen as something also folded by the event of the baroque. Should we presume, then, that we are now experiencing a modulation of the baroque, unfolding in the present hybridization of code and organic matter being wrought by information culture? Are cyborgs the inheritors of an early modern predilection for medico-scientific freaks and monsters?

The relationship of baroque folds to contemporary superfoldings impinges on a broader theoretical issue concerning the invocation of the past in the present, and furthermore, of *which* past is solicited in relation to *what* present. This is not simply an issue of what conditions the present, but of how history, whether it be medical history, a history of ideas or art history, can be produced *so as* to impinge upon us now, to bend the lines of force figuring the present. We need to understand here a reworking of the concept of event in which occurrences, eras, epochs do not simply proceed from start to finish. The latter is a perception of the event dear to contemporary Western media societies, which are obsessed with presenting discrete, packaged information. Instead, an event lands one in the midst of processes that have their own mode of continuation and discontinuity beyond the arbitrary cutoff points of art histories or social histories.

We are not simply playing out some baroque inheritance by encouraging aesthetic forms of production based around multiples—the trailer that becomes the movie that is connected to its Web site and re-released into a DVD—made excessively available for consumption through digital manipulation. Nor do I wish to draw a parallel between baroque ornamentation (and its use of devices such as *trompe l'oeil*) and postmodern simulation, although, inevitably, there are comparisons to be made. Rather, I am interested in the strategy of appealing to the baroque in the context of contemporary productions of self, embodiment and artwork, particularly those productions hinging upon the interface, or fold, between corporeality and informatic code. Although there is no clear line of connection between the baroque and the digital, there is some strategic mileage to be gained by nominating the fold as the operative concept for both.

By choosing to start with baroque folding in the context of thinking through information aesthetics, a series of events or folds opens up for investigation; folding is a philosophical concept, then, that forces one to craft thought along certain genealogical lines.[35] The fold becomes a strategy for dealing with history or time from the point of view of the present: a way to read events not as historical inevitabilities but as pliable possibilities for the present. The question becomes not *what* is the fold, but rather *how* does the baroque unfold, *how* does the present enfold, and so on. This vibratory notion of the event can set up transhistorical relations between its operations, cutting across neat periodizations such as the placement of the baroque between the renaissance and neoclassicism. Thinking through the baroque as an unfolding ongoing event allows us to see its virtual and actual relations to computational culture and therefore to understand culture according to new modalities. Nevertheless, the transhistoricism of the fold or the event does not mean that we should forgo the differential topology that marked the baroque and situated it historically. Rather than an aesthetic period, the baroque can be circumscribed as a "plateau" of folding.[36] There is a sense in which a certain set of intensities, or internal qualities, are played out in many of the philosophies, arts and sciences of the early modern period. The fold is both a transversal and a specific concept. Its transversality bears witness to its vectorial tendencies to cut across the confinements and limitations of predefined social, aesthetic and philosophical histories. Yet each cut and traversal across socialities, thought and aesthetics gathers up new relations among these and singularizes the way in which a specific intensification of folds produces new perceptions and affects at a particular time. Invoking Manuel de Landa's schematization of the processual relation between the virtual and the actual, the baroque could be thought of as a virtual force that impresses itself upon and shapes the contours of digital culture.[37] But equally the processes through which this virtual tendency plays out are concretized specifically and mark out the actual topographies of either baroque or digital times. What these different topographies might look like will become clearer if we begin to trace the distinctive contours of their respective aesthetics.

The Sensory Folds of Baroque Aesthetics

Aside from his metaphysical contributions, Leibniz also made a number of forays into the territory of aesthetics. He was interested in the exploration of sensory perception based on what emerged from indistinct and minor perceptual experiences occurring at the margins of responsiveness to the world. Jeffrey Barnouw argues that Alexander Baumgarten's mid-eighteenth-century coining of the term "aesthetics" as a field demarcating feeling and experience owes much to the continuum of perception conceived first by Leibniz.[38] Leibniz's reply to the Cartesian separation between indistinct and confused sensory ideas and ideas formed with clarity through the deployment of reason was to concatenate clear and indistinct perception as a series. Thus the "illuminated" idea valued by Descartes was for Leibniz only part of a process of formation through which minute, marginal perceptions gradually differentiated into sensings of the world. The perfectly distinct and clear perception of the world was not evidence of perception freed from sensation but rather a folding of perceptual awareness that has turned toward consciousness and light. This serial composition of perception that saw it unfold out of a sustained relation to the sensate body also allowed for the conscious moment of illumination or self-awareness to enfold or decompose back into the margins of darkness and the infinite variety of indistinct perceptions. In fact, for Leibniz, perception and sensation operated as two distinct if entwined differential processes. Auditory perception, for example, emerged as a qualitative extraction of sound from the infinite variety of sounds "murmuring" in perpetual concert with each other, almost "beating" our ears into particular rhythms of listening.[39] Leibniz famously used the example of the murmuring of waves to call up the infinite variation in perception suggested by auditory events. He maintained that the perceiving "soul" would remain confused by this variety if it were unable to qualitatively discern one particular aural perception from among them. The baroque universe of Leibnizian perception is one of vibrating events and murmurs impacting upon one other, one in which distinction occurs as a result of bodies contracting particular and clear perceptions into their local spheres. Perception and sensation are held together through a relation of divergent analogy, a relation that I would suggest holds them apart yet is also connective: folding.

We can begin to characterize the baroque aesthetic as a deep ripple that disturbs the firm opposition between clear and confused perceptions. Resisting the assignation of a periodicity to the baroque and moving toward this more textural understanding might also allow us to grasp how its aesthetic forces refused to be hemmed in by classicism. This latter direction had already begun to gather speed in the physics, optics and philosophy of Descartes before it regrouped around the twin vectors of empiricism and rationalism during the enlightenment. The baroque could be seen as a particular kind of artistic, scientific and cultural "war machine" at odds with the program of classical science. In Deleuze and Guattari's topography, the war machine can be any cultural or political movement that aims at producing a different kind of spatiality, one involving flux, heterogeneity and differentiation.[40] This is produced outside of the forces of the state, which aim for classified, discrete, and calculable space that can be easily territorialized. From the viewpoint of classicism, the baroque resists the dominant current of seventeenth- and eighteenth-century Western rationalism through its deployment of infinite regresses, its appeal to the ambivalence of allegorical interpretation, its pursuit and delight in multiple layers of visual artifice, and most importantly its aesthetics of seriate continuity, developed between the senses and consciousness in its articulation of perception. Christine Buci-Glucksmann calls the baroque an excessive "other" to classical philosophy, literature and art: "the baroque presents from the beginning quite a different, 'postmodern' conception of reality in which the instability of forms in movement opens onto the reduplicated and reduplicable structure of all reality."[41]. Buci-Glucksmann foregrounds the distorting aspects of baroque visual space, with its emphasis on anamorphosis and use of allegorical devices, such as the ruin and the labyrinth, that favor fragmentation over unification.[42] Yet we need to be careful not to simply produce further oppositions here—the baroque as "other" to the dominant strands of rationalism and classicism in modern Western culture.

The notion of a stylistic duel taking place between classical aesthetics, philosophy and science, on one hand, and the voluptuous, effeminate and sensual baroque, rococo or mannerist cultural productions, on the other, is a common motif used to impart periodicity in art history.[43] The problem with this approach is that it tends to assign a place for baroque style only within the confines of classicism's own system. The baroque and its various derivatives then begin to appear as cultural symptoms of the cracks and ruptures opened up when dualities fail to maintain their due distance from each other, and when the perfect symmetry of renaissance form destabilizes. The baroque returns, as it were, whenever faith wavers in the tenets of reason to resolve its own crises. One can see those elements—effeminacy, excessiveness and artifice—resurface to signal the rumblings of repressed thought or "baroque reason."[44]

This argument, which assigns interiority to the baroque within classicism and rationalism, is not recent. Henry Wolfflin, the nineteenth-century art historian, saw the baroque as delimited by the renaissance on the one hand and classicism on the other.[45] Arguing that for two hundred years the baroque entailed a dispersion of and reaction against regularity, completion and stability, he argued: "The baroque never offers us perfection and fulfillment, or the static calm of 'being,' only the unrest of change and the tension of transcience."[46] Wolfflin attributed the predilection for massive and disproportionate form that Italian baroque architects displayed in much of their religious architecture to an indication of "art in decline."[47] Similarly, he found that his own nineteenth-century *fin de siècle* malaise exhibited a "baroque sensibility"; in other words, a tendency toward excess, effeminacy and the grandiose that had been precipitated by a crisis in reason and its classical aesthetic supports. The underlying logic of these readings of the baroque construes it largely as reactive and oppositional; it manifests itself in terms of rupture along the fault line of Western reason's abyss or void.

But greater than these images of splintering and crisis, the baroque offers a kind of sumptuousness, amplitude and mannered affectation that does not necessarily resonate with rupture or automatically imply the presence of a rational center against which it competes. If there is a crisis in classical reason, then the baroque is not simply the negative answer to that schism in being. It is instead an attempt to shift an understanding of the world away from essence and its adjuncts of subject and non-subject and toward belonging. World and self, thought and sensory perception, science and matter do not stand apart from each other as separate substances but rather emerge in a seriate fashion.

The rationalist legacy of the Cartesian system is driven by the desire to erect truth upon a pure essence—rational thought—that has been detached from anything that would disrupt its clarity. But Leibniz, as exemplary of baroque thought, is preoccupied with how different substances, body and soul, animal and human, organic and inorganic, can belong, in their continuity and in their differentiation, both to each other and to the same world. The "other" is not so much what one confronts across a divide or what one uses to define the rational self against; the baroque "other," in fact, is already implicated by living in the world. This is a world in which humans must have bodies in order to express and perceive and in order to be receptive to the actions of other bodies. But these bodies also "have" other bodies (the animalcule revealed in microscopy, for example), which contain the bodies of other animals ad infinitum. This is a relation of bodies to each other contoured in terms of a series that encloses, envelops and *enfolds,* but it is equally a series moving in an alternate direction, unfolding outward toward its next undulation.

Substance is thrown into flux and movement by Leibniz's interconnected monads. This maneuver also resonates with both the seriate and the ascending movements prominent in Bernini's and Borromini's sculptures or in the dramatic religious paintings undertaken by the various Spanish and Italian baroque schools. Here the eye sweeps around the canvas, rolling from the bottom of paintings upward through angels and clouds to be almost carried away as virgins and saints are assumed into the skies. The billowing of clouds, the undulation of folds in fabric and the rippling of anatomical muscles in a painting such as Juan de Valdés Leal's *Assumption of the Virgin* (1659) all assist in energizing the image into a flurried movement (figure 3).

But things do not simply turn into an undifferentiated fluxus. Following the logic of the fold, matter must be thought of not simply as what occupies space (geometrical extension) but as what space "belongs" to, what intrinsically maps out a spatiality according to its own qualities or texture. The qualitative relations that inhere in matter provide it with its capacities, power, and force. According to Leibniz, the capacities of matter do not maintain the identity of substance (the ontological requirement for essence) but instead produce change and difference: "Accordingly, there must always be presupposed something which continually acts or spreads out, as the white color of milk, the glitter, malleability and weight of gold, the resistance of matter. . . . Hence I believe that our thought of substance is perfectly satisfied in the conception of force and not in that of extension. Besides, there should be no need to seek any other explanation for the conception of power or force than that it is the attribute *from which change follows and its subject is substance itself.*"[48]

Inasmuch as the Leibnizian system implies both an extrinsic unfolding toward others—shifting the solitary identity of the contained monad—and an intrinsic folding of the twists and surfaces of all matter, a continual displacement of essence occurs. It is a question of asking not what the individual thing is or is not but rather how the capacities of different substances force their unfolding, their production of a particular kind of spatiality. Furthermore, how is one topography of folding different from another? Not what *occupies* space, but what twists and folds of substance can occupy space, and therefore *spatialize,* in different ways? What relations are made compossible by the simultaneous folding/unfolding of different substances?[49] Thus the baroque cannot be viewed merely as the set of signs marking discord within classical reason. It is a different concep-

FIGURE 3. Juan de Valdés Leal, *The Assumption of the Virgin*
c. 1658/1660), oil on canvas. Samuel H. Kress Collection, Image
© 2005 Board of Trustees, National Gallery of Art, Washington.

tual and aesthetic space that may develop alongside and interact with or
even precipitate these crises, yet it is not reducible to them.

The political forces of convergence ultimately close the infinite differential of individuation and belonging that the baroque of seventeenth-century
Europe conjures. Rather than a continuing series of folds, differentials and
modulations comprising the world as a folding, the baroque is actualized as
a smoothing out of creases through accord, harmonization and the reintegration of fragments. With Leibniz we encounter his *Theodicy,* a justifica-
tion of the world of absolute monarchism as the best of all possible worlds;
teleology emerges to direct provisional curvature toward the legitimation of
a definite socius and polis.[50] Within music the dissonant chord, the differ-

ential in the chromatic series pursued in the *basso continuo* of European baroque music, is always subsequently resolved harmonically at the end of a chordal series.[51] As José Maravall has argued, the absolute monarchy of European states became the instrument for hampering the forces of social mobility and flux and the sense of self-conscious despair and crisis threatening to run amok during the early modern period.[52] The state succeeded in maintaining political stability. Hence we could say that the early modern baroque is piloted by a virtuality in which the world continuously unfolds, in which aggregates of matter shift toward each other and in which a mode of existence is forged through the intersection of infinite lines fleeing toward animality, the senses and, as we shall see in the next chapter, the inorganic. But equally unfolding in this baroque were the questions of sovereignty and the emergence of the nascent nation-state. These relations produce the actual baroque of seventeenth- and eighteenth-century Europe by closing down and recontaining its virtuality through the theology and moral philosophies of necessity and destiny and the politics of absolutism.

A Folded Sense of the Digital

Do the dominant ways in which we presently configure our relations to others and to what continues to be named as "other" (corporeality, animality, racial difference, machines, to name only a few) remain indebted to the forces of classicism? In the tropes we use to depict our relations to digital technology, above all the term "interface," we have continued to deploy a mode of separating ourselves from materiality, thus recalling the classical separation of mind and matter. The interface appears as a figure to rejoin what has already been separated out from and hardened against the flux of material existence. The machine is conceived as something that we confront across the void of the world and that we can only ever connect with through a "face to screen" confrontation or communication. This meeting attempts to erase the interval between different substances, human and machine, through instrumentalism, which is popular in cyberculture, or a reductionism in which the digital machine is configured anthropomorphically as a supermind.[53] Or else, as is common in corporate hype, the new technological machine becomes the conduit for connecting a disparate, dispersed world. This comes at the cost of laying cables right across its diasporas, suggesting that a new kind of technological absolutism might be at work. Here, interfacing with technology comes to be seen as the instrument for global social reintegration. This classical inheritance that the digital maintains has been well documented by a number of writers, themselves critics and practitioners of contemporary technologies.[54] But railing against digital technology's antecedents is not enough; other forces are at work here, forces not just of stasis, consolidation and control but also of movement and becoming. If the baroque is not simply a delimited epoch but can be seen as a set of forces crafting a differential topos, then it becomes politically exigent now to trace the folded topography yielded by entwined embodied, aesthetic and technological relations.

In Kim Cascone's CD *Dust Theories,* released in 2001, the audio travels in undulated forms, as if squeezing itself into and pushing itself out of the signal processing to which it has been subjected.[55] Continuing to craft compositions with "residual" sound—using artefact and stripped-back audio generated during digital signal processing—Cascone reroutes the already fragmented audio through software called MAX/MSP. MAX is a programming environment that allows users to create their own software out of various "objects" or media behaviors joined together as "patches" (figure 4).[56] Digital media signals from audio to text to video can be processed through the MAX environment, and an increasing number of new media artists are using it to create complex real-time interactions between sound and visual elements. MAX/MSP denotes an audio signal processing environment, and Cascone has used this extensively to produce the qualities that inhere in his *Dust Theories* tracks. Cascone's audio oscillates in an expanding and contracting manner along the edges of fullness and imperceptibility. At times the signal sounds almost organic, like fermenting liquid, but as it develops it immediately falls off, tapering away into an increasing compression. Using a patch he built in the MAX/MSP environment, Cascone produced the tracks by mixing down four different audio players that were being fed random sound files from a database on his computer. The result is a playoff between signals that have been processed according to a particular behavior—a filter, a type of compression—and a sense of indeterminacy generated by the random grabbing of the various files. Of this modulated audio topography, Cascone states:

> A lot of people have said that they hear insects, or birds . . .
> I guess there's a little bit of the misty bog kind of thing, this
> natural synthetic habitat. That's the other interest of mine—
> I'm not really into narrative, I'm really into different kinds of
> space. I don't particularly like to have a point A, point B, start,
> finish—I just like to throw you into a space. I like for people
> to build their own narrative, whatever they want to do with
> that space. If they want to envision themselves in a field, or
> there are crickets, or birds, or what have you, I think I'm

more comfortable with that than A, B, C sharp. I'm not really into loop-oriented performances for non-beat-oriented music, either. I find it kind of boring. I like to keep things moving.[57]

Here we get a sense of the movement and production of spatiality that are characteristic of an aesthetics underpinned by the operations of folding and unfolding. Furthermore, as is becoming typical of artists working with new media technologies such as MAX, the *Dust Theories* CD contains tracks by other artists—Ben Neville and DJ4′33″—who have remixed Cascone's audio. The CD also includes the MAX/MSP patches used in their remixes, and these can then be reused by others to mix again. Thus the potential for producing and remaking audio is opened up beyond the limit of the audio product *Dust Theories*. Instead, the audio functions as an ele-

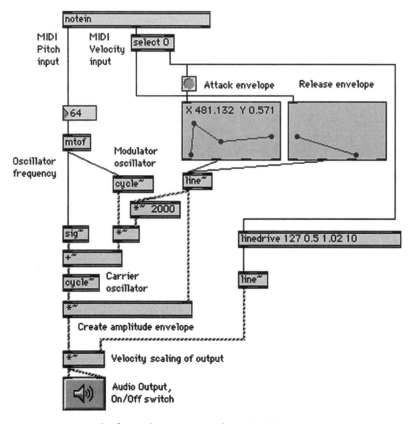

FIGURE 4. An example of a "patch" written using the MAX/MSP programming environment. MAX © 1990–2005 Cycling '74/IRCAM. MSP © 1997–2005 Cycling '74.

ment in a larger "information environment" that involves the artist, the signal, the software tools, other artists and a potential field of other unknown users. The *Dust Theories* tracks start to behave like digital monads contracting audio spaces into themselves while also opening up onto an entire system of information aesthetics.

We cannot expect to experience a direct mirroring of the serially connected textures of baroque fabric, knowledge and matter in information aesthetics. But we may be able to trace a trajectory that begins with the differential movement of baroque folding and reverberates through a contemporary machinic superfolding. What if, alongside the reduplication of the Cartesian schematic of mind over body that has dominated many conceptions of cyberspace, virtual reality and the body-machine interface, there might also be a Leibnizian world of serial continuity enfolding through divergence? This mode of folding pushes us out toward a realization that "humanness" or "machineness" are nodes comprised of wound-up spaces, and that the inside of each—although folded in on itself to demarcate an individuated space—also nestles against the outside of another node.

The point is to maintain a sense of the differential here: how do we both individuate and connect within a folding that seems, in terms of information technologies, to be accelerating temporally and diminishing spatially? Can we continue to think through differences as they become increasingly infinitesimal and threaten to become less divergent and then pass merely into fluctuations of a universal code, genetic or digital? The digital has been described in terms of its nondifferentiation of cultural and aesthetic spaces.[58] Yet by focusing on emerging aesthetic spheres, such as microsound composers or recent explorations in the field of hyperarchitecture, we can see how both convergence and divergence in the digital fold play themselves out within information topographies. This suggests that digitization is not of necessity a process that erases difference in the translation to code but that it can in fact again open up the legacy that the baroque interval bequeaths us.

The fold and its terminology of pliancy, flexibility, complexity and emergence have become part of the new processes, practices and conceptual apparatus for a range of architects and designers, including most notably Greg Lynn, Bernard Cache, Jeffrey Kipnis, the work of UN Studio architects Ben van Berkel and Caroline Bos, Foreign Office architects and Asymptote.[59] There is a broader shift that has transpired in the wake of the formal conflicts and fragmentations that marked the peak of deconstructivist architecture and its theorization during the 1970s and 1980s.[60] Brian Massumi has termed this shift "topological" to describe the way in which architecture itself transforms and follows the variable deformations of spatial form along the temporal unfolding of a series.[61] Coincidentally or not, this topological turn has also been accompanied by the widespread use of computer-aided design and by architects exploring the three-dimensional modeling software, such as Form Z, Alias and Maya, used initially by special effects animators from the film industry. These programs operate within the usual Cartesian grid space of the x, y, z coordinate axes. Yet they also allow for the surface manipulation and deformation of 3-D models through Bezier curve formation and drawing tools. Hence, enclosing or opening surface grids can generate volumetric models. By selecting a series of weighted or "spline" points around which the wire-frame mesh of the form is built or calculated, the model's geometry can remain volumetric but be transformed at the level of pure surface manipulation. Another kind of space or geometry, embedded within the unifying and extensive space of the Cartesian system, emerges. This is an immanent space produced differentially by continual variations performed on the surface that subsequently *creates* the volumetric space.

Although topology and its complex geometries preceded computation by a good century, the visualization of three-dimensional non-Euclidean spaces, in which curvatures cut across, fold back upon, twist around and stack upon each other, has been accelerated by these digital modeling processes.[62] During the early 1990s, much of the deformation of form in architecture took place only within the computer. Cyberarchitects such as Marcus Novak produced spaces for navigation and imagination, but they were not then realizable.[63] Increasingly, the effects of digitally generated topological and complex geometries are being realized as built form.

In 2002, the team of Foreign Office architects completed their design for the Yokohama Port Authority. Not only did the modeling for the pier require the use of complex topological geometries but the actual cutting and molding of many of the materials also needed computer-aided programming and prototyping. Although it is wildly contrasting with almost all previously realized pier and harbor architecture, the Yokohama Port Authority does not simply produce a confrontation between computational and physical environments. The spatial orientation of traditional pier architecture reflects the functionalism of the pier's place within industrialized societies. In this context, a pier should function as a space of maximum efficiency, with two directions, out and in, for shunting goods and people from the city into the world and vice versa. A pier's narrow linearity out into the harbor and hub of transportation should—in this functionalist approach—streamline the movement into a double flow, outward and back again. But the Yokohama Port Authority building invents a new space for the pier with its folding and cutting planes and surfaces. The physical environment of air and water are folded into the interior of sections of the building; likewise, part of the building's roof dips down and meets the ground, narrowing its internal spaces.

Although characterizing a shift in architectural practice toward topology is useful for thinking about these new spatial conditions, we need to acknowledge a tension in the spawning of these folded surfaces that also inhabits the virtuality of any digital aesthetics. It comprises an unfolding toward an outside that is radically different—whether this be organic matter, human subjectivity, or other heterogeneous elements such as the physical environment—together with an enfolding of external elements back into a form of codification enacted via the digitized sampling of differences. Architecture's topological turn, imbricated as it is with digital technologies, stretches across a field drawn by these tense directions. The more it veers toward folding external elements into computational variables, enabling the convergence within an abstract information space of all of the properties deforming and exerting pressure upon that space, the more it tends toward digital formalism. This formalism seeks coherence across any series of differential changes.

In Greg Lynn's computationally produced project *Embryologic Housing* (1996), a prototype of prefabricated housing is modeled in three-dimensional space. This is then animated, and a new form is selected at each stage of the animation, giving rise to a series of differentiated forms. The series is produced by applying deformational forces that are *internal to the computational space*. These forces are generated by codifying both the properties assigned to the forms themselves (for example, forces of attraction or repulsion preassigned to the meshes and activated by the deformations) and external variables. Some of these include estimations or calculations of, say, the environmental pressures that might be exerted by proximate automotive movement upon the surface of the building in the environment into which it will be built. So, although the computational form is produced in relation to external differences in its future environment, these differences are nevertheless reduced to fluctuations that can be translated into informatic code.

On the one hand, computational space in the hands of "topological" architects demonstrates the potential to become a dynamic space of interactions. Aggregate forms emerge through the interaction that the calculated properties of models exert upon each other in a localized field. Across a number of these interactions, or through a deformation applied temporally to the aggregates, these forms unfold as differently inflected entities maintaining some measure of continuity. On the other hand, the resultant renderings of such transformations are themselves simply new "blob" forms that, taken out of informational space and the temporal unfolding of dynamic process within the computer, threaten to become simply static representations of a new architectural style that flaunts differentiation as a mere variable of digital process.[64]

This tendency toward the aesthetics of purely formal, computational space is, however, offset by the assemblages—commercial, built environment, governance and urban planning relations—through which architecture necessarily actualizes itself, a point made by both Massumi and Stephen Perrella.[65] Through the conversion of the external world into digital parameters, the computer is privileged as an abstract space that accommodates processes of differentiation. To what extent would this reduce to mere calculable variation the indeterminacy introduced into this digitized aesthetic by such elements as environment, bodies passing through space or the uses to which design and built form are put? The informatic space must continue to extend outward toward the concrete thing it is destined to become without accounting for, and hence assimilating, every potential concretization.

In addition, there are architects and designers exploring the intensive differentiated space of digital aesthetics who foreground the interval or gap in their work. This interval opens wherever digital spaces extend into assembled spaces with external environments, other bodies, and other matter. For Bernard Cache, an interior and object designer, the differential calculability enabled by computer-aided design is not the end point to be achieved through the process of folding. His digital manipulation of the surface and curvature of objects through the infinite variability of the computed topological inflection of forms allows him to produce a series of actual objects that are nonstandardized in shape.[66] For Cache, computational design becomes a means of moving away from automation and the use of the computer-designed model as a predictable prototype. He moves instead toward exploring the variations to which informatic objects can be subjected. Produced as wall panels, tables, shelves and chairs, his furnishings fix attention upon curvatures and finish, drawing out the grain of their materiality and drawing across this materiality with computationally directed lines for shaping their forms. The result is the formation of an abstract meandering of cut and shape across the surface of wooden objects, recalling topographical maps or complex, unnavigable geometries. The object exists at the space of the fold between its own matter—wood, plastic, metal—and the directions left by a more abstract space, the information-scape embedded within its form.

Cache has himself referred to the importance of the inflection point: that twist through which a curve changes its direction toward convexity or concavity.[67] This is the single most variable point on a curve, the point at which it is most differentiated and most liable to vectorial change. This inflection can move the curve in a completely different direction, and yet it speaks of continuity as well, remaining within a general geometry of curvature. For Cache, this point of inflection evokes a baroque stylistics that follows the twists of a continuous yet varying curve from obscurity to clarity, monad to world, gravity to weightlessness, floor to ceiling. Furthermore, it is the inflection point that sets the course for the kind of spiraling vertigo that sometimes seems to be the dominant affect of the baroque arts. In these twists and turns of the fold, direction itself slips: we lose the ground that globally embeds space and give ourselves over to the slippery, pleated spaces of surfaces themselves. We could also say of Cache's objects that they are riven with these kinds of inflections; his furniture seems to follow the folds of its own material composition yet suddenly gives its form over to the production of impossible lines. The cuts and curves in his objects take us back into the digital universe of infinite manipulation, where any kind of space might be possible. Cache's objects operate as inflections themselves, folds that extend impossibly across the divergent directions of the concrete and the informatic.

We need some new operative concepts to challenge the notion that contemporary digital culture only ever completes the project of classicism, concepts that unleash those intricate degrees of differentiation posed by the baroque without collapsing them into a universal connectionism. Having set the stage for a nonlinear folding of baroque aesthetics and perception into digital culture, I now wish to explore more fully the relations between knowledge, sense and bodies peculiar to the baroque arts and sciences. Long overdue is a loosening up of some of the well-worn assumptions about the domination of science over nature, mind over body, and knowledge over sensation and matter that accompany our understanding of the seventeenth century as the genesis of modern science. This will help to untie the connections with classicism and enrich our understanding of digital assemblages of information, matter and machines. We can begin to stake out a space instead where one of these need not claim dominion, to the exclusion of the others, over the organization of contemporary aesthetic and cultural experience.

Here is the Sceletus of a Man on Horse-back, of a Tigar, and sundry other creatures: The Skinns of Men and Women tentur'd on frames and tann'd: Two faire and entire Mummies, Fishes, Serpents, Shells, divers Urnes; the figure of Isis cut in wood of a great Proportion and Antiquity; a large Crocodile; the head of the Rynocerous; the Leomarinus, Torpedo, many Indian Weapons, Curiosities out of China, & of the Eastern Countries; so as it were altogether (impossible) to remember all, or take particular notice of them . . .   — JOHN EVELYN, 1641[1]

On page eight, there is a story about computers and chips controlled by the Japanese; on page nine, about the right to keep frozen embryos; on page ten, about a forest burning, its columns of smoke carrying off rare species that some naturalists would like to protect; on page eleven, there are whales wearing collars fitted with radio-tracking devices . . . On page twelve, the Pope, French bishops, Monsanto, the Fallopian tubes, and Texas fundamentalists gather in a strange cohort around a single contraceptive.   — BRUNO LATOUR, 1993[2]

2 natural history and digital history

Naturalizing the Digital

Although it may seem unordinary to couple the natural and the historical, the idea of digital *history* is altogether more pernicious. The digital, as we are constantly reminded, is a new technology, and its newness seems to stretch out toward a future, deemed either dazzling or terrifying, rather than backward to the settled dust of the past.[3] Even if we can successfully locate the beginning of digital technology in computer science and the construction of a calculator capable of storing the programs it was given to run, we have already leapt into 1947.[4] The changes that transform digital technology into digitality—a culturally embedded set of technologies producing new kinds of perceptual and affective experiences—do not follow directly from the introduction of a piece of technology such as the microprocessor. For this to have an effect and to signal the broader cultural phenomenon of a "personal computer revolution," for example, other factors must come into play. As Felix Guattari has suggested with regard to understanding technologies generally, we need "universes of reference" to which computers defer that create the social, cultural and political assemblages that *are* digital technologies and information culture.[5] These assemblages would include the development of standardized programming languages, the rise of venture capital, the rise of 1970s counterculture attitudes toward the democratization of computing technologies and the production of a "need" for every consumer to own a desktop computer. Although, taken as a social-technical ensemble, this approach to understanding digital history does present us with a rich set of problems, *natural* history comparatively possesses a more illustrious past, one able to be traced all the way back to Pliny's *Natural History*.[6] This makes the digital's claim to being treated historically appear somewhat paltry by contrast.

Yet adjacently situating natural history and digital culture can infuse the latter with a broader set of concerns than that offered by locating its genesis in the mid-twentieth century birth of computational machines. Natural history can infect the digital with the rambling practices, discourses and institutions that constituted the early modern projects for conceiving of the natural world. Using a genealogical approach that resonates with the previous chapter's discussion on folding, I will examine more closely the wayward directions at the "origins" of natural science itself. I want to bring its folds between the areas of science/knowledge and the natural world into conjunction with the folding of digital code and biology into each other. These historical baroque folds may provide us with a mode for negotiating contemporary relations between new media technologies and corporeality.

The ways in which history—natural, cultural, social and so on—might be received and understood are being changed by the use of new media in museum environments. There has been significant criticism of multimedia in museums, ranging from the claim that this erases the material artefact base of the museum to the broader claim that the material specificity of history is itself erased in the spectacle of simulated display wrought through digital visualizations.[7] But increasingly museums themselves are branching out into new ways of effectively *making history* by using online interfaces, relational databases and rich media environments to extend and change their modes of display. I want to propose that the use of new media in a number of museum contexts reopens the incipient unruliness of early modern natural history collection and display. The information aesthetics of new media in the contemporary museum context rejoins a baroque aesthetics of nature folding into artifice and of visual conceit entwined with the material world.

Both museums and artists have been using the relational capabilities of new media to evoke pre-Enlightenment museum culture. In an initiative of the Smithsonian Institution's online and new media branch, the *Smithsonian without Walls,* an online prototype exhibition was launched in 1998 called *Revealing Things.*[8] Concentrating on presenting digitized images of everyday objects in the Smithsonian's collection—television sets from different periods of twentieth-century design, or patched jeans, for example— the online site assembles anecdotal fragments, historical knowledge and images into one visual plane. The personal and one-off images of the objects open onto more generalized but perhaps little known historical information. A plain dress, stitched from a sack of flour, can also be accompanied by commentary on the history of fashion: "As the practice intensified during the lean years of the 1930s and 1940s, manufacturers began to print sacks in attractive colors and patterns. The high-quality sacks became a source of barter, and women took charge of selecting feed in order to obtain a desirable fabric."[9]

The difference between the online display of such information and the same kind of information in a physical museum environment does not turn upon a distinction between dematerialized information and the material artefact. Rather, *Revealing Things* is characterized by a sense of movement that traverses the online viewing space, alternating between clustering and flowing snatches of information. This oscillation can also be created in curated exhibitions in physical museum or gallery spaces. In fact, I will suggest later in this chapter that early modern museums were designed around this exact affective experience. What is different about the online space of *Revealing Things* is that the pace, and the tendency toward clustering or flow, is moderated by the actions of the user who navigates it. By rolling the onscreen cursor over thumbnail images of the objects, the user causes a scrolling visual field of objects to pass across the screen. The user then unfolds further information by selecting individual images and thereby "revealing things"—textual fragments, audio files— about the objects. But what is actually revealed as the user becomes more accomplished is not so much things as *relations.* These relations comprise the predetermined datasets constructed in the design of the online display—how an object might call up both anecdotal and broader historical information about its everyday use and its place in catalyzing or playing a part in a series of larger social and cultural events. But these relations also operate at the level of sensation and affect, as tendencies and currents peculiar to user-initiated and modulated rhythms of information flow and the spatialization of information fragments.

The software used to produce the *Revealing Things* prototype is a data visualization program called Thinkmap.[10] This program provides a visual and customizable interface between relational data sets (which can comprise text, audio, images, digital video, Web sites and so on) that is quite different from the goal-directed nature of information search engines. Rather than present users with data they know or believe they want to know, the relational nature of the visualizations concentrates upon making visible relationships among data that the user may not know existed: "Low-level data relationships are defined as part of developing a Thinkmap application, and Thinkmap then depicts the relationships. It is in these depictions, however, that users oftentimes discover relationships, patterns, and meanings in the data that would otherwise not have been apparent."[11] A program such as this is facilitating not simply the formation of relations among data but also the production of a mutable set of relations among code (the developed application), the aesthetics of information (its visual interface) and the specificity of the user's actions and interactions (the navigation of the interface to reveal relationships).

What is missing here, however, is the concrete insertion of the user— her body, interests or passions—into the information environment. And it is precisely this catapulting of the user into a dynamic of participation in digital spaces, in ways that situate the specificity of her actions, perception and corporeality, that is the province of new media art. In George Legrady's installation *Pockets Full of Memories* the physical museum and gallery space is reorganized by information space *and* by visitors to that space (figures 5 and 6).[12] First exhibited at the Pompidou Center in Paris, Legrady's work required visitors to literally empty their pockets and then to scan one of their personal objects into a database. These small memory-laden bits and pieces hold meaning for their individual owners, yet their absorption into the work's database is partially serendipitous. They signal the meeting of a technology for ordering and categorizing with the day-to-day reality of whatever happened to be on a visitor's person the day they visited the center. Once her item was loaded into the data set, the visitor then became a "moderator" of the information connected to the object *and,* often unwittingly, of the relations and patterns in the visual arrangement of the objects as they were redisplayed on a large projected "map." The visitor/participant added a title, descriptive information and a short "story" about her object but also set a series of sliders into place that described degrees of quality concerning the object: old/new, soft/hard, natural/synthetic, disposable/

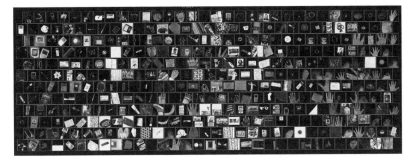

FIGURE 5. *Pockets Full of Memories* 2D visual map of contributed objects organized by the Kohonen self-organizing algorithm. Exhibition at Cornerhouse, Manchester, UK Winter 2005. George Legrady © 2005. Courtesy of the artist.

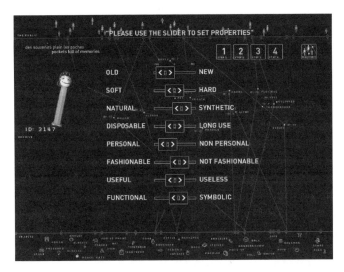

FIGURE 6. Attributes Screen of *Pockets Full of Memories* Questionnaire. George Legrady © 2001. Courtesy of the artist.

long use and so on. In providing this information, the visitor entered into a participatory relationship with the databases, determining where her object—on the basis of its qualities—would be displayed in relation to other participants' objects: "An algorithm classifies the scanned objects in a two-dimensional map based on similarities in their descriptions."[13] The map is organized like a grid of objects; however, because for the duration of the installation new objects are being scanned and added to the database, the visual clustering in the display of the images is constantly changing, creating new patterns and relationships among the individual elements. It is as if each visitor's presence has become a small participatory fold in the larger unfolding of an idiosyncratic information space within the management of information in contemporary museums and galleries. *Pockets Full of Memories* is not a chaotic aggregation of personalized and random information, nor is it a systematic ordering of information into purposeful arrays. Instead, it functions as a production of information space that reverberates with baroque relations between the monad and the universal.

A more common way in which "the natural" has functioned with respect to digital technologies and digital culture is as an embedded mode of ordering and accounting for the "ascendency" of information societies. So, for example, Paul Levinson, in *The Soft Edge,* purports to present a "natural history" of the information revolution: "Information and the structures that disseminate, preserve, and thus shape it are, in their very origin, natural: what else is DNA, and the living structures that it both shapes and is shaped by, if not a system of information technology *par excellence?*"[14] The reduction of the digital to technology, and this technology to informatic code, helps to erase the intervals and disjunctions between the information universe and the natural world. Returning to the years surrounding the development of EDSAC (Electronic Delay Storage Automatic Computer), we first witness the separation of information from matter in the then-reigning discourse of cybernetics.[15] The return to nature in rhetoric about digital culture permits information to reenter the organic world as a cybernetic helmsman. All matter is now steered by the desire to acquire information; it then requires further information input to sustain its closed cybernetic system of life. We are implicitly dealing here with a "natural" system, oriented toward an informatic growth that is directed by information input and output rather than "natural" processes such as nutrition and decomposition. As Levinson states, "the amoeba that lacks information about a noxious element in its vicinity may well embrace it and die."[16] If life is life-threateningly dependent on information, then life's history, *natural* history, can only ever be conceived in terms of events that have occurred internally in information systems. Hence a two-way sleight of hand is contrived, in which the development of information technologies is framed through a concept of natural development: "We should not be surprised, then, to find in the history of information technology, and its current configurations and future projections as well, an evolutionary dynamic in many respects very much like that of the literally natural, organic world."[17] And, simultaneously, the natural world becomes increasingly dematerialized and cybernetic. But where, in Levinson's natural and digital history, has the actual, organic world gone? It functions only as an after-thought; the matter of the universe is configured as an unintended by-product of the information-seeking behavior of code.

In these types of narratives, the recourse to evolutionary agency to account for the temporality of natural history and the emergence of digital life is *naturalizing* rather than natural. There is something comforting about placing nature, however denaturalized, at the genesis of digital events. Henceforth, biology can ultimately be unraveled as code, and code, behaving as code, is only "natural." Levinson's edge is not soft but doubled: it sustains the phasing out of matter and the making of information into the only matter of importance.[18] My intention in revealing the two-way, reductive arguments of digital naturalists such as Levinson is not to sweep out nature. Rather, we need to revisit the histories of both the natural and the digital in nonreductive ways. By doing so we will find that introducing natural history to the history of digital culture produces an enriched account of the aesthetics of information. The ridding of natural *matter* from natural histories of the digital is caught up in an aversion to what is located at the critical genetics of natural history itself—life understood as expanding and contracting, folding and unfolding in a myriad of nonsequential, nonlinear modes.

Genealogy is here to be understood not as a tracing of successive historical stages issuing forth from the fact of a single origin but as the struggle of a relational complex that produces the history of something. This relational complex of forces is paradoxically indeterminate *and* responsible for the genesis of that history. Consequently, the kind of history that a genealogical inquiry produces is differential. It does not follow a fixed trajectory but emerges as the changing outcome or derivative of continually varying quantities of force. In Nietzschean terms, these forces may be expressed as affirmative or reactive, "noble" or "plebeian," strong or weak, and the question for genealogy is to evaluate "the rank among values."[19] That is to say, genealogy must address which forces, which values, have succeeded in taking possession of something, and how the differential of these forces has contributed to the particular formation of the thing. For Nietzsche, Western thought has generally been dominated by reactive, base forces in which knowledge, reason, and philosophy attempt to limit, judge and observe life. Thinking is rarely framed as the possibility of creating or inventing new forms for life or new ways of living. Genealogy acknowledges the material contributions made by perspective and interest yet insists upon the realism of historical events. An effective history would take apart naturalizations or essences such as self, body, the organic, code and technology in order to rethink these as the outcome, the *differential* productions of various systems of subjection. Michel Foucault has called these productions "the hazardous play of dominations."[20]

Embodying the Digital

Rather than foreclosing the relations between matter and machines, perhaps we could ask what "interminglings" between the two are made possible by yoking a sentient body to a computer terminal. In this frequently conjured image of the demise of human activity and the transcendence of "natural evolution" by the incorporeal information universe, the microformation of new modes of corporeal engagement frequently gets neglected. For example, we could ask about the intensive changes in speeds of this mass of carbon matter (the body) that come about through an intensified relation with increasing masses of data. As data increases and the time and space of processing it become ever smaller, so too does the relative sedentariness of a human's body seem to advance. Yet there is also a speeding-up of digital dexterity and a possible intensification of retinal flickering. This is not to suggest that the body is now becoming more like a computer.[21] Instead, the distribution and range of human corporeal movement may have shifted into the interstices of infinitely smaller but more concentrated spaces. There is a *becoming* carbon-silicon, matter-machine, human-computer up for grabs here, which I referred to in the last chapter as a *superfolding*. We might now further modify this concept by terming it "recombinant folding." The finite, extensive qualities of bodies—the feeling of occupying fixed, extensive, physical space—are recombined via the introduction of a differential: the intensive, infinite forces of computational culture. We become moveable points on sliders, like Legrady's scanned pocket objects, resting momentarily between the physical space and duration of the corporeal and the patterns and flows of the informatic universe.

Katherine Halyes has provided a useful distinction between "the body" —a normalization of idealized corporeal representation at any given moment—and "embodiment," which is always situated by the spatiotemporal coordinates of particular cultural practices, climate and physical circumstance.[22] For her, information technologies extract, through abstract gestures, the body from embodiment. And yet, as I have suggested, both the spaces and the times of digital life are themselves particular. These, it seems to me, are enmeshed with and situate the sensations, perceptions and affects of our bodies, at one extreme converging with the lightning speeds of metabolic and perceptual processes, and at the other diverging from the slowness of habit or producing their own tardiness in the slow accretion of masses of junk data. As Hayles herself suggests, "During any given period, experiences of embodiment are in continual interaction with constructions of the body."[23] Although it is not simply a replication of the perfectly operating, "coded," sequenced and thus retrievable data body, digital embodiment cannot be considered without recourse to these vicissitudes of code.[24] For Hayles, the distinction between the body and embodiment implicitly overlaps with the dynamic between information and materiality. The first is an abstraction that can be organized/sequenced and regulated/programmed; the second is in flux (lived) and exceeds (interferes) with ideal representation or pure signal transmission. Through her conception of embodiment, Hayles allows bodies to escape from their capture by a reductive sociopolitical program, such as we find in Levinson's erasure of the difference between the organic and the digital, which reduces matter to code.

And yet, if we are looking for something specific in the embodied experiences we might expect to result from the relations *between* information and materiality, Hayles's framework only takes us so far. Although she acknowledges that new technologies must affect how people corporeally experience space and time, she does not provide an account particular enough to circumscribe the kind of interaction that occurs in the relation between new media technologies and bodies. This is because Hayles's conception of interaction rests on the assumption that information and materiality are pregiven formations. Both arise from specific practices and more general cultural influences, which then come into interaction with each other: "changing experiences of embodiment bubble up into language, affecting the metaphoric networks at play within the culture. At the same time discursive constructions affect how bodies move through space and time, influence what technologies are developed, and help to structure the interfaces between bodies and technologies.[25]

Rather than focusing on the predetermined nature of the interactants in the code/body dynamic, I want to propose that we shift our attention to the outcomes of the interaction itself. This will be a somewhat messier procedure, as we now enter the territory of emergent and provisional rather than substantial and resolved entities and of indeterminate, aleatory relations rather than predictable outcomes. I want to conditionally present some contours for the kind of spacetime that comprises an embodied sense of information aesthetics. We can posit that a continuum of sharp transformations emerges as a result of the oscillation between polarities through which information and corporeality interact. At one extreme is the movement of doubling or reproducing corporeal image, sensation and action, such as we find in computer gaming when avatars engage their embodied corollaries in replicating physical action in digital space. At the other extreme is the splitting of aspects of corporeal activity from daily, habitual life across cyberspace/time, as is exemplified in many forms of on-line activity. Here cognitive attention, sensory-motor repetition (continually clicking a cursor, for example) and affective absorption separate the inter-actant from the immediate and everyday physical environs. Activity is directed instead toward a universe constituted primarily out of information.

It will become evident as I summon more specific examples highlighting these oscillating aspects of digital embodiment that corporeal-code interactions can comprise both doubling and splitting phenomena, and that the capacities to split and double are not confined to the relation between information and bodies. These polarities or zones are inflected by the other elements—commercial, ideological, scientific, historical—that enter into the broader mix of information culture. But by attending to the interactions that take place within the field delimited by the parameters of multiplication (doubling) and division (splitting) that currently shapes code and corporeal relations, we start to grasp an active conception of how digital embodiment is produced. It is an ongoing process of interactions between corporeality and code that is governed by a logic of differentiation. Further, the movements and speeds specific to these relations begin to unfold as well.

Digital embodiment, then, is a differentially produced mode of living or experiencing the body. It is constituted across the folded interval that extends and opens up as the times of organic matter come into a relation with the speeds of information. Its space stretches across a series of constant deformations as the organic alters its rhythms and tempos in order to align itself with the mutable morphology of code, and as information twists itself into strange configurations that temporarily animate it. The temporality of digital embodiment comprises not simply moving toward absolute speed but also a stretch of asynchronicity punctuated by lags or intervals. These delays occur because both code and the body fall short of the other's speeds. This logic of differential engagement is not unique to information culture but is already prefigured in the baroque relations articulated between the organic world, natural science and aesthetics. Before I move to a consideration of this, a contemporary example will better illustrate this sense of the differential interval punctuating my idea about digital embodiment.

The way in which new media art has often sought to convey the affective possibilities of digital embodiment has been to encourage asynchronous relations between bodily and machine rhythms, and to split, layer and aggregate the differing series of technical and organic bodies. In the 1999 video clip for Björk's song *All Is Full of Love,* directed by Chris Cunningham, a semi-automated representation of Björk clones a robotic double of herself. She accomplishes this while remaining attached to the giant machine arms guiding the assemblage of her "other" body. Rather than a menacing vision of a technological future in which bodies, sensation and feeling have disappeared, this intermixing of organic and industrial/cybernetic elements—the expressionless faces of the two Björks reaching their robot limbs toward each other, the heavy machinery set against splashes of milky liquid, the noise of the automated factory overlaid by the lyrics of a drum'n'bass infused ballad—is whimsical, erotic and joyful.[26] The Björk clones do not represent a reduction or erasure of the organic body's relation to the cybernetic, replicating machine. Instead, Cunningham draws our attention to the differential produced, to what remains at the conjunction of two kinds of speeds. These speeds traverse the visual field of the video clip as the organic speed of liquid splashes and melting flesh meets the mechanical jerkiness of the robot's cybernetic limbs. The twin Björk robots flutter their eyelids, get hot and steamy and eventually melt together with a long slow kiss. Yet their mechanical limbs make it impossible for them to entwine. Their robotic bodies get in the way of each other and subsequently thwart the ideal of perfect lovemaking, in which two become one. Although we might understand the video as a comment on the human narcissism at the core of anthropomorphizing machines, Cunningham's clip undoes a naïve two-way reduction of both humanness and cybernetics by unleashing affect. Against the promise of ecstatic fusion that utopian imaginings of a cyborgian merger of flesh and technology have sometimes promised, Björk's "fullness of love" is replicated *and* displaced. This is brought about by the difference Cunningham highlights between machine speeds and movement in relation to organic ones.

In Cunningham's clip the failure of both robot and corporeal speeds to catch each other and combine in the technological fantasy of futuristic union becomes the differential force of movement that takes charge of the video's aesthetic economy. What we are left with is not the cyborg as a sign that represents the merging of machine and human but rather the cybernetic organism as ongoing assemblage produced and regulated by the relations between slowness and rapidity, heaviness and lightness, and spasm and flow. We are no longer dealing with an aesthetics of representation—of the cyborg as the sign of the future. Here, instead, the cyborg becomes machinic, releasing itself as a qualitative field of multiple and possible connections and disjunctions with the organic. The figure of Björk the clone in *All Is Full of Love* can be accounted for not in terms of a mimetic economy between machine and human but rather as the compounding of desire through doubling and serializing that is achieved in a culture of abstract informationalism. Yet Cunningham's refusal to allow the convergence of cybernetic and organic speeds at the moment the robots kiss leaves just that disparity in the sign of the cyborg to render it as a moment of indecision, an ongoing problem or space for further differentiation.

In his reading of the Deleuzian concept of sensation and the role it plays in aesthetics, Daniel Smith has suggested that it is precisely the role of the sign in a work of art to be the bearer of a problem.[27] We encounter this aesthetic sign not by recognizing and understanding its meaning but as a kind of agitation of sensation directly affecting the nervous system. In the encounter between Björks, new affects are generated in the act of aesthetic composition, in the connection between different modes of intensity, both robotic and human. Every aesthetic composition harnesses forces and brings them into relation: magnetic forces, geological forces, corporeal forces, forces of gravity and anti-gravity and so on. The particular forces harnessed and composed depend upon the material used in sustaining the artwork and the particular sensation an artist is attempting to wrest from her material. New media art must contend with composing the differential forces of information: equilibrium and entropy. Cyborgs, clones and robots can all be understood as protosubjectivities, nodes that actualize these forces by creating certain kinds of assemblage between the informatic and the organic. Cunningham's insight is to indicate that actualization does not necessarily result in dissolution, in the loss of sensation to the entropy of information or the transcending of the organic by the cybernetic. He offers us instead the tension of unresolved desire that is produced out of a differential of technical and organic forces as that which remains to reignite, propel and be recaptured.

The Waywardness of Early Modern Natural History

We cannot conceive of these new possibilities for bodies and machines if we conceive of natural history only as a science designed to order the complexity, dirt and disrepair of "matter." Extending this conception of the natural or of natural history into the digital realm devalues the strength of the natural history tradition, even though this is how we more frequently encounter the relation between the digital and the biological.[28] But what if natural history were not itself a closed system, one mired by the teleological directions of current models of posthuman digital evolution? What if we begin to think about the natural outside of its contemporary imprisonment in these relays between genetic and digital code? Rethinking natural history through a genealogical approach allows us to conceive of the digital-matter relation as a more open proposition, one resonating with the early modern European conception of natural history as organic artifice. This opens up a set of multidirectional tendencies at the genesis of natural history itself, one of which provides us with a "line of development" from natural history to digital culture.[29] A critical genetic moment for natural history can be located during the seventeenth and early eighteenth centuries in the tension of forces that give rise to it as narrative *and* nature, visual culture *and* organic world. This moment precedes the stratification of natural history into a classical science, which marks its later development in the eighteenth and nineteenth centuries.

I will turn now to sketching out the three main areas that signal these errant directions at the heart and foundations of the early modern scientific project—a project ostensibly seeking to establish true and certain knowledge of the natural world. The first territory is circumscribed by the debates surrounding reason and the passions in the seventeenth century. During this period, the discussion of wonder and curiosity as passions and their relation to a scientific worldview suggests that natural science did not necessarily emerge from a disembodied, mechanistic view of the world. Given the productive relations made possible between passion, knowledge and matter during this earlier period, it makes little sense to see the culmination of natural history as a superseding of nature by science or natural selection by artificial evolution, as is featured in contemporary fantasies of postbiological life.

These early modern debates intertwined with, supplemented, were fueled by and reacted to the practices of collecting and constructing cabinets of curiosity or *Wunderkammer*.[30] This second territory indicates pastimes that, although not unique to the seventeenth century, had come by then to be more than aristocratic pursuits, laying the foundation for private and institutional resources for the museal collecting of the natural world. Here the desire to classify matter according to an abstracted and externally imposed order was not necessarily foremost. Instead, early natural science was as much embroiled in aesthetic concerns, in the amassing of the history of nature as anecdote, and in its tendency to revel in the bizarre and unnatural as it was concerned with demonstrating the presence of the underlying laws of the world. I will suggest that this concentration on the wonders and curiosities of the world, on the way that both artificial and natural objects were perceived to relate to each other, their collectors and their viewing audiences, implied that early modern science was capable of entertaining passionate relations to, and encounters with, the material it was nonetheless arranging. This produces a story different from the narrative of a scientific revolution, which instigated a disinterested and increasingly distanced perspective upon the world. It is not simply that passions or wonders grafted together the two distinct realms of nature and artifice. Instead, the antinomies of cultural/artificial, natural/ material and scientific/epistemological were produced in proximity to each other. As John Sutton suggests in his discussion of the animal spirits that were presumed to activate the passions of early modern European bodies: "What some lament as 'confusions and contaminations' across discourses and levels of explanation involving the spirits can instead be seen as rare proximity between theory, culture and phenomenology."[31] Furthermore, it is this mode of relation that resonates with contemporary digital embodiment. Proximity is a form of connection that results from differential relations, that is, relations in which the ongoing variation of things from each other produces both convergence and divergence. Proximate relations provide a mode for understanding and living in the world as a folding out onto other things—something edging close to something else— but these things do not quite line up with the objects they are attempting to reach. Indeed, they are only approximations, and they fold back upon themselves. It is the folding of the world rather than the ordering of space that the early modern *Wunderkammer* embody.

Third, I will argue that these forces of convergent and divergent folding are not completely crushed by the march of classicism in the late seventeenth and then throughout the eighteenth centuries. Although it is possible to see natural science increasingly developing in the direction of an orderly mathesis through the implementation of the universal taxonomy of the Linnean system, nevertheless classicism was not epistemologically exhaustive.[32] The natural sciences continued to intersect with the development of an *ars memoria*. Frances Yates has argued that early modern science did not dispose of the Hermetic tendencies of the arts of memory, which were associated during the renaissance with magic and a belief in divine names, symbols and powers, but instead transformed the memory tradition: "amongst the new uses to which it [*ars memoria*] was to be put was the memorizing of matters in order so to hold them in the mind for investigation. This would help scientific inquiry, for by drawing particulars out of the mass of natural history, and ranging them in order, the judgement could be more easily brought to bear on them."[33] Leibniz, in particular, believed that images and symbols of a thing joined to that thing, or to a concept, could provide the basis for a mnemonical system. In his 1666 work *Dissertatio de arte combinatoria*, the idea of a universal art for solving all problems (the basis of his notion of calculus) was first put forward.[34] Here, lists of the mnemonic symbols he had drawn up would be used, according to various rules of combination, to resolve mathematical, philosophical and even moral problems. It is Yates's suggestion that Leibniz was influenced by an interest in and perhaps involvement with Rosicrucianism, thereby bringing an entire mystic tradition to his mathematical project for dealing with the world.[35] Whether this is the case or not, his conception of the natural world and of the scientist/philosopher's relation to it does not neatly divide between science and reason on the one hand and nature and the senses on the other.

This third territory, in which artificial and natural objects are arranged through both classificatory systems and the aleatory characteristics of human memory, can be explored as a source for generative concepts for the great eighteenth-century projects of encyclopaedism. Positioning these projects in turn as the ancestors of digital modes of collecting and systematizing the world yields a richer and less predictable computational lineage. This is especially so if we place at the very genesis of encyclopædism a reliance upon the fragile and less predictable machinations of human thought, such as memory. Engaging with and thinking about the natural world in these early modern ways reveal that there was no steady capitulation of nature to reason and of the world to instrumentalist science, and that there was no necessity to the emergence of a disinterested and disembodied cogito out of the scientific endeavor. By reasserting the passionate, proximate connections of natural history as a mode of knowing the world, we might also inject a degree of passion into the way in which digital processes likewise capture and encounter objects and matter.[36]

Wonder as an Early Modern Passion

The second half of the seventeenth and the early part of the eighteenth centuries, a time often thought by historians to represent a consolidation of natural science as a system for ordering the world, also saw a proliferation of publications and debates about wonder, secrets and curiosities.[37] An entire literature around rarities and the anomalies of the natural world had accumulated by this stage, as had the practice of collecting them. Wonder and the sense of surprise furnished by the "discovery" of the strange and unusual objects that populated and constituted nature were due for some serious philosophical reflection. This they received in Descartes's *The Passions of the Soul*, Hobbes's *Leviathan* and Spinoza's *Ethics*, as well as a multitude of smaller treatises on natural and moral philosophy.[38] Although these authors' views on the role of wonder and curiosity in relation to natural science were varied, they nevertheless concurred that it warranted discussion for the specific relation it held to reason.

I want to draw attention to Descartes's discussion of this relation primarily because he is the philosopher to whom the abiding schism of mind and body in modern Western thought is frequently attributed. Referring to Descartes's most celebrated works, *Discourse on Method* (1637) and *Principles of Philosophy* (1644), diverse contemporary critics have admonished his inauguration of a harsh, ontological dualism in Western thought.[39] It is to the Cartesian system and method that many cybertheorists trace preoccupations such as the hankering after disembodied digital spaces and the forgetting of the body as a necessary precondition for entering these realms.[40] And, as we saw in the introduction, Descartes can also become an unlikely champion of computer geek culture. Although *Cartesianism* may certainly have developed in this direction, it is not so clear, across the entirety of his work, that Descartes himself ever decisively split matter from the powers provided by reason to judge, observe and classify it. In his last published writing in 1649, *The Passions of the Soul,* Descartes revisited the relation of matter to reason via a discussion of the passions.[41] Descartes's work on the passions can be seen as part of a much broader debate on passion, motion and feeling that took place throughout the seventeenth century.[42]

Passions, in seventeenth-century philosophical parlance, were not synonymous with emotions, nor can they be brought into equivalence with the twentieth-century notion of "feeling." They were largely conceived as perceptions or states of the soul caused by the external world acting on the senses. The passion was a mediating representation of these externally produced sensations and was directed toward human reason. It provided the mind with an opportunity to understand the "raw" sensation's potential benefit or harm. It was the task of any moral philosophy to curb and bridle those passions that could destroy the powers of reasoning and to cultivate those passions that increased reason's power.[43] In Descartes's schema, which were common to many treatises of the time, the passions caused a direct physiological effect on the body, promoting a rise in the blood's temperature, an increase in the heart rate and a rush of his infamous "animal spirits" through the body: "we may define them generally as those perceptions, sensations or emotions of the soul which we refer particularly to it, and which are caused, maintained and strengthened by some movement of the spirits."[44] Passions manifested themselves corporeally, changing expression, demeanor and gesture in their bearer.

For Descartes, the primary passion for humans was wonder, which was capable of assisting the mind in pursuing its powers of reasoning in part because of wonder's effect on human physiology. As wonder arose through an encounter with an object in its novelty or unfamiliarity *before* its potential benefit or harm was known, Descartes believed it did not lead to changes in the heart or body's blood but to a rush of animal spirits straight to the head, hence affecting the brain alone.[45] A passion could be judged to be helpful because the sudden alertness and concentration it brought about helped the mind to retain a knowledge of external objects, which in turn laid the foundation for a systematic knowledge of the world: "Wonder is a sudden surprise of the soul, which brings it to consider with attention the objects that seem to it unusual and extraordinary."[46] Thus, for Descartes wonder suggests a conjunction of body and mind under the guise of a disinterested but not *dispassionate* journey to discover the extraordinariness of the world.

Wonder, then, is something of an anomaly among the passions in the Cartesian schema, deemed to have less of a physical effect than other passions, producing a reaction only in the head and therefore providing less of a distraction for reason. It seems to provide the bridge and balance point between reason and the senses: a rationale for the passionate and exhilarating pursuit of a life given over to understanding the principles and laws of nature. But, as is the nature of all passions, wonder, according to Descartes, can occur in excess, leading us to look beyond the reasonable and toward the unusual, unnatural and strange. Wonder can become destructive of reason, if it is overindulged, and lead to an endless quest for the ever more curious instead of helping reason to wrestle the strangeness of things in the world into their place within the natural, ordered schema of the universe: "This is what prolongs the troubles of those afflicted with blind curiosity, i.e., those who seek out rarities in order to wonder at them and not in order to know them."[47] Having acquired the basis for a scientific knowledge of the world through the help of wonder, then, we must nonetheless curb its passionate tendencies and free ourselves through reason from the inclination to surrender to it. The passions in the Cartesian schema thus represent not the simple subjugation of matter and the senses to the mind but rather the difficult and delicate territory of a negotiation to be worked out between the two.

As Susan James, the contemporary philosopher of seventeenth-century passions, argues, the status accorded to wonder during this period indicates the problematic situation of placing *scientia* in proximity to the knowledge of the world gained through the assistance of the body.[48] This territory becomes even more complex when we take into account Descartes's notion of "intellectual emotions." These are emotions that arise internal to the self as a result of the actions of the soul rather than through the impact of the external, sensory world. This origin distinguishes them from passions such as wonder; they include instead the emotions of joy and desire when stirred by the pursuit of philosophical reason. Although Descartes does not say as much, wonder, employed reasonably and moderately, sits somewhere between the five other passions and his concept of an intellectual emotion. Unlike the other passions, wonder has no opposite, so if an object fails to surprise the mind then it excites no passion at all. In such circumstances we may contemplate it under the cool and disinterested light of reason; that is, as an intellectual "passion of the soul."[49] As the first of the passions, wonder oscillates delicately between reason, emotion, soul and passion, the senses and the external world. How to understand Descartes's elaboration of the faculties as proximate territories to be negotiated by the work of wonder, rather than as realms divided from each other, then becomes the question.

Through the latter part of the twentieth century, we developed a habit of conceiving Descartes as the representative of an insidious dualism. Yet his discussion of the passions is more bound to questions of degree than duality. The emphasis in his treatise is not upon separation or exclusion but on moderation. Where, in the flows and connections that allowed the animal spirits to move from the head to the heart from wonder becoming too untamed and spilling over into curiosity, could one maintain the degree of reason necessary for living in such proximity to the sensory world? Although Descartes's methods for contemplating a world distinct from matter and the senses still stand as the linchpin of the split between being and knowing, his moral and physiological writings place him very much within the event of baroque thought. As Timothy Reiss argues, Descartes's work on the physiology of memory actually referred to the visual appearance of the folded cranium to delineate the traces where memory imprints could be held in the human body.[50] Folded matter both attracts the baroque eye of Descartes and becomes his means of elaborating the differentiating mark of the mind's operations at a bodily level: "As for the species preserved in the memory, I imagine they are not unlike the folds which remain in this paper after it has once been folded; and so I think they are for the most part in the whole substance of the brain."[51] This labyrinth of folded matter that bore the imprint of memories was, for Descartes, a corporeal topology to be negotiated—not denied—by reason.

Of course, important philosophical arguments and controversies divided Descartes from Leibniz. Yet both men were preoccupied with the question of degree, particularly as it pertained to discussions of perception and passion; that is, to matters directly concerned with baroque articulations of how one saw, experienced and conducted oneself as a bodily being in the world. This concern does not suggest an ethos wrought by principles of unification and exclusion, but one experienced as overwhelmingly proximate. Zones of life in which art and nature were adjacent, zones posing the difficulty of discrimination between wonder and curiosity, zones spawning an experimental science that rested upon a continuum between tactility and the visual. This was a world teeming with trees that groaned, perfectly formed double-headed humans, mythical gryphons gracing the pages of natural history catalogues, as well as all manner of anamorphic jokes and surprises crafted deliberately to trick the onlooker.[52] If wonder were close to reason for Descartes, then it was situated equally in proximity to the body. What, he mused, provokes one to the corporeal activity of laughter other than wonder?[53]

Wonder and the Passion for Collecting

Descartes's discussion of wonder and its dangerous tendencies to stray into curiosity and astonishment was in part a reaction to the frenzy of collecting, a frenzy also assisting the development of natural science during this time. But we should not automatically view Descartes's comments about taming the excesses of wonder as an indication that this passionate embrace of natural and artificial objects excluded a systematic ordering of the world by reason. Rather, as I have argued in relation to Descartes's own philosophy, thinkers in the seventeenth century did not necessarily cast reason in an oppositional or hierarchical relation to matter, sensation or emotion. Moreover, those arts deployed in the pursuit of collecting, such as the arrangement and display of objects and the furnishing of spaces and cabinets for their exhibition, were not seen by natural historians of the period as sensual distractions that detracted from the demonstration of an underlying organization of the universe. The artifice deployed, and the passions of astonishment and wonder such collections provoked, provided "an educated culture" around viewing natural objects.[54] Historian Kate Whitaker notes the use of measurement and scale in illustration and the detailed description and careful cataloguing accompanying most of the European *Wunderkammer* as indications of a visual display dedicated to the pursuit of obtaining knowledge. Thus we could postulate that a conception and practice of ordering emerged through these collections that was amenable to the bizarre, to provoking passion and inciting humor, and to emphasizing the aesthetics of contrivance. But even the encroaching eighteenth-century conceptions of order and system, which drew the practices of collecting curiosities into a taxonomic ordering of the world, were flexible. Ultimately, baroque practices were retained, indicating a sensitivity to the degree and variation in order rather than an inflexible principle of division between things.

If we look at illustrations of the most famous baroque *Wunderkammer* in Europe, which form frontispieces to their museums' inventories, what first strikes a contemporary viewer is their seeming *lack* of order. In, for example, Olaus Worm's *Museum Wormianum* (figure 7) and Ferrante Imperato's *Historia Naturalae* (see figure 1), the rooms are crammed with specimens, seemingly arranged in a rambling and chaotic fashion.[55] Yet this method of display was an aesthetic contrivance that drew attention to the wonder of natural diversity, which was further highlighted by being amassed within a confined space. Barbara Stafford argues that information about both nature and its matter were treated as openended conglomerates of knowledge about the world in these spectacular cabinets.[56]

FIGURE 7. Frontispiece to Olaus Worm, *Museum Wormianum Seu Historia Rerum Rarariorum* (1655). Courtesy the Wellcome Library, London.

They were not considered inert resources, waiting for a transcendent order to be imposed upon them. It is perhaps surprising to note that one of the great natural history treatises of the baroque, James Petiver's *Historiam Naturalem,* combines a classificatory method for detailing phylum, genus and species with the usual rambling commentary concerning location, materiality and anecdotal information about the curiosity or ordinary natural object being illustrated (figure 8).[57] In the captions accompanying images in Petiver's text, contemporary assumptions about "scientific" classification give way as he titles his tables with combinations of actual and mythical specimens, for instance, "gryphon, leaves, moths and fruit."[58] As in the *Wunderkammer,* objects pile on top of each other because the natural world was conceived of as a kind of vast plane that could accommodate

FIGURE 8. Table xlv in James Petiver, *Opera Naturalem Spectantia or Gazophylacium,* vol. 1 (1674). Courtesy of the Wellcome Library, London.

the proximity between the ordinary and the extraordinary, and between what had been observed and what had been gathered merely through anecdote and hearsay. Knowing *about* an object required a knowledge that involved a *getting to know*: a familiarity with its location, the stories one could elicit from and about it, and its own association with a wide range of other objects in the world. As Nathanial Crouch's 1685 treatise tells us: "My self and many hundreds of ingeneous men have seen at St. Edmonsbury in Suffolk, a groning piece of wood, it was of an elm tree sawn in the middle, as I conceive and guess it to be of a very great age, as soon as a hot iron was put in this piece of wood, it groaned like a dying man, so that it might be heard a great way."[59] Curiosity, surprise and wonder arose from the relation of objects to their location, from their capacities and from their proximity to similar or different objects. We are here in the midst of nature being understood through the engaging of passionate, corporeal relations to the world, through the modulation of these passions by reason, and through the relation and individuation of this object to all other matter in the world. What the *Wunderkammer* and its imbrication in a burgeoning natural history indicate is that baroque relations between perception, affect and thought were relations of force and degree, not separation and exclusion.[60]

If we look at one of the most admired and respected baroque cabinets of its day, Frederick Ruysch's Anatomy Museum, we can see the extent to which natural science and one of its fundamental branches, anatomy, contributed to an "art" of corporeality.[61] Prior to Ruysch's appointment as Doctor of Physic at Leiden University in 1664, the university's Anatomy Theater had already achieved European renown as a center for both the burgeoning new science of anatomy and its display of curiosities.[62] Commentary upon Ruysch's extraordinary displays emphasized the remarkable artifice of his work, as can be seen in the 1740 entry in Robert James's *A Medicinal Dictionary*: "He mingled groves of plants, and designs of shell-work, with skeletons, and dismembered limbs; and that nothing may be wanting, he animated, if I may so speak, the whole with appropriate inscriptions taken from the best Latin poets."[63] Ruysch's considerable contribution to the advancement of anatomical learning in his development of specimen preservation through venal and arterial injection methods was not removed from his practices of collection and visual display.[64] His cabinet exuded a preoccupation with aesthetic concerns that were simultaneously pedagogical, inquiring and moral. In the plates illustrating his *Thesaurus Anatomicus*, an ongoing inventory of all of his cabinet's contents, we get a glimpse of the bizarre dioramas he created for his museum.[65] Ruysch used foetal skeletons, dried membrane tissue, gallstones, kidneystones, stretched stomach lining and injected and preserved arterial and venal systems, among other bodily bits, to create embodied tableau designed to depict the transience of the mortal world. Although the argument can be made that his work fits squarely into the serious *vanitas* tradition, a sense of grotesque delight and humor flows from these displays. Perhaps this is because they were also demonstrations of the heights to which science, as an art turned toward the wonderful, could aspire. Ruysch's collection certainly seemed to contain not just the wonderfully constructed but also the mightily curious, as for example "a box of fly eggs obtained from the anus of a 'distinguished gentleman who had sat too long in the privy.'"[66]

The Return of Wonder and the *Wunderkammer* in Information Aesthetics

More recently, the hybrids crossing our contemporary terrain have revisited the possibility of a more corporeally engaged and situated relation to the dematerialized world of information and knowledge. In areas as diverse as cabinet making, museum display and interactive and Internet art, the notion of the *Wunderkammer* has resurfaced as a structuring device to collect what I described in the last chapter as the unfolding, endless production of information into spaces imbued with tangible meaning. Helmet Lueckenhausen, a designer and maker of contemporary cabinets, for example, reconnects his practice to seventeenth-century cabinets of wonder.[67] This provides him with a way to think about design outside the model of the universal template that imposes itself in a top-down fashion upon the materiality of the object. For Lueckenhausen, as for those architects and designers preoccupied with the topology of the fold, physical space and matter exert inverse forces as strong as those of the technologies such as CAD and computer-controlled laser cutting, that proffer precision and control over the material world.[68] The *Wunderkammer* and its visual assertion of the teeming materiality of the world can act to complicate and enrich a digital lineage that has often taken its cue from a conception of technology as an instrument for the sanitized operations of modern science.

One could argue further that as an "origin" of digital information spaces, Enlightenment "information science" was more a practice of radical incompletion, opening itself out toward the world instead of pretending to capture it. Contrasting the overt order that grand projects for knowledge collection such as the *Encyclopédie* expounded against the textual methods they actually deployed reveals that the former closed-system model tended to break down. *Encyclopédie* editor Jean Le Rond d'Alembert expounded the virtues of a proper scientific order for collecting and distributing information in its preface, proclaiming the encyclopaedic method as the perfect tool for arranging and then navigating a sea of knowledge: "a chain with which one can descend from the first principles of an art or a science to the most far removed consequences, and to reascend from these consequences to their first principles, as well as to pass imperceptibly from this art or that science to another; and if I may express myself in this manner, to go, without losing one's way, for a voyage around the literary world."[69] And yet Denis Diderot, the *Encyclopédie*'s other editor, chose to work with an alphabetical order rather than follow the pathways of scientific classification and logic. In his entry "Encyclopaedia," submitted to the *Encyclopédie*, Diderot, with the hindsight of being an editor, indicated an awareness of a number of different orders operating simultaneously through the entire project.[70] As Hugh Davidson argues, the *Encyclopédie* was an ongoing collection that over a period of time was forced to deal with the changes wrought upon its systemization by the polyvalence of the living language and culture it was attempting to collect.[71] Diderot apparently had great difficulty maintaining the separations and order of the headings for entries, because new perspectives, both cultural and political, were constantly impinging upon the content of the collection. Cross-referencing developed into a system that multiplied the connections between entries rather than mooring them to a demonstration of scientific order. The *Encyclopédie* made extensive use of cross-referencing, not simply as part of its erudition or to aid the recombination of its parts back into a scientific order but also to take the political heat off entries that would have attracted state and church censorship. The reader would be directed to seemingly innocuous entries where often more controversial political and theological views were covertly stored.[72] The *Encyclopédie* may appear to be a prototype for universal knowledge collection and hence the genesis for contemporary impulses to store the world through digitization. Yet examining it as a complex set of collecting practices inflected by discursive and institutional forces reveals how a collection's order is always shaped by the contingencies of the practices of collecting.

One prominent direction in new media art in recent years has been in database design, visualization and interaction. If George Legrady's *Pockets Full of Memories* highlighted the potential to sustain relations between material artefact and information pattern through the database styles of new media art, then his installation at Seattle's Public Library, *Making Visible the Invisible* (2004–5), works with multiplying and interrelating variable orders of information. The public display of the work consists of six plasma screens behind the librarian's reference desk that are projecting constantly updated information that visually maps out, on a daily and an extended basis, the circulation of nonfiction books through the library.[73]

What a library—or, one might speculate, a museum collection, a multimedia CD-ROM, or an Internet search—represents to an individual borrower or user is a kind of minefield of information through which they must navigate. From the perspective of the librarian, these users need to be steered through this field, and there exists a correct order for doing so: the Dewey system. Yet what this arrangement in effect sustains is the idea that information is a kind of entity that floats or sinks between two bookends: the borrower/user and the librarian.

In *Making Visible the Invisible* information becomes a set of collective and changing productions that is negotiated at the individual level of transactions between the borrower and the collection but is never entirely reducible to them. Legrady visualizes ways in which information can be ordered, sets that embody these transactions in terms of their collective, impersonal, aesthetic and individuated aspects. In the hands of the new media artist, there is not *one* order that provides us with access to information. Information is mutable because it is always produced through dynamic, contingent yet sustained relations between people, technologies, locations and institutions. Legrady offers us four modes of visualizing what the Seattle community is reading: "best hits," which compares three time periods of books in circulation according to broad reading categories ranging from "General Management" to "Poetry"; "Dewey," which visually scrolls through the Dewey decimal categories of "1: Knowledge" to "999: Extraterrestrial Worlds" and accounts for the number of these items in circulation; "Concept," which gives a time and scale set of artistic images that maps different reading patterns through temporal and growth phases; and "Daily," which provides a precise readout of book titles for each day's borrowing list. None of these modes transcends the others; none is more useful, more systematic, more categorical. Each order is instead dependent upon other information parameters, upon context and upon what one might initially seek. Hence what Legrady's installation reveals is that information is only ever made meaningful through social and cultural context and communal transactions. Suddenly the library is no longer a storage house that must be navigated and from which something must be retrieved. It is a hub of transaction and of pattern formation and decay, of people converging and diverging in their interests and participating in the visualization of nodes of habit, preference and transformation.

The database approach in new media art draws attention to the ways in which information flows through nodes and concentrations of interest clusters, institutions, habits and transformations of all of them. It provides us with a sense in which data, users and designers—and hence information and knowledge systems—are not things or endpoints but are dynamically *networked*. Likewise, direct reference to the cabinet of curiosities has been made in the context of contemporary networks of information to situate the user as a co-creator of knowledge who thus changes and develops accordingly. The Web site for Australian Museums Online, a nationwide Australian initiative, arranges its information architecture into what it calls "three cabinets of wonder."[74] These "cabinets" are in fact search engines organizing the navigation of an intranet of approximately 70 percent of Australian museums' collections. Sarah Kernderdine, the network's information architect, discusses the efficacy of the *Wunderkammer* metaphor to conjure up and accommodate the enormity of textual and graphic information attached to this wealth of objects.[75] In effect, the cabinet has become an interface metaphor for the experience of searching a museum in a networked environment, one that shifts the emphasis from the official ordering of collections through organized narratives of progress and history to the role of the user as an eclectic "curator" of knowledge. Kernderdine explicitly draws upon recent debates within museum studies that have addressed the destabilization of the museum's modernist foundations through the digitization of historical artefacts and the integration of user-activated displays within museum spaces.[76] Here, knowledge no longer resides in the object alone but must be produced through the differential relations each user's particularized pathways create while finding and acquiring data. These pathways, like the mesh that wove together anecdote, visual display and direct observation in early modern natural history, have the effect of bringing context and localized meaning to aggregates of digital data. Kernderdine suggests that sites such as Australian Museums Online function as information *meta-centers,* in which museum-like objects and processes might be renegotiated rather than simply presented in the form of polished displays to a viewer.

How would the information metacenter be comparable to a cabinet of wonder? The implication is that the *Wunderkammer* offered a kind of perspective upon the world, a commentary elicited in the relation of cabinets to one another, of objects to one another within the cabinets, and of the viewer to the objects. The early modern museum visitor did not simply receive predetermined knowledge about the world but actively created this knowledge through the admiration of the cabinet's contents and in their marvelous, unfolding modes of display, modes that included incongruence, humor, surprise, illusion, visual amplitude and trickery. In what way, then, could we say that this contemporary digital equivalent, the information meta-center, resonates with these kinds of baroque modes of commenting upon the world?

It resonates with the cabinet of wonder in the latter's emphasis upon a materiality that resides in the *relations* produced between objects and viewers. Networked museums can only be thought of as offering dematerialized and disembodied experiences if materiality is assumed to lie solely with either the museum object or the viewer/interactant's body. But if knowledge of the world is understood to be an ongoing process resulting from negotiation among the materiality of objects, the representation and display of those objects and the affective responses of the museum's visitors, then these processes can also occur in incorporeal information spaces. Yet the idea of the meta-center is also caught in the tension between knowledge as an ongoing process and a known outcome. This is perhaps the very same tension that arose in the transition of the museum from cabinet of curiosity to encyclopaedic project for storing the world. The concept of the information metacenter draws upon debates and design strategies concerning information architecture and its relation to the organization of museum resources.[77] In implementing the use of "metadata" tags in the marking-up of resources in online spaces, Web designers, and especially those working upon relational databases and resources such as online museum sites and collections, have sought to increase the visibility of their information objects for search engines. Metadata tags allow search engines to easily locate information about online objects, including as their overall location within a site, the name of the site in which they are housed, and any other information associated with the object. This subsequently impacts upon the display of the object or site within an online search engine index and can provide added visibility for it in search results, depending upon the structure of the engine's indexing facilities.[78] The effect of couching an information object within metadata structures is to make it more accessible within the information universe. Here, the information meta-center departs from the sensibility of the *Wunderkammer* by privileging the accessible and the visible over the curious and obscure. In doing this we move away from the strange and folded pathways of the baroque and toward a classical conception of the world as ultimately knowable.

Without explicitly recalling the *Wunderkammer* tradition, many experimental artists' interfaces for accessing and displaying digital relational data inject the labyrinthine quality of a baroque aesthetic into the digital. Accordingly, digital space becomes less an integrated and knowable space with encyclopaedic promises of total access and retrievable information than a heterogeneous set of spaces, full of gaps, accidents and lags. In conjunction with the collaborative online group c5, artist Lisa Jevbratt has constructed the database project 1:1.[79] The database contains a collection of 2 percent of the sampled IP (Internet Protocol) addresses of all possible host servers existing online at the time of the sampling. "Crawlers" or software robots undertake the task of sampling. Major Internet search engines also sample IP addresses using crawlers. Jevbratt executed this crawl of IP addresses in 1999 and 2001 and again in 2004 on a smaller scale in order to update one of the interfaces.

Various pixel color values are assigned onscreen to display the requests made by users when interacting with a particular interface. What the user sees as the colored patterns of the interface are visualizations of the stored database information—"snapshot" images of the Internet at a particular moment in time. However, rather than a map that contains all of the information, or, indeed, orderly information, these images provide us with aesthetic terrain that can itself be explored. This in turn gives us a visualization for accessing data that is very different from that gained by using a standard Internet search engine. Each user attempt to search and retrieve information about an IP follows a visual pathway and produces a different contour for the user's sense of the map. The interfaces function as both navigation and display, and they obscure the simplistic mapping of image to external referent or information. As Jan Eckenberg from c5 states:

> The Internet requires an interface to be experienced. The title of this project: 1:1, as in scale 1:1, suggests that a map, or a model, has the same size as that which it refers to. When this occurs, the distinction between the abstract "Geography" and the tangible "Empire" becomes vague. First we encounter a collapse between the map and the interface. But the post-photographic practice of the 1:1 project makes the implosion even more severe. The interface becomes not only the map, but the environment itself.[80]

Instead of an equivalence between information and knowledge, 1:1 offers information byways through aesthetic connections guided by color and luminosity. The outcome of an interaction with the project in the original interface for the 1999 manifestation of 1:1, "petri," arranges previous user attempts at access into aggregates of similarly colored pixels (figure 9). These color conglomerates beckon the newest user toward the brightest area of the "map." And yet there is no guarantee that these iridescent

FIGURE 9. Screenshot of the "petri" interface from *1:1* by Lisa Jevbratt/c5 (1999).
Courtesy of the artist.

clumps will yield any concrete information outcomes—that is, any actual
IP addresses. A frequent experience of using the *1:1* interfaces as both cartographic and navigation tools is that the user ceaselessly finds servers that
do not respond, do not permit nonauthorized access or are not available to
an "http" protocol request. *1:1* leaves the user with the feeling that pathways to information are not transparent, that they instead require a kind
of cryptic or even secret knowledge in order to gain access. The Internet
begins to feel less like an organized network of ordered information and
more like an infinite field of small nodes clustered into localized areas of
access that drift together and fall away from each other. By using the technologies and sciences of statistical sampling and databasing, *1:1* shows us
the limits of the database as a model for definitively knowing the world.
Rather than being a representative collection of real spaces—people's
homepages, institutions, corporations and companies' sites—*1:1* gives us
the interface to the Internet *as* the web of connections and disjunctions
themselves: "When navigating the web through the database, one experi-

ences a very different web than when navigating it with the 'road maps' provided by search engines and portals. Instead of advertisements, pornography, and pictures of people's pets, this web is an abundance of non-accessible information, undeveloped sites and cryptic messages intended for someone else."[81] The significance of a project such as *1:1* for an alternative aesthetics of new media, an aesthetics that incorporates affect, recognizes context and contingency and operates through differentiality, lies in the way its gradually changing visual contours trace engagement and the changing nature of the collection itself. The individual who accesses *1:1* maps a series of their own affective responses of surprise and disappointment in their attempts to connect to an Internet address. In the "petri" interface used in the 1999 manifestation of the project, *1:1* actually becomes an emergent map of the different interactions of users with its data collection. Here we have a digital inversion of Leibniz's monadology, in which each monadic substance represents a different view of a singular universe. In *1:1* we have the optical illusion, through one of its interfaces, of a singular and accessible universe of information, dependent for its very production as well as its useability upon the activity of thousands of local, singular engagements.

FIGURE 10. Screenshot of the "every" interface from *1:1* by Lisa Jevbratt/c5 (2001 and ongoing). Courtesy of the artist.

Yet this is no demonstration of the "new biology" of digital systems, in which order evolves inevitably out of a swarming chaos. In using the interface "every," the arbitrary nature of the system of pixel assignation is revealed to the user: green equals an accessible address, red an inaccessible one, and so on (figure 10). Each colored pixel in the interface represents an IP address stored in the database and is arranged from the top left of the screen to the bottom right in ascending numerical order. And yet the visual qualities of the interface itself resonate aesthetically with an image of electronic noise. Again, the statistical ordering of information cedes to an aesthetic engagement as the user is drawn to areas of color and brightness in the interface. *1:1* maintains the element of wonder by refusing to reveal a "natural" order for this data world. Instead, wonder stirs in the modulated play between finding and losing connections to other Internet presences, in the astonishment of, after dozens of thwarted connections, actually returning a successful connection to the user's request, signaling another presence in the vast sea of numerical combinations that comprise actual and potential IP addresses.

The challenge of producing an aesthetic experience through new media must take into account the incorporeal conditions of working within information spaces. But a more expansive conception of materiality can help us to understand the sense in which digital aesthetic experience operates to draw intensive connections between the actions and affects of bodies and the forces of digital code. The information universe is not one determined by the same forces as the natural world, nor does it transcend matter, the domain of nature. By tracing the differential histories of "natural history" we can also signal how this countergenealogy assists us in apprehending a more contemporary digital "nature." Natural history as the science of ordering matter has simultaneously been a terrain textured by its objects and held together by the divergent proximities of passion, knowledge and matter. In this respect, it belongs to an ongoing experimental aesthetic project for constituting contemporary nature through digital artifice.

My body wasn't in the computer world I could see around me, but one of my hands had accompanied my point of view onto the vast electronic plain that seemed to surround me, replacing the crowded laboratory I had left behind where my body groped and probed. — HOWARD RHEINGOLD[1]

Beyond the relations of actualized forces, virtual ecology will not simply attempt to preserve the endangered species of cultural life but equally to engender conditions for the creation and development of unprecedented formations of subjectivity that have never been seen and never felt. — FELIX GUATTARI[2]

3 virtuality
actualizing bodies, abstracting selves

Virtuality, Reality and Digitality

Catherine Richards's 1993 installation *The Virtual Body* is seductively named, having appeared at a particular time in the history of new media arts and entertainment and being deceptively simple in its realization (figure 11). If the culture of information and its aesthetics were dominated by any two tendencies during the late 1980s to mid-1990s, they were virtuality and interactivity. The virtual, more than any other quality or dimension associated with digital technologies, has promised to leave the body and its "meat" behind, as minds, data and wires join together in an ecstatic fusion across the infinite matrix of cyberspace. But Richards's installation asks us to focus upon the body in relation to the virtual just as the rhetorical hype about the body's disappearance

FIGURE 11. Installation shot of *The Virtual Body* (1993) by Catherine Richards. Photograph by Herman Van Aerschat. Courtesy of the artist.

through cyber-apotheosis was reaching a climax. But what kind of body might this be if, as she specifically directs us in the work's title, it is now inseparable from that very condition that is everywhere disassembling it—the virtual? *The Virtual Body* is not what one expects to find, given that slick, real-time, three-dimensional immersive environments are what first come to mind in association with virtual reality (VR) technologies. Initially realized for the Antwerp '93 Festival, the installation sits in a nineteenth-century rococo-style room in Belgium's Centrum Voor Beeld-cultuur, literally translated as the "center for picture culture."[3] A heavy crafted wooden and glass box with a viewfinder positioned centrally on top and a steel-ringed hole on one of its sides is mounted waist-high on a polished wooden plinth. As Richards comments, the piece is not an overt reference to technology, at least not *new media technologies,* and it lures the viewer visually into a world of optical instruments that might now be found in a museum with its "alluring, warm, fine materials, reminiscent of the column stereoscopes of the mid-nineteenth century."[4] The cabinet on top of the plinth is in fact a miniaturized representation of the room in which the work is installed. It uses glass and a video projection up through the "floor" of the little room to create the illusion—popular from the baroque right through to the late rococo periods—of a room within a room. The contemporary viewer can both peer into the room through a viewfinder on top of the cabinet and place her hand inside its space from the cabinet's side.

Although not immediately obvious to the participant, this dislocation between *looking* at one's hand and *experiencing* one's hand in receding motion is similar to the designs of the early 1970s and 1980s for single-person interaction in VR environments. This is further enacted in Richards's piece by the triggering of a moving image due to the insertion of the participant's hand into the miniature room:

> The floor pattern on the monitor begins to scroll. In a few moments the spectator begins to sense a body illusion: a displacement of the body, an illusion of motion. One's hand appears to be infinitely traveling away from the body. Then the arm begins to take the body with it. It is as if miniature space is folded into infinite space, as if stillness is folded into motion. The body loses all references: inside/outside, giant/miniature, spectator/object, part/whole.[5]

What is fascinating about the sense of virtuality evoked in Richard's work is that, despite the strange displacement produced between having an arm that feels attached to one's body and looking at/experiencing an arm simultaneously departing from the rest of the body, this does not produce a *disembodied* digital experience. Richards suggests instead that a folding occurs between pairs of dissonant experiential states and spaces. This discord leads to a loss of extensive and locative referentiality for the body. Bodies may no longer be sensed as anchor points in information culture. Yet, as *The Virtual Body* suggests, the heightening of corporeal and affective experiences through the very dispersion of bodily location has become a key aspect of information aesthetics.

As I will suggest in this chapter, in spite of VR and indeed much of the late-twentieth-century cyberculture's disregard for the body, virtuality does not exist in a realm beyond or transcend corporeal experience. Rather, to borrow John Beckman's phrase, there is a "virtual dimension" to digital embodiment.[6] So far I have concentrated on the relation between the baroque and the digital from the perspective of what early modern relations between matter, aesthetic perception and a new scientific knowledge of the sensory world offer the reactivation and rethinking of contemporary body-technology relations. From this point, the baroque will become a force within contemporary information aesthetics as we enter the spheres of virtuality, human-computer interaction and globally networked information. My argument throughout the remainder of this book, and the examples I draw upon, will be more firmly planted within present times, bringing the concepts of folding, differentiality and machinism to bear directly upon themes within information aesthetics and culture.

During the 1990s, VR technologies became almost synonymous with the quintessence of digital research and development; they both represented the high end of military-industrial and entertainment advances in technological simulation and promised bubble worlds of techno-utopian enclosure and escape. In Hollywood depictions of virtual reality such as the films *Lawnmower Man* (1992) and *Disclosure* (1994), in countless theme park rides in Disney, Universal Studios and game arcades, and in the less publicly accessible domains of medical and military simulation, enormous quantities of capital were invested in high-tech body prostheses. These prostheses all promised alternate or "out of body" experiences for the "operator," as virtual world participants have been called.[7] Invariably these depictions and realizations have taken the virtual to be both an extension of and a supplement to the real. As Howard Rheingold's detailed observations of the state of VR research in the early 1990s remind us, virtual experiences of this kind strive to replicate human perception and provide an added metaphysical dimension to sensory experience.[8] One effect of the hyperbolic rhetoric and representation of VR was to cast a shadow over everyday reality, which in contrast comprised the inadequate qualities of daily life and human corporeality. Virtual reality, while striving technically to duplicate the complexity of everyday life, nevertheless undertook to exceed it through the offer of neverending accumulation: more than the physical extension of the body, it offered greater movement, more freedom, the plunge into a future of pure consciousness.

Many theorists of cyberspace have remarked upon a gap that seems to structure the relations between cyberspace and physical space. Alluquere Rosanne Stone, for example, characterizes virtual systems in terms of their split between projected electronic space and everyday physicality: "Cyberspace is a physically inhabitable, electronically generated reality, entered by means of direct links to the brain—that is, it is inhabited by refigured human 'persons' separated from their physical bodies, which are parked in 'normal' space."[9] For her, virtual/real splitting initiates a schema of projected proprioceptive movement that accompanies navigation through the cybersphere, such that one feels exclusively caught up in and affectively immersed within the virtual environment. But at the same time she acknowledges that these noumenal affects produce a growing distance from the substance of the organic, stationary body. Although Stone seems to offer us an enriched version of virtuality, one in which the virtual mind is accompanied by its virtual body, her actual, physical bodies subsequently undergo a demotion. They continue to run but really only take up space back at the parking bay; their "motors" are not really running.

On the face of it, then, technological virtual worlds seem bent upon enlarging the gaps that separate them from the coordinates of the material world, coordinates that require us to have bodies in order to have experience. Indeed, VR has achieved much of its notoriety and criticism from the claim that it can disconnect consciousness and perception from their anchors in living human matter.[10] Although virtuality and the digital are not synonymous, they are nonetheless imbricated. Three terms circulate in proximity to the virtual: the actual, the possible and the real. In digital configurations of virtuality, the real is most often invoked as its partner, simultaneously imbuing virtuality with the modality of possibility and its concomitant task of *realizing* possibilities. It is not that this is the wrong configuration of these terms, which, as Pierre Lévy has suggested, form poles that are immanent to each other.[11] Rather, the problem lies in this configuration's creation of only one actualization of virtuality: that is, to make real possibilities that have already been prefigured, whether as imaginary or mimetic manifestations.

But the virtual is not of the order of representation; that is to say, it does not proceed from reality. Nor does it precede the real as ideality, model or simulation. It is, rather, a set of potential movements produced by forces that differentially work through matter, resulting in the actualization of that matter under local conditions. To return to Richards's *The Virtual Body*, the virtual dimension for corporeal experience evoked here lies in the way it poses the potential for *embodied distribution as a condition of experience for information culture* by dislocating habitual bodily relations between looking and proprioception. Virtual forces are vectors that pulse through the contours and directions of matter. They may or may not break off into other directions, connect with other lines or encounter other forces and matter that cause their flows to be blocked. As Lévy suggests, drawing upon Deleuze's virtual-actual counterpoint relationship, the actual is a particular response to a set of virtual forces rather than the realization of a possibility.[12] Virtuality and actuality form a differentiated continuum of force and materiality, promising to move according to one set of tendencies, then encountering the forces of differentiated matter and actualizing in both foreseeable and unpredictable ways. The virtual-actual relation has the advantage over the virtual-real partnership of draining the theological flavor from virtuality. If conceived as a possibility waiting to be made real, as is the case with much initial VR conception and design, the possibilities themselves feel like preordained scenarios waiting for the right conditions under which to unveil their destiny.

But how does the alternative use of the virtual-actual pair and trajectory help to explain the movement of technosocialities in what appears to be the inverse direction, toward virtualization? How can we account for the breakup of the structure of private and interiorized subjective experience or the informatic transformation of the referential world, both of which were hastened by the dematerializing tendencies of electronic media and now computational processes? Although the claims for the disembodied nature of VR can be attributed to the dependency of the digital upon Cartesianism, the strangeness of embodied technological experiences—in which, for example, VR environments produce both dematerialized senses of the self *and* intensified corporeal sensations or actualizations—remains underinvestigated. Rheingold himself implicitly drew attention to virtual splitting by convincing himself that he had left his inept corporeality behind him when he suited up and toured virtual environments, yet he nevertheless noted that he was trailed by "one of his hands." This hand had miraculously managed to attain a double identity as both part of his inert body and part of his virtuality. As Janet Murray has remarked, it is this relation between a virtually perceived and felt body and an actually lived body (that is, embodiment localized in a place and through duration) that captivates us in digital engagements: "When the controller is very closely tied to an object in the fictional world, such as a screen cursor that turns into a hand, the participant's actual movements become movements through the virtual space. This correspondence, when actual movement through real space brings corresponding movement in the fantasy world, is an important part of the fascination of simple joystick-controlled videogames."[13] Murray's argument concerning correspondence here is not premised on resemblance to the real. It is, in fact, more in line with the virtual-actual relation I have been arguing is crucial to understanding even a digital virtual experience that rigidly seeks an aesthetic of realism. For, as she points out, the spaces we have come to regard as virtual in contemporary culture are not simply steeped in realism but are also simultaneously perceived as imaginary, fantastical spaces. If we look at where VR is most readily consumed, it is predominantly in terms of entertainment: amusement rides or cheaper versions that appear as games in video arcades or home computer entertainment. Of course, one could argue that this only accounts for one area of virtualization. Taken as part of a technosocial trend, as Lévy argues it has become, the virtual condition engulfs all spheres, turning our notions of work (the virtual office), science and medicine (telesurgery) or the economy (speculative currency) upside down.

Yet Murray's argument has the merit of being able to account for why virtual experiences involve a degree of making strange in the experience of digital embodiment. She argues that virtual spaces are culturally demarcated through their separation from everyday experience. The animated VR ride one experiences in Disney World as a trip through the marketplace of Aladdin's land has an exit and entry point that announces it as "a ride." One formally enters and exits the virtual world, just as one starts and finishes a computer game: arrival is indicated by the "loading" progress bar or bay, and departure from the world usually spurs a series of computer prompts/announcements asking the user if they wish to leave or save their exit point. Immersion, for all its realist trappings, is also an unreal place, in which bodies are distributed between the fantastic and the actual, moving around impossibly in one sphere and feeling movement in the other. This splitting and doubling produces a relation of correspondence between differential fields, and *this* is what makes VR an affective aesthetic experience. Yet it remains one for which we really have no cultural vocabulary to adequately describe those affects.[14]

The reductive maneuver of situating digital technologies as the cause of virtual experiences can be detected in the early cyberculture frenzy surrounding high-end VR technologies. But it has broadened into an ascription attached to the general effect of digital imaging processes and immersive online and offline graphic environments. The task of this chapter will then be to disinter the virtual dimension from its status as a byproduct of digital media alone. I will also examine the contribution virtuality does make to sensory engagements with digital technologies. By exploring the virtual dimension within the time of the digital, we shall then see that one of the wider aesthetic implications of processes of digitization has been to impinge upon and give a certain form to manifestations of the virtual. This threefold set of tasks will be steered by the hypothesis that, at a general level, computation brings to our cultural, aesthetic and corporeal engagements with technology a mutable and conditional measure of abstraction. Computation, especially within the arts, allows for the visual, sonic and spatiotemporal production of the conceptual modeling of data: visualizations of conceived, potential environments might be, for example, another way to describe VR spaces. Computer space is in many ways a kind of cognitive space for problem production: within its parameters concepts can be sketched, planned, tried out, tested, revised and erased. Yet the very mutability of data—the infinitely reconfigurable arrangements of code as varying responses to user interaction, and as results of nonhuman interactions (networked communication with other machines, infrastructure and technologies)—means that the abstract elements of computation are constantly subjected to external transformation and rearrangement beyond their programmed parameters. This process subjects the abstract space of information and its relationship with purely conceptual operations to the contingencies of corruption, nonstandardization, incompatibility and accident.

Thus we need to qualify the more general aspect of the hypothesis by adding a second qualifying level, in which we can propose that computation duplicates, through fluctuating degrees of variation, the general mutability and contingency of sentient life. Contrary to a strong cultural tendency within computational aesthetics that is oriented toward realistic representation, this form of duplication is not one that *resembles* reality. It is, rather, one that *corresponds* with—in the sense of exchanging missives— the actual, sensory world. The abstract quality of digital processes apparently disengages us from immediate corporeality and the physical environment. Yet there is nevertheless a set of corresponding points, tendencies or capacities between computation and the everyday world that produces zones for sensory and affective engagement with, and interaction between, computers and humans.

The universe of computational spacetime both differs from and repeats the coordinates of human corporeal experience. The two universes form orders that are serially connected to and differentiated from each other: the abstract informational world engages the virtual dimension of human experiences; the sensory and contingent plane of living bodies is doubled and variably reconfigured through computational schemas. The virtual dimension of computation moves us toward abstraction and the infinite reconfigurability of algorithmically produced space; the actual processes of computation, as they form assemblages with concrete circumstances and activities, comprise and compose facets of contemporary embodiment. We should not imagine that these two orders simply support relations of aggressive superimposition or maintain a benign coexistence. The virtualization that computation moves us toward is not, then, a replacement of materiality, bodies or humans but a process that can combine with and multiply the virtual propensities of all of these. In order to grasp the digital's impact upon virtuality as it shapes and inflects it in ways that cannot be reduced to realist representational trajectories, we need to look to the breadth of digital culture itself. Many instances of VR environments and technologies can be revisited by engaging the dynamic between virtual and actual processes to enrich our somewhat paltry understanding.

The Digital Production of Virtual Time

One set of corresponding tendencies between the virtual, abstract computational domain and actual embodied experience lies in both orders' potential for producing temporal compression and simultaneity. Digitization has been said to produce cultural historical amnesia through areas as diverse as computer gaming and digital museum display. In particular, digitally produced and manipulated worlds appear to seamlessly assemble past, present and future moments and artefacts. The effects of recreating history might be considered exemplary of a more general propensity to "virtualize" the past if we consider processes such as three-dimensional software modeling and compositing between fictional and archival footage, as showcased in movies such as *Jurassic Park* (1993) and *Forrest Gump* (1994). The past is dusted off, as it were. Any material phenomena providing it with distinctive historicity, such as context, decay and the unreliability of memory—all of which forestall exact replication—is filtered out through computer processing.

But does a digital reconstruction of the past necessarily entail a disengagement from the material world? In fact, we might surmise that repetition, in cohorts with decontextualization, is actually doing something new to history, producing a deliberate reimagining of the past rather than a faithful but tired attempt to authenticate through resemblance. When the digital is harnessed to the forces of realism it inevitably fails to match up to the past, becoming either a poor imitation, as can be witnessed in the countless museum projects for digitizing Great Masters collections, or else too perfect, erasing the material and cultural differences that constitute the differential rhythms of temporal experience. But if we recast the digital as an aesthetic force capable of producing new kinds of sensations and affective responses, we might instead see it as belonging to the activity of imagining. This is what Brian Massumi has termed "felt thought" in reference to a relation between thinking and affecting rather than to representing the real.[15]

The six-part English series *Walking with Dinosaurs* (1998), produced by BBC Television, is ostensibly concerned with the prehistoric past.[16] It uses the genre conventions of nature documentaries, such as authoritative voiceover combined with close-up location footage, to speculatively reconstruct the behavior and habits of extinct species. Yet all of the episodes are aesthetic masterpieces, equal parts metaphysical speculation and sensory aesthetics. Of the 180 minutes of total television footage, 132 minutes are computer generated; the remainder of the dinosaur footage uses animatronic models. Alec Knox, the senior technical director of computer animation for the series, gleefully admitted that the animators invented behavior in order to build up a "lifestyle" for the creatures.[17] On the one hand, then, the shows present a monumental endorsement of the power of digital technologies to erase the "real" evidence of palaeontology, telling us little about the known life lived by and between species of dinosaurs. But on the other hand, the pedestrian notion of the digital's virtual dimension as a flattening and dematerializing force cannot account for what is so captivating about the programs.

What is affective about *Walking with Dinosaurs* lies in the juxtapositions that arise through its compressions and decompressions of time, in which the long lost past is brought into immediate relation with the coordinates of contemporary technology. The series achieves this through animation, modeling and imaging techniques, dwelling on vibrant images of prehistoric viscerality: reptilian skin that drips with the slime of some primeval swamp; ripped flesh clinging to the jaws of a velocoraptor, a winged dinosaur. The detailed imaging of digital dinosaur viscera may be the result of exhaustive 3-D texture-mapping, but it has the effect of introducing into the somewhat anthropomorphized narratives an utterly nonhuman, almost alien, element. From the perspective of what digital imaging offers us aesthetically, *Walking with Dinosaurs* reinvents natural history as imagining—as "felt thought"—about the potential of the past to reenter into sensory relations with the present. Past, present and future, the factual, actual and digital, fold in and out of one another in a sensory mélange that is fascinating and unnerving and affects the very seat once thought to be responsible for producing affect: the guts.

This kind of "virtual" telescoping of time accompanies the "loss" of spatial orientation in cyberspace, with each feeding into a frenzy of accusations about its disembodying propensities. Peter Lunenfeld speculates that the lack of spatial referentiality and the compressed scale of liquid, digital spaces when compared with everyday proprioceptive space may be the reason for a proportional loss of duration for users in virtual environments.[18] In this understanding of the digital production of virtual time, a participant's movement through digital space is responsible for driving an unfolding sense of digital time. The problem here is that we resort to modeling movement in digital space upon an imagined, indeed already virtualized, experience of spatial navigation. Anyone who has observed a user immersed in a full head-mounted VR situation will immediately recall the amusing image of a body whose blinkered eyes are negotiating a complex terrain but whose limbs spasmodically jerk around, limited by their VR prostheses. The virtual/actual spatial discrepancy underlines the fact that digital space does not unfold in direct relation to the bodily traversal of it through time. Instead, digital spaces are moebius-like, comprised of asynchronous feedback that loops between a doubling of and a splitting from bodily awareness. These loops bind and differentiate the experience of immersion in VR from everyday proprioception. Furthermore, there is a technical production and specification of spatial coordinates in VR prior to any corporeal engagement with it. The experience of virtual space for the user is a negotiation between this digitized spatiality and her own habituation to ordinary, everyday embodied movement. Likewise, digital virtual time is technically constituted *prior* to an engagement with VR environments. Hence, the VR environment pulls the user into a negotiation between the time of its technology and regular experiences of duration. The "loss" of experiential time reported needs to be understood at the juncture of these processes of negotiation between technically produced and corporeally habitual space and time. Digital technologies pull temporality through a pre-designated coordinate grid, processing it as if it were a quantitative effect of traversing digital spaces. Yet almost counter to this capability, the digitized processing of space and time allows temporality to be experienced in a qualitatively different way, recalling modes that resonate with the non-linear processes of human cognition and experience such as memory.

Much of VR is described in terms of spatial perception; that is, in terms of the navigation of virtual worlds or an immersion in computer-generated graphics and sound. But the full VR perceptual experience gained by wearing a head-mounted display is in fact generated via temporal manipulation. The effect of feeling immersed in a computer-generated 3-D graphic world is produced by alternating the left and right eye views of the small monitors mounted in front of the immersant's eyes. This process, known as "time multiplexing," literally shuffles alternating images every one-thirtieth of a second or even faster to produce the illusion of stereoscopy.[19] As VR experiences have become increasingly sophisticated, time multiplexing has also been used as a solution for providing individuated visual perspectives for multi-user VR experiences. Here, alternating "world views," combined with other technical features, ensure that each user of the system is presented with an image correctly corresponding to the body-tracking information that the computer has received for that participant.[20] Although the subjective experience of VR is filtered by a representational image layer of traversable terrain and accompanied by action modes such as navigation that utilize the everyday metaphors of physical space, it is digitally realized by breaking time down into discrete states and quantities.

This quantifying vector produces movement in digital virtual space as a succession of alternating instants in time. Thus we might see the technology of VR as part of a direction that has always haunted time-based media: movement captured by stitching its instances together. This direction picks up speed through postindustrial forms of automation, channeling the virtual dimension through ever more rapid and minute processes of quantification. The perceiving body becomes aligned with this general economy of quantified time. It does so by "buying back" its own perceptions as storable instants always available for access: think of the Polaroid Instamatic camera, home video and now the databanks of images being forwarded around the world from cell phones. This commodification of time into instances is exactly the scenario presented to us in the film *Strange Days* (1996), directed by Katherine Bigelow.

In the film, which is set on the eve of the second millennium, the relatively unobtrusive headset device donned by the characters provides, for a hefty black market fee, access to the full sensory recall of their recorded and stored memories. In an early scene Lenny, a trader in virtual memories on the black market, replays and accesses emotional and sexual fragments from his lost relationship. The film revisits a memory of a romantic outing with his girlfriend, in which Lenny's first-person perspective of his lover whirling and ducking on roller-blades is contrasted with the present reality of his lonely and groping body attempting prosthetically to recapture the movements of past sexual desire. The sequence comes to an abrupt end as the data on the memory disk corrupts and his virtual past world crumbles into pixellation. It is as if the futuristic peepshow the film's audience has paid to drop in on suddenly exhausts its line of credit.

But this conception of memory as a perfectly formed illusion of full and present perception is not just futuristic fantasy. It haunts the contemporary relation between virtuality and reality as well. As Lev Manovich argues, the quantification of virtual experiences in digital culture delivered through paid connection time online means that produced "reality" will soon be manufactured and exchanged through digital technologies in the global marketplace like any other product: "The bottom line: the reality effect of a digital representation can now be measured in dollars. Realism has become a commodity. It can be bought and sold like anything else. This condition is likely to be explored by the designers of virtual worlds. If today users are charged for the connection time, in the future they can be charged for visual aesthetics and the quality of the overall experience."[21] One direction new media produces for virtual time, then, is toward quantification, particularly where virtual experience is construed as a replication of real experience.

Yet the temporal telescopy that is foregrounded within the aesthetics of digital realism also allows other kinds of virtual time to emerge. In fact, if we take note of the kind of movement that occurs when we engage with virtual spaces—whether in nonimmersive encounters such as Internet surfing, semi-immersive environments using Virtual Reality Mark-up Language (VRML) and computer game interfaces that offer 180-degree spatial interaction or fully immersive simulated environments—what is happening more closely resembles a traversal between levels and interfaces. All kinds of nonsequential and multidirectional negotiations of temporality are necessary to sustain these activities. Computer gaming, for instance, will often require a user to take a "timeout" to return to a check screen and account for "fuel" use, verify supplies and reload for further action. Online interaction is similarly made up of returns to index pages, revisiting in boxes and retracing hyperlinks. In VR environments, this coming and going is extended to all axes of the spatial coordinate system, ensuring that large stretches of time are spent just flailing around in the virtual surrounds. This multidirectionality qualitatively changes any straightforward narrative of temporality from present back to past or toward the future; time is instead compressed into vertical strata of nonlinear, simultaneously existing layers. The loss of time experienced during computer absorption and immersion can be better described as a temporal encounter comprised of these nonsequential modes, where instants are compressed and rearranged into levels, layers and intervals, becoming multi-accessible from any given single moment. Instead of going anywhere, or moving purposefully in a way we can "account for," experiences of digital virtuality are made up of this "lost" time.

Just by tracing the complex array of potential user movements that is generated through our engagement with new media as a database or an information environment, we reveal the presence, even if in a rather weak form, of nonlinear, virtual time. A stronger understanding still of virtual nonlinearity sees it emerging as the differential outcome of many kinds of interaction between human rhythms and information flows, in which abstract informatic times mingle with embodied forms of duration. The experience of nonlinear time, emerging from the dynamic between computational compression and layering and the correlative durational capacities humans already have to function in nonlinear modes, is a key aspect of information aesthetics. Indeed, it may be that new media can reacquaint us with temporal experiences that are lost in the march of time to the tune of industrial and postindustrial quantification. Here we need to remind ourselves that the differential unfolding of new media—played out in this field of immersive and computer-mediated environments through the relations between the virtual propensities of information and the actualizations of information in concrete social-technical assemblages—can tend toward both convergence and divergence. Wherever new media is actualized aesthetically so as to quantify and sequence time, it converges with and contributes to the production of a commodified information society. Where it displaces and destabilizes temporal and spatial habitual experience *yet continues to work with and transform our embodied selves,* new media has the potential to produce a diverging virtual ecology.

In Deleuze's interpretation of the Bergsonian concept of duration, he presents an understanding of memory in which time is no longer conceived of in a linear manner as the succession of the past by the present.[22] Instead, past and present can coexist simultaneously. A recollection, for example, does not take us backward from the now to the then; it can only occur if we make an ontological leap into "pastness":

> We have to put ourselves into the past in general, then
> we have to choose between the regions: in which one do
> we think that the recollection is hidden, huddled up wait-
> ing for us and evading us? We have to jump into a chosen
> region, even if we have to return to the present in order to
> make another jump, if the recollection sought for gives
> no response and does not realize itself in a recollection-
> image. These are the paradoxical characteristics of a non-
> chronological time: the pre-existence of a past in general;
> the co-existence of all the sheets of the past; and the
> existence of the most contracted degree.[23]

Rather than an independent memory residing within us as a recollection or preserved within objects and data, as is depicted within Lenny's virtual memories in *Strange Days,* we exist coterminously with active temporal processes of memory construction. There is a nonlinear complexity composed by shifting from any moment of the present to coexisting regions of the past and then back to present moments again. Biochemist Steven Rose has a different way of formulating the operation of nonchronological multiplicity that manifests itself in human processes of recollection: he suggests that memory is multimodal.[24] In a mundane example drawn from everyday temporal experience, Rose foregrounds the way in which one's recollection of items from a meal consumed the evening before involves modes for transforming the menu's printed information. These modes range from sensory memory to cognitive work done upon memory to processes of selection and semantic translation: "Information in the printed text of the menu was transformed into recollections of earlier tastes, then the spoken order to the waiter, and then the material reality of the food and its actual taste. And now when I tell you I ate broccoli soup and salmon I neither offer you the printed menu nor the food—still less do I expect you to taste it directly—instead I further modify last night's experience by translating it into a few spoken words."[25] When broken into its different modalities in this way, the "processing" of information through various means of accessing the past—via sensation, linguistic recall, chronological ordering and so on—seems phenomenal. And yet this is part and parcel of our daily negotiation of the world. It should come as no surprise then that as organisms we already have the capacity to shift laterally, to follow biurficatory paths and to move in tandem with the phase/state/mode transitions of the nonlinear nature of computational culture.

To return, then, to the issue of an experiential loss of duration experienced in virtual reality environments, we are in a better position to begin to account for this if we accept that the time we sense in computational immersion is not primarily successive instants but is composed of nonlinear periods and cycles. In digital manifestations of nonlinearity, such as we might find in editing time-based footage nonsequentially, or even in the compressed representation of various ancient worlds in a computer game such as Tomb Raider, multiple versions of the past can coexist with the present and be accessible from any given moment. And for every different edit of past and present together, or every sequence of accessing levels within a game, another future begins to unfold. Something of this potential for multiple coexisting sequences of time also forms the experience of the VR user who can reaccess and repeat sequences of the virtual environment that then affect the outcome of future experience within it. Indeed, VR occupies a strange place that, from the perspective of the user, sits partway between computer gaming and digital time-based editing processes. At the same time, engagement with virtual environments from gaming to VR involves a new habituation for the body and contributes to the formation of new kinds of motor-sensory memories. The digital production of virtual time can also therefore be said to operate multimodally. Temporality is sequentially compressed, and yet new types of rhythms become part of the virtual experience. These many modes and regions are stretched out across a flattened instant, such that time seems to no longer move backward or forward but rather sideways. It is perhaps this lateral rearrangement that accounts for the extended present moment as the frequently experienced duration of digital virtual time. Time is not so much *lost* as compacted into stacked and varying rhythms. And although the quantification of time by a particular sociotechnical regime pulls the virtuality of information toward temporal sequencing and quantification, digital virtuality nevertheless retains its aesthetic dimension: the potential for imaginative virtualization through the underscoring of the existence of many durations.

The Digital Production of Virtual Space

In the majority of fully developed immersive virtual environments, spatial axes and properties such as gravitational pull operate to provide a navigational transition between the user's physical environs and the terrain of the virtual world. Once immersed and familiarized with the head-tracking or data-glove interface commands that will execute virtual movement, relatively ordinary spatial navigation and negotiation of the virtual space can commence. As Murray has noted, immersive virtual environments owe a debt to the shaping of digital space through spatially flattened interfaces such as the Pacman game, playable on Atari computers through the 1970s and 1980s.[26] The first fully interactive virtual environment, Aspen Movie Map, designed by the Architecture Machine Group from MIT in 1978, was literally a cartographic navigation of Aspen, Colorado. It assembled photographic images of the city's streets, shot at three-meter intervals. Although VR was further developed using 3-D graphics by Scott Fisher's work at the NASA-Ames workstation in 1989, the visualization of virtual spaces owes a considerable debt to the coordinates and conventions of Western mapmaking.

Yet maps are not, nor have they ever been, replicas of physical spaces. Instead they deploy a multitude of codes, from scale to color and orientation, to produce representations of space, which in turn affect the way we conceive of and navigate our way back through the places they depict. In their extensive investigation into the cartographies of cyberspace, Martin Dodge and Rob Kitchin put it the following way: "Maps are powerful graphic tools that classify, represent and communicate spatial relations . . . a method to visualize a world that is too powerful and too complex to be seen directly."[27] But, as they further argue, cyberspace is space in the making: it does not exist prior to its myriad visualizations, and hence the very process of imaging forms its contouring and construction. The digital production of virtual space, like virtual time, oscillates between two socio-technical-aesthetic poles: the fabrication of space through familiar strategies of realist representation such as continuity, directionality and referentiality, and the creation of largely unvisualized spaces that operate according to a combination of discontinuity, nonlinearity and distributed connection. Hence virtual spaces are also governed by these two vectors of convergent enfolding and divergent unfolding.

There are a number of historical and political reasons why the first of these poles seems to dominate the cartography of virtual space. Positioned as representations of physical spaces, the new media technologies that have enabled the visualization of virtual spaces are intimately connected with the simulation of terrains constructed for military training and the enactment of combat scenarios.[28] But it is not simply an act of recent historical complicity that brings together virtual spaces and military operations. The relation between the military and cartography is an old one, discernable in the visual economy that belongs to both enterprises: surveillance. Military surveillance involves the stakeout, keeping an eye on the target subject or area, assessing the terrain ahead of time, as it were, and taking into account any contingencies that might unfavorably impinge upon the goal to be achieved. Surveillance thus produces space as terrain to be navigated through for the purpose of accomplishing a particular goal or task. The military heritage of digital virtual spaces has therefore also provided contemporary cyberspaces with cartographic practices that lean toward techniques of surveillance. It is little wonder, then, that most digital virtual spaces exhibit directional, goal-oriented spatial qualities. In the commercial data project MapBlast! an entire server is devoted to cartographic information that can be used to pinpoint locations using a series of zooming techniques that recall the movement of satellite surveillance cameras honing in on their targets.[29] The data can be manipulated to create various maps available to be navigated interactively onscreen. On the demonstration available through the project's Web site, it is possible to enter a global street name in a text field and to generate a zoomable, interactive map, displaying options for differently scaled views of the street. As it happens, there is a more direct connection between these virtual street cartographies and military surveillance. The street maps are graphical facsimiles of data collated from satellites. The GPS (Global Positioning System) satellites were initially set up by the U.S. military, and the data gathered was later sold to corporations, who now find everyday commercial uses for it.

Cybergeographers, VR developers and digital theorists have all argued that virtual spaces need to draw upon the codes of cartography and habits of negotiating proprioceptive space in order to guide the user through the unfamiliar territories of data negotiation.[30] Yet there are also other modes of negotiating space, particularly urban space, that comprise an alternative cartographic tradition in Western culture. In these strolls and wanders that appear in the literature of Baudelaire, the cultural criticism of Walter Benjamin and the polemic and aesthetics of the Situationists, new modes of charting and moving in space then compose new kinds of spaces and new abstractions of the embodied self. The idle sauntering of the *flanêur,* the rapt absorption of the modern human absorbed in panoramic spectacles of consumption and the breaks and disjunctive collages of the Situationist *dérive* or "drift" come close to mapping experiences of engaging with and losing oneself in virtual spaces. Although many of the more commercial or instructional examples of virtual environments have emphasized navigation and task achievement, there is no necessary reason to construe data space in this way.

Furthermore, in spite of all of the requisite cartographic markers, virtual environments, particularly in the case of VR, nevertheless induce experiences of disorientation. This disorienting propensity, which we might more positively understand as the emergence of new and unfamiliar forms of spatiality, has been explored more often by artists who have chosen to produce spaces that negotiate the loss of boundaries, direction and mission. I want to examine some different approaches to the aesthetic production of digital virtual spaces, approaches that both intervene and experiment with the conception of cyberspace as easily navigable. These are exemplified by the practices and writings of the artists discussed below, but I believe they also form the basis for formidable alternative cartographies of cyberspace. These approaches are based upon the idea of virtual *dérive,* in which a number of contemporary artists using VR, the Internet and mixed-reality media have begun to create a form of drifting that not only signals a different kind of movement through, but also a different production of, digital spaces.

The mid-twentieth-century images and theories of Unitary Urbanism, the *dérive* and a critique of the everyday, all exemplified by the Situationists and associates such as Henri LeFebvre, were a series of actual and representational experiments with urban space.[31] In the hope of abandoning official demarcations of the city's districts, images such as street maps that delimited one district from another, and the class distinctions that marked off and distinguished various quarters from each other, groups of Situationists would walk and move through different zones of Paris and Amsterdam. Equipped with walkie-talkies for traversing road and communication spaces, they would attempt to bring disjunctive areas of urban experience into contact with each other. In 1957, Guy Debord published his alternative map of Paris, *Naked City*, which he constructed by ripping up and randomly collaging fragments of a street map of the city that were then linked together with arrows. The *dérive* experiments were both critical and productive: on the one hand, they worked to reveal the way in which images of the city, whether as maps or as government impositions of urban planning, created a simulacrum of seamless space. This construction of space masked the realities of urban dissonance as they were experienced on a day-to-day level as class and ethnic ghettoization and conflict. On the other hand, the Situationists attempted psychogeographical reconstructions of the cityscape that produced spaces of coexistence between people communicating with each other through low-tech devices. For the individual traversing the city in this manner, experiences and memories were subjectively activated and conjured by negotiating the city's disjointed districts. For the Situationists, the drift was a mode of radically overhauling experiences of urban space, which had been historically unmoored from the actual lives of people and had come to be imposed upon, rather than composed by, them.

Throughout the 1990s and into the twenty-first century, the idea of the *dérive* has inspired a number of artists to experiment with and through digital virtual spaces. British artist and activist Heath Bunting has produced several works that appear *dérive*-inspired, including *Underground Movement* (1994), *Visitor's Guide to London* (1995) and *BorderXing Guide* (2001). Bunting's art is interesting because he works between physical and digital spaces and media, sometimes combining physical movement with digital mappings and other times choosing to work exclusively in one space or the other. Hence, the notion that virtual spaces proceed from or replace actual locations in contemporary culture has little relevance to Bunting's work. He moves relatively easily and rapidly between both and pulls his audience and participants across the hype and disjunctions that might be presupposed to divide them. In *Underground Movement,* for example, the artwork comprises a performance by Bunting in which he traces the letters of the alphabet by moving through the London underground tube system. The trace of this performance remains accessible through Bunting's Web site as an image representing the rearrangement of the official transport map that he produced. But the piece is more than a performance and an image; it invites a conceptual interaction in which we begin to rethink what it might mean to disentangle a system of urban movement that was designed to facilitate mass transportation (yet all the while dismally failing and growing into an increasingly convoluted sprawl) into a system for textual communication such as the alphabet. Bunting foreshadows the transformation of material space by information systems but manages to chart the nonsensical element that this also heralds; his performance ultimately provides only letters arranged into a preordained system that is itself devoid of meaning. If there is sense to be derived from Bunting's work, it lies, as it did for the Situationists, in the personal and political act of moving through the representations and imposed chartings of spaces themselves. This physical experience leads to the discovery of the restrictions placed upon openings that are nevertheless still available for human movement within systems of ordered information.

In *BorderXing Guide* Bunting attempted to cross the twenty-eight borders of Europe without legal papers (figure 12). Here, a direct form of sociopolitical *dérive* comes into play, for Bunting's point is that although incorporeal and informatic flows are constantly crossing the lines between nations, producing what we have come to think of as globalism, the physical movement of humans has been increasingly monitored and restricted.[32] This tension has become a point of critique of and intervention in information culture by a number of artists, Keith Piper, Shilpa Gupta and the collective Mongrel, who have variously experienced the colonial legacy of nation-states as enduring in spite of the so-called freedom brought

FIGURE 12. Screenshots of *BorderXing Guide* (2001) by Heath Bunting. Courtesy of the artist.

about by the information age. I will return to these artists in chapter 5 in order to examine the critical and aesthetic relations between movement, globalization and new media that their work signals. Bunting does not simply point to the tension but multiplies it through a process of reversal and restriction. Viewing the sites he both crossed and was unsuccessful in crossing can only be done by either visiting their physical locations or accessing their full documentation at publicly maintained IP addresses. These include a number of art and educational institutions that maintain public access to their Internet servers. A list of authorized online viewing points can be found in the Web documentation of the project and a request to be listed as an authorized point of access can also be made online.[33] Access points to geographical borders are increasingly surveyed in order to regulate the movement of people in and out of nation-states for the purposes of shifting migrant labor forces to areas of postindustrial production and for closing down access to those without working visas or independent financial support. Public or state points of border access are thus put into the service of the private sector. Our "freedom" to roam the great information superhighway is bluntly called into question by Bunting's reverse gesture, as it is only by our being verified as a virtual private citizen with a virtual private address (and a credit card) that we enter the virtual space of restricted information servers in the online world. Bunting's selection of online public access points for his project attempts to build an alternative form of public space through information technologies themselves. Moreover, Bunting's physical negotiation of alternative places to cross the European borders reads like a "how-to" manual for asylum seekers and illegal immigrants. His descriptions and images documenting each crossing detail the physical labor undertaken in order to perform and endure such actions. This is a reminder that migration, especially undertaken on the run, is never easy and involves immense pain and hardship.

Einstein's Brain, the collaborative and ongoing project between Alan Dunning and Paul Woodrow, produces a different kind of virtual space, one given over to flux, chaotic journeying and disorientating sensations. Directly referencing the Situationists, one element of this project, titled "Dérive," produces an explorative, immersive space for the interactant that is accessed through the physical interface of an anatomical model of the human body (figure 13).[34] Tracing the contours of the model with their hands, participants activate sensors to visually navigate the projection of a night sky filling the four walls of the installation. As with other phases of *Einstein's Brain,* random image sequences begin to be projected as the participant selects a point to focus upon in the journey around the body/

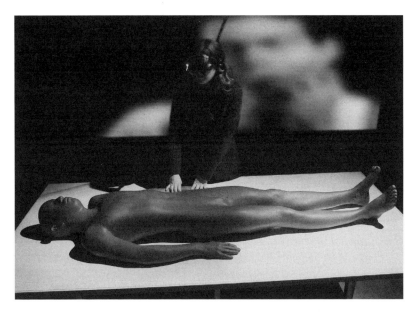

FIGURE 13. A participant interacts with Anatomically Lifelike Interactive Biological Interface (ALIBI). From "The Madhouses: 2001–2004. Pandaemonium" by Alan Dunning and Paul Woodrow (The Einstein's Brain Project, 2002). Courtesy of the Einstein's Brain Project.

map. Dunning and Woodrow play with formal and historical image conventions, suggesting visual and social memories and compositional formulae. But the visual space that is produced never allows an order, purpose or task to clearly emerge for the participant:

> The worlds that are invoked provide a 360° immersive experience in which participants find themselves disoriented and misled by the usual visual codes. These nested worlds present situations and environments, sometimes architectural, sometimes organic, sometimes textual or audio, sometimes hallucinatory, that suggest an understanding of a world in flux, sustained only by the flimsiest of signposts and the most fleeting of memories.[35]

The illusion of user navigational control in virtual space rapidly gives way to the patterns of color, texture and movement emerging and collapsing around the participant. The work signals two trajectories for spatial reconfiguration. First, a drift occurs between the participant's body in actual space, the anatomical representation of the body as interface, and the effects that the sensations of the digital images arranging and rearranging themselves in virtual space produce at a corporeal level for the participant. Neither distance from the body nor full immersion occur: instead, a series of loops traces an iterative cartography, sometimes covering the same ground, sometimes opening new spaces. Second, VR is not conceived as a map of the world that is knowable or accessible outside of human perception and movement. Like the *dérive*, virtual environments can become experiments for changing the meaning and value of space for us. The resultant experience is one in which the corporeal experience of perception and the social codes of visual representation are thrown out of alignment:

> We are developing worlds in which the raggedness of the
> virtual reality systems are exaggerated and invoke those dys-
> functions of perception associated with brain damage and
> mental illness. Vision is blurred, detail is shifting and in-
> constant, slower or faster frame rates suggest a rendering
> engine behind the scenes, left or right hand sides of stereo-
> scopic vision blink out, depth perception is lost, objects only
> appear when one is in motion, the edges of the worlds visibly
> reinvent themselves.[36]

Rather than seamlessness and integration, effects that digital audiovisual technologies often attempt to sustain, marginal perception and the edges of visual space occupy the visual field of *Einstein's Brain*. And here we return to the idea of perception as a continuum from the peripheral to the orderly, and to the way in which new media might actively help us attend to the emergence of visually coherent worlds out of chaos. We detect the resonance of the differential aesthetics of baroque perception.

Virtual Selves—Actual Embodiment
On the face of it, digital virtuality has seemed bent upon enlarging the gaps that separate its times and spaces from the coordinates of the material world, coordinates that need bodies in order to have experiences. It has achieved much of its notoriety and criticism from the claim that it can disconnect consciousness and perception from their anchors in living human matter. As we have seen, artists have used strategies of reversal and subversion that promote drift and disorientation over the navigability and task-oriented character of more mainstream virtual spaces. Yet what is nevertheless forming across all kinds of virtual environments, those where time compacts and space intensively unfolds, is the production of a new kind of embodiment.

In Scott Fisher's description and schematization of NASA's early investment in a VR model and system, the user's body seems so encumbered by technology that it disappears beneath the hardware:

> When combined with magnetic head and limb position tracking technology, the head-coupled display presents visual and auditory imagery that appears to completely surround the user in 3D space. The gloves provide interactive manipulation of virtual objects in virtual environments that are either synthesized with 3D computer-generated imagery, or that are remotely sensed by user-controlled, stereoscopic video camera configurations. The computer image system enables high performance, realtime 3D graphics presentation that is generated at rates up to 30 frames per second as required to update image viewpoints in coordination with head and limb motion. Dual independent synchronized display channels are implemented to present disparate imagery to each eye of the viewer for true stereoscopic depth cues.[37]

This detailed description has become a seminal diagram for the relation between VR hardware, software and the user's body (figure 14). And yet, like virtuality itself, this diagram adds a dimension. But it is one that is difficult to visualize or perhaps just to spatialize in ordinary Cartesian terms. It comes closer to being circumscribed by lines of connection and direction than by anything else, lines that are virtual, as they are not all quite there. These lines cut across the captive body of the VR user, the prosthetic clothing worn, the exterior, interface devices, and the representation of 3-D surround sound and images, and they traverse and couple all of these areas with each other. These lines suggest to me the criss-crossed complexity, rather than the predesignated nature, of virtuality. They are the best thing I can find for signposting the more subtle relations coalescing in Fisher's model between materiality and information, actual and virtual, the human and the machinic. For rather than rising above or beyond the matter of our bodies, rather than disappearing past the horizon of the actual, even hyped and overly technophilic notions of the virtual, engage transversal relations to materiality.

As the NASA model shows, the user/immersant's body acts like a kind of power point. For all of its technological trappings promising freedom from this world, VR interfaces eventually lead back to the ground of embodiment from which they claim to depart. But because most versions of VR are inclined to wish away this ground, they tend to restrict the range of

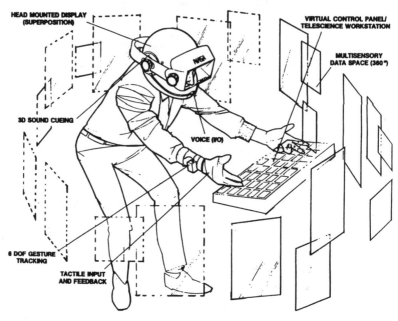

FIGURE 14. Virtual Environment Workstation Project (VIEWlab) at NASA Ames Research Center, 1998. VIEWlab system included helmet mounted display with 3-D sound, speech recognition, and datagloves. Project Director Scott S. Fisher. Photo: NASA/S. S. Fisher, W. Sisler, 1988.

impact and activity of their foundation, loading the body of the user up with wires and sensors and thereby turning it into a joystick for the machine's operations. Yet we can nevertheless begin to think about the lines of connection that cut across the virtual production of the self in digital spacetime and the actual corporeality of the user in its perceptual and social dimensions as an emergent technological embodiment.

The limitations on human movement produced by the restrictive nature of VR experience and representation have led, more recently, to attempts to produce different technical experiences of the virtual. Noting the restriction of bodily freedom that wearing a head-mounted display creates, MIT technicians during the mid-1990s developed the CAVE project.[38] The user and other participants enter a cubed room made up of 3-D sound and moving image. Instead of all of the cumbersome clothing, there are only slimmed-down head-tracking and hand sensor devices that allow repositioning of sound and graphics in real time on the four surrounding screens in relation to the viewpoint of the main user. In somewhat naïve adulation for this alternative "room" as compared to the encumbered VR platform, Michael Heim has suggested that a virtual environment such as this adds to and amplifies corporeal experience: "Because the user's body is immersed without having to adapt to the system's peripherals (heavy helmet, tight data glove, calibrated earphones), the CAVE immersion does not constrict but rather enhances the user's body."[39] More radically, the Canadian artist Char Davies has developed a VR interface for her works *Osmose* (1995) and *Ephémère* (1998) that senses both the breath and the balance of the user, deploying them to move in a floating form of navigation through her world of luminous and transparent 3-D images.[40] This, she claims, simulates the experience of scuba diving and facilitates a sense of both space and embodiment that removes one from the sphere of everyday life but not from the corporeal.

Both Heim and Davies make ontological claims for these forms of VR, suggesting that they return their participants to a renewed sense of "being in the world." This term they both appropriate somewhat haphazardly from phenomenology to refer to the bridging of mind and body enabled by new negotiations of VR. Here, nature and the material world are supposedly augmented rather than replaced, and technology functions to center and resubjectify rather than instrumentalize and objectify the world for the immersant. Heim and Davies pay tribute to the Heideggerian critique of technology by focusing on the phenomenological experience of body and self in VR. In its military/industrial/entertainment version, VR can be seen as symptomatic of the brutal modern "enframing" of the world as nothing more than a resource. According to Heidegger, bodies, human or otherwise, are here merely a "standing reserve" to be wrenched from their present and/or historical contexts and used up in the frenzied race to continue to sustain technological systems.[41] A non-instrumentalist deployment of technology within an aesthetic VR environment would allow modern technology to reconnect with *technē*, Heidegger's reworking of the ancient Greek relationship between technology and technique or craft. For Heim and Davies, this can be achieved through the magical gesture of adding the body back into the virtual picture. In spite of our historical experiences, and hence habituations, of living an instrumentalized relationship between technologies and matter, the assumption made by Heim and Davies is that embodiment in its "natural" and rightful state can somehow be revitalized via "care-full" recombination with technologies. We have returned here to the notion that bodies and technologies are constituted components *prior* to their interaction.

How is it that critics, revisionists and apologists for VR all reach almost identical predictions for both its normative and potentially subversive uses and impact? Perhaps in these visions of VR, technology is consistently conceived in a transcendental relation to the body. Contrary to any overt declarations of re-embodying the world, the body in all of these accounts is either perceived to be an impediment that a prostheticized technics must help to overcome or a supplement to be added back into a technology that has lost its "way."[42] This brings us back to those dividing and connecting lines that begin to form as we conceive of different ways of seeing new media technologies as modes of living our embodiment. Lines, I have already suggested, are difficult to spatialize, perhaps partly because VR is frequently theorized and manifests itself as a problem of solving the relations of four-dimensional space/time (lived corporeality) through what is essentially a 3-D sleight of hand (the visual illusion of immersion). The line, on the other hand, is more of a two-dimensional problem that is always threatening to collapse back, fuse or actualize itself in a completely singular way. Turn a line on its side—look at a line from the point of view of its depth, its third dimension—and it is nothing more than a point. The line and its relation to points of singularity may provide us with a way to think of embodiment and virtuality together, as a set of relations between elements simultaneously joined together and deforming as they intersect at certain points and move apart from each other following various vectors or lines.

In Fisher's diagrammatic sketch this singularity is produced, paradoxically enough, in a transversal manner. At least three "incorporeal universes of reference" intersect with each other.[43] Incorporeal universes of reference can here be understood as fields such as the arts, the media, or political or economic forms such as late capital, which exist as ontologically prior to a specific formation of subjectivity or to the production of actual technical objects. Subjectivity experienced as disembodied is thus an actualization that occurs through the intersection, and hence singularization, of several of these universes. In the case of the Fisher model for VR, a number of universes are singularized through transversal relations and thus allow for the actualization of the technical object VR—for example, an incorporeal, electronically mediated universe of 3-D sound and image; a technological universe that makes, via silicon, the material production of the former feasible; and the universe of the gestural and performative human body. And, of course, to keep these fields at just three cuts short the trajectories of these lines. Already we can see in this conventional model for body and technology in virtual reality the sense in which these vectors move beyond the confines of this VR space, this platform, this room, pointing toward an outside, a connection to yet other universes of reference. These might include a political/economic universe that finances VR, an imaginary universe desiring the concretization of VR based on the familiar territory of Cartesian space, and so on.

What is interesting about these lines of connection between universes of reference is the extent to which they override the distinction between spheres such as the material and the immaterial, the real and the virtual, the corporeal and the technological. They draw our attention toward the ways in which bodies and new media technologies are beginning to operate conjointly. But they simultaneously make us aware of the gaps punctuating this conjunction. Technologies of VR, viewed from this framework of transversal singularity (a gathering of points that cross each other to form divergent lines), can offer an understanding of the mutations that machines and bodies are currently undergoing. They cannot, however, provide a technological fantasy ride into a sublime, virtual realm, nor do they simply represent the culmination of modern technology's inexorable march toward the ultimate in dehumanization: corporeality as instrumentalized objectified experience. Rather, to paraphrase Guattari, they are actualizations of machines of virtuality.[44]

What is important in focusing on the diagrammatic aspect of VR as a means of thinking of virtuality is the ontological shift this brings about. We move away from the subject as self-synthesis of the sentient, and technology as the transcendental subject of history. But, as Brian Massumi has argued, diagrams do not give us a plan of the virtual any more than the 3-D immersive graphics of the NASA-Ames workstation do.[45] Virtuality, as such, cannot appear but can only be inferred through the relations between the elements of a diagram. Lived corporeality is not a state but a flux that flows in and out of the other fluxes of the social machine, technical machine, art machine and war machine. Massumi's insight is to suggest that topology—a geometry of the changes affecting both the alteration and the retention of the morphology of the diagram—provides the contours of the virtual. The fluctuating diagram that might appear in the wake of this virtual tracing would signal both the qualitative changes undergone by parts of the assemblage body-VR and the qualities that also persist and remain impervious to changes.

We would now need to resituate the role of the embodiment of the VR user as centrifugal to the Fisher model. The forces impinging on a user/operator of VR technologies produce a series of sensations that are experienced as continuous, qualitative changes for her or him. It is the analog experience of living a body in relation to the forces that impinge upon that body that produce those fleeting sensations of virtuality. Massumi indicates the importance of both affective embodiment and the domain of the analog in relation to the virtual. But the digital, scaled down from its commodified hype, may also be a mode of setting off the pulsations, repetitions and multiplications that our bodies, analog compositions that they are, can use to transform themselves and become virtual selves. Analog/digital relations are interdependent rather than separate. With this interdependency also comes the acknowledgment of the interrelations between corporeality and technology, actuality and virtuality. These interdependencies trace out various actualizations of virtual subjectivity. As Hayles has argued, VR technologies may allow us to experience subjectivity that does not remain bounded by our bodies but rather is distributed across our physical bodies and virtual selves.[46] These are doubled in VR environments, games and many other forms of new media interfaces.

Another way to picture this trajectory is to think outside the notion of line as direction or movement toward a finite state of resolution—virtual reality—and to see virtualization as an expanding and contracting field of differentiation, an enfolding of matter by informational incorporeality. Hayles suggests that this trajectory has led to a restructuring of Western culture's ideas about the material world, such that we now see it as inextricably bound up with the immaterial patterns that constitute code: "*Virtuality is the cultural perception that material objects are interpenetrated by information patterns.*"[47] But the way that this "condition of virtuality" is currently understood is in terms of a weighting toward the immaterial. Materiality is conceived of as the carrier for what is ultimately more essential: the information it houses. Information needs something through which to pass in order to transmit its flows. The material is not perceived as a force of equal strength in relation to virtualization but rather as the difference from which the virtual cannot quite seem to escape. The interpenetration of materiality by information is not generally acknowledged to result in interdependency but consistently remainders matter as smaller and smaller differences that effectively no longer matter. Hence we might think of dominant manifestations of VR as a kind of blocking of the virtual elasticity of human carbon bodies (their ability to become other than static, weighty impediments) by an overinvestment/overdetermination of the informatic universe by capital.[48] In this light it has seemed almost "natural" to assert the importance of the "body" or "embodied experience" as an antidote to this movement toward virtualization, as Heim and Davies do. But the point is not to continue to pit body against technology, actuality against virtuality; rather we must address the question of how to actualize the virtual in ways that take into account the virtual, incorporeal capacities of matter.

Virtualization, understood through transitions and transactions between information and the materiality of our bodies, involves a multiplication of affect, of the capacities of conceptualizing, perceiving and feeling embodiment. It incurs the strange situation, for example, of learning to negotiate a three-handed body, for instance. Two hands occupy ordinary spatial and specular relations with our eyes, while another, split from us via the mediation of the digital, extends an invitation to jump across the physical environment to the information sphere. The virtual dimension of matter, that is, the capacity of bodies to enable this transition, is really an ongoing question: how can our biology continue to become different? This dimension, elaborated through the virtual lines that I have been following in Fisher and Guattari, traces embodied relations of chaotic, biotic, interior flux all the way to emerging thresholds of complex organization. These verge upon and fold into outside forces and forms, such as technical machines. Guattari's lines of virtuality, like the lines in Fisher's diagrammatic sketch of VR, struggle to be registered at the level of representation, but this does not mean they do not register at all. As Massumi notes in his work on affect, these are virtually impossible lines to trace; they happen too quickly to register in our current cultural vocabulary of separating the world into either/or relations: "The virtual is a lived paradox where what are normally opposites coexist, coalesce and connect; where what cannot be experienced cannot but be felt—albeit reduced and contained."[49] What we feel as our ordinary everyday embodiment is only one actualization of intersecting sensory and proprioceptive virtuality, concretized over a period of time into habits and recognizable rhythms. Virtual reality environments can affect those habits by disrupting the speed, rhythm and direction of movement and stasis. This disturbance may temporarily make us feel that we have moved outside of or beyond the boundedness of our bodies. These environments frequently alter our perceptual and spatial relation to the horizon and play with our sense of bodily scale. In Char Davies's works, users learn to travel through vertical, virtual environments by focusing on the rising and falling rhythms of breathing instead of navigating through space organized through the conventions of perspective and so on. Davies's experiments with VR could therefore be rethought in terms of what they offer as new modes of techno-embodiment, rather than simply as a return of the body to virtual reality.[50] But if VR as a digital technology has something to say to us in the register of existence, it is to underscore the fact that bodies in many kinds of experiences are in the process of becoming virtual; VR is only one among countless other organizations of virtuality.

The issue is not so much one of accrediting new media technologies with the dematerializing of the body; bodies are constantly extending toward an incorporeal dimension as they become virtual. Rather, the problem is the extent to which these technologies claim virtuality as a property unique to themselves, and as the only possible way of organizing the virtual. The problem with VR is its claims for technologically managed and delivered ontology. Frances Dyson signals the extent to which, according to this techno-being, the virtual self is reduced to a predicate of new technologies: "Thus the 'ontology' of cyberspace does not imply the being of some thing or another, rather it signals the attempts to assign Being as an attribute to these new forms of media and communications."[51] As a result, other virtualities, other becomings pass by unnoticed as VR is accorded the status of technologically altering our fundamental modes of being and hurtling us into the next millennium. This is an ethical or political problem in which certain forms of technologically enhanced environments are attributed with more value and hence are invested with greater funding, infrastructural support and expertise than others. Although we cannot actualize the technical object VR outside of the social machine that creates it as an ensemble of disembodied prosthetics and quantifiable spacetime, we might momentarily exploit the paradox engendered by this set of conditions. This paradox lies in the ability of VR to also contribute to the production of technologically embodied experiences.

Furthermore, we might look for these curious moments, mainly highlighted by new media artists, that unfold embodiment as an ongoing and incomplete proposition. In arguing for virtuality to be viewed as a differential in relation to its current and potential actualizations, I have suggested that folding can be made concurrent with the concerns of contemporary aesthetics. Folding now emerges as a discontinuous line of force(s) that brings together informatic selves and organic bodies into a proximity to which they strangely or contingently belong. Where the baroque arts and sciences produced a *scientia* entwined with history, local anecdote and passions to draw the viewing subject into an aesthetic relation with the matter displayed before them, information aesthetics now needs to invent an affectivity for its culture from the sensations and perceptions that its technologies produce. This may better help us to understand the dynamic of information and bodies, of the plastic incorporeal and the extensivity of material life.

An interface is a contact surface.　　　— BRENDA LAUREL[1]

An interface is an obstacle: it stands between a person and the system being used.　　　— DONALD NORMAN[2]

4 **interfaciality** from the friendly face of computing to the alien terrain of informatic bodies

The Interface and the Problem of Facialization

Between the two seemingly opposed approaches of Brenda Laurel and Donald Norman to the design of computer software and hardware, an even playing field defining the dominant relations between humans and computers has been mapped out over the last two decades. Laurel, who has had considerable influence in the areas of software interface design, digital theory and digital art practice, evokes the specter of the inhuman, alien computer.[3] Held at arms reach, it stretches across to our world, making contact with the human at surface points only. Here, the interface functions as glue, tenuously holding together the incompossible worlds of the machinic and the organic. It desperately seeks out some common ground of communication in order to unite them. Norman, who lays the foundation stone of cognitive psychology's contribution toward relations between computers and humans, signals a desire to erase this surface. He craves instead the seamless, convenient integration of the computational universe into the friendly but inept world of the "user."

A rather different approach emerges from the experiments in interface design conducted by artists using new media. The field of information interface design in artistic and more pragmatic arenas is vast, covering all manner of objects and environments, from screen to haptic interaction. I am mainly concerned in this chapter with the ways in which humans' bodies have been both specifically engaged by new media artists and elided by so many other forms of design for body-computer interaction. I want to suggest that new media artists concerned with body-computer interaction have simultaneously designed evanescent *and* palpable interfaces. In departing from a preconception about the interface as the requisite representation or translation of computer architecture or functionality for an inept human user, these artists have opted for dynamic interfaces. These emerge as shifting arrangements through actual engagement and interaction between participants and computational machines. What I will be arguing in this chapter is that the body-computer interface in new media art can be more readily grasped through concepts such as the fold and the differential. Where the fold designates the interface as a topology and movement of extension and envelopment between body and computer, the differential of this engagement indicates that interfaces remain the domain of an irresolvable relationship between material and incorporeal forces.

In artist David Rokeby's work, interfaces are at once nonspecific, invisible sites that are tangible and pervasive. Rokeby began work on *Very Nervous System (VNS)* in 1986, developing a new media sonic interface environment using video cameras, image processors, computers, synthesizers and a sound system (figure 15).[4] The piece is very much an experience, and if one were to look for the *VNS* interface, it would be hard to pinpoint its location. Rokeby has set up the installation in both gallery and public spaces, including the street, and from a distance a *VNS* participant might look engrossed in their own private post–dance party ritual. Working on fast feedback between the body's motion and its position, captured through image data and sent to audio file databases, a participant in the *VNS* space learns to trigger, play and sculpt an array of sound samples through corporeal kinetic engagement. And yet the fluidity of both the sound—there is a range of tonal and atonal scales, beats and textures available to mix into the space—and the movement involved turns the *VNS* environment away from a goal-directed activity such as controlling the audio space as if it were an instrument to be mastered. Instead, as Rokeby suggests, the interface is a space for improvisation, and the more one improvises in its space, the more the space develops its shifting topography:

> The active ingredient of the work is its interface. The interface is unusual because it is invisible and very diffuse, occupying a large volume of space, whereas most interfaces are focused and definite. Though diffuse, the interface is vital and strongly textured through time and space. The interface becomes a zone of experience, of multi-dimensional encounter. The language of encounter is initially unclear, but evolves as one explores and experiences.[5]

And yet *VNS* intensively focuses the participant's attention onto her body. The point is not therefore to lose one's body and enter into a limitless communion with computational space. Once again we see a key motif of new media aesthetics emerging in this seminal work by Rokeby, which reminds us of the continuity of perceptual experience first noted by baroque thinkers, scientists and artists. Corporeal experience (or aspects of it) extends and intensifies and, in so doing, splits, folds or inflects away from a sense of the body as bound and closed to the outside world. Hence the

FIGURE 15. David Rokeby in *Very Nervous System* (1986–90). The interface is installed in a street in Potsdam. Photo: Lambert Blum. Courtesy of the artist.

body-computer interface in new media art is typically both intensely embodied *and* diffusely abstract.

Artists have frequently responded to the so-called dematerializing tendencies of information culture by bringing bodies into direct contact with computational hardware in their work. In Diane Ludin's performance and database installation *Memory Flesh 2.0* (2004), a performer sits calmly suturing her leg while images, originally obtained from the Internet and now stored in a database, are generated into collages on an adjacent monitor (figure 16).[6] The stream of image collages is comprised of journalistic and scientific texts statements and visual content engendered and published on the Web upon completion of the Human Genome Project (HGP). We are confronted with the public discourse and face of the HGP—a scientific endeavor that transforms "the body" into sequences of dematerialized information—in immediate proximity and jarring contact with the intimate and overtly painful gestures of skin penetration and body modification.

As it turns out, the suturing is only a performance; the woman stitching away at herself is piercing nothing more than a pair of nylons. A bend sensor is attached to the needle so that while the suturing takes place, the signal generated by the performer's gestures can be cross-processed and used to generate the database image collages.[7] The point in *Memory Flesh 2.0* is not so much that the suturing is fake but that it is a performance; it gestures toward something in a metaphorical manner. For Ludin, the metaphor of penetrating the body's surface with a technological device helps us think about the ways in which information—especially information from something as regulatory and managerial as the HGP—literally gets under our skin. Equally, the visceral body, that body sitting just below the epidermis, becomes the source from which dematerialized versions of an informatically organized body are first generated. An interesting correlation between Rokeby and Ludin's understanding of body-computer interaction arises in the interstices between 1980s high-end dedicated hardware interfaces and the new media interfaces of the new millennium. In *Very Nervous System* Rokeby drew our attention, to the extent to which computational interface design derived from a tradition in which the "body" had been removed. In 2004 Ludin made this very same observation and used it as a starting point for the juxtaposition between a startling body-based performance and the continuing shuttered sensibility of information technologies: "The Internet and information as well as computer technology are all about restriction. Because this is the case, representations of the body have to be extreme and exaggerated to begin to reflect something of power, something of experience/life that we are used to outside the com-

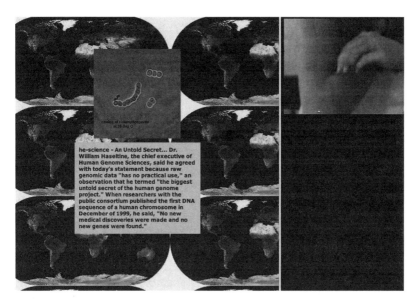

FIGURE 16. Screenshot of *Memory Flesh 2.0: A Micro Media Record* by Diane Ludin (2004). Courtesy of the artist.

puter."[8] Body-computer interaction in both of these cases is not accomplished through the seamless transmission of information from one dislocated space to another. Surfaces and volumes, contours and folds may be hooked into each other through information circuits, but frictional and resistant interfaces emerge from these interactions.

In the more traditional approach to human-computer interaction (HCI), Laurel and Norman's positions on the interface have, since the late 1980s, set the outer parameters of our interactions with computers. Both Norman and Laurel belong to a loose network of software and hardware designers from influential institutions such as MIT, the NASA-Ames Research Center, Xerox-Parc, the Carnegie-Mellon Robotics Institute and Apple Computer. This looseknit group has been responsible for the development of such computational design features as the desktop, the Windows, Icons, Mice and Pointers interface design style and the development of early immersive virtual environments.[9] Designing interactions between humans and computers has a much longer history and can be traced to work done by J. C. R. Licklider, Douglas Englebart, Ivan Sutherland and others from the late 1950s to the 1970s. Nevertheless, we will focus here on the consolidation of HCI from the 1980s onward, because a number of key issues structuring the way we have come to think about relations between bodies and digital machines come into clear view from this time. In fact, Laurel and Norman are not really at odds with one another's design concerns and methodologies. Norman's emphasis on the user's goals as the start and end point of the interaction between computers and humans can be seen as a guiding principle for a generation of younger designers such as Laurel. What has ultimately been at stake in this design field is the attempt to map the interface from an anthropomorphic perspective.[10] The emergence of an almost fanatical concern with interfaces that are "user-friendly" and with machines that do the bidding of humans by the end of the 1990s comes to the foreground in the useability discourse of Web design aficionados such as Jakob Nielsen.[11]

There is a more profound sense in which the symmetry of these two positions—the one advocating the filling in of the interstices between human and computer with the interface, the other doing away with the requirement for contact altogether as the two spheres become one—is apparent. The premises of HCI filter into and arrange our everyday engagements with digital technologies, such as sitting in front of a computer-keyboard interface. They also support the development of certain directions in interactive digital art, setting up a closed and reflexive circuit between the human and the computer in which one party is attributed with the qualities of the other. I will suggest in this chapter that the force I call interfaciality organizes these premises and has permeated the broader experiences in which interaction between computers and human bodies occurs. This has guided the trajectory of our relations with new media technologies along a particular line of subjectivation. The notion of subjectivation implies the production of a certain kind of position that the human subject assumes or becomes, and it implies that this position is always produced through the play of power relations. The idea of assuming the position of the "user" with respect to the computer is therefore not about taking control of digital technology. Rather "users," as the artwork of both Rokeby and Ludin reminds us, have their movement restricted by computation. Sitting in front of a computer monitor and interacting with an interface intimates a certain form of bodily posture and gesture that is clearly demarcated. The "user" greets or confronts a screen and thereby interacts with the "face" of the computer; we are as much placed and used by this ergonomics as we are users in it.

We can think through the development of HCI as a twist in a particular line of subjectivation: facialization. Facialization is a system of codifying bodies according to a centralized conception of subjectivity or agency in which the face, literally or metaphorically, is the conduit for signifying, expressing and organizing the entire body.[12] Because the computer also comes to figure as a "subject" in HCI, it too takes on facialized attributes and qualities. The *body*-computer relation is effectively erased and what is deemed to take place instead is a communication exchange, in the form of friendly or authoritative "face-to-face" conversation, between the user and the computational software or hardware.[13] The emphasis on conversation, user-friendly design and facial iconography, such as the happy and sad Macs that were a sign of system operation and failure in Apple's operating system up to Version 9, are all examples of the codification of digital technologies through this system of facialization. Structured by these facializing mechanisms, computers invoke a particular kind of subject position for themselves in the form of the conversational agent or a subjectivation for the user—the conversant with control (or not) over the machine. The differences that bodies contribute to interactions with technologies are subordinated to these two poles of facial subjectivation. More fundamentally, Deleuze and Guattari have argued that information theory—and its reliance upon the discrete on/off switching that characterizes binary digital logic—is also codified by a "machine" of faciality.[14] As I will argue later, new media establish very specific modes of facializing or *inter*facializing, in which particular kinds of subjectivations are invoked. I will refer to these as, first, a subject defined as pure surface; second, a posthuman subjectivity; and third, a programmatic subjectivity. In total these interfacializations aim to overcome the differentiation always at stake in body-computer interaction, by eradicating the distinction between human and machine. This is achieved by ignoring the material conditions of human-computer engagements and by "elevating" this interaction to a communicative, cognitive level. Interfacializations also bequeath certain powers and even proto-subjectivities to computers, such as the helpful servant or the suprahuman conquering race of future robots.

As we saw in the case of virtual reality, however, by locating the forces that have taken hold of and organized a particular area of digital technology it is also possible to see that relations between bodies and computational machines might become other than facialized ones. In this chapter, a field of relations—HCI—will become the object of productive critique in order to open up a space for thinking about other ways that the interface between bodies and computational machines might be conceptualized. From this point we will then need to turn directly to experiments within new media art in which the interface is experienced as a dynamic, enfolded relationship between information and the sensate body. There is, then, an alternate trajectory to be taken by attending to body-computer interaction within the sphere of new media art. This is signaled, I argue, through artworks that utilize informatic renderings of the body while simultaneously situating their audience within immersive technological environments. I will suggest that the potential of this work lies not in the reduction of bodies to information but in the disjunction these art interfaces open up between code and matter. These interfaces organize computers and bodies through productive, differential relations. Furthermore, new media art has opened into the biotechnical field, in which the artwork has turned into matter itself, but a new kind of matter that is imbued with code. Biology, produced and understood through the technologies of tissue culture, cloning and recombinant gene therapy, has become a critical concern for an emerging group of artists. The predominant use of information theory when applied to biology has, arguably, resulted in a reduction of corporeality to an effect of code.[15] The interface between bodies and technology, it could be argued, has disappeared in these works not by eradicating matter but by becoming it. Yet these directions in information aesthetics offer the body-computer interface another trajectory where machine or digital code and matter are mutually constituted through relations of symbiosis and differentiation.

Friendly Faces and Disappearing Humans: The Two Poles of Interfaciality

During the late 1980s interface design underwent something of a rethink. Having lived with the desktop as a standard in user-friendly interface design from the 1984 Apple Macintosh onward, many designers were criticizing this metaphor by the end of the decade.[16] In giving the user virtual objects that seemed to resemble real objects—desktops, trashcans and windows, for example—various "unfriendly" aspects of the machine had been inadvertently unleashed. The assumption that the computer would act according to the representative status of its icons had led to problems in the smooth translation between the physical and the digital worlds. So, for example, placing a file icon on top of a folder icon in a virtual desktop subsumes the file into the folder, which is not how items on a desktop in physical space behave.[17] These kinds of failures in correspondence often led to user difficulties in navigating systems and utilizing software. Because the relation between the digital and the physical seemed to break down at a metaphoric level, many designers assumed that the interface, as the space of both representation and action, needed serious readjustment. The fault seemed to lie with a failure to produce digital systems that were friendly or comprehensible enough for the user. This was partially blamed on the poor translation metaphor offered. Only metaphors that mapped an exact translation between the interface and the physical world should therefore be deployed. As one designer stated: "To the extent that an interface metaphor provides users with realistic expectations about what will happen, it enhances the utility of the system. To the extent it leads users astray, or simply leads them nowhere, it fails."[18] Interface design moved in two directions that led to its current configuration under a regime of facialization. First, designers and system architects ceased to think of computers as objects that simply required a friendly face. Yet they completely facialized the activity of digital systems by conceiving of computational processes in terms of agency. Nicholas Negroponte wanted to release the interface from its role as the face of the machine, as it had appeared in the desktop model of HCI.[19] He imagined digital technologies as distributed media that would be fully integrated into everyday life. But for him, computers are simply technological processes under the control of (sub)human agency, robots constituting a servant class dutifully performing tasks for the user. The disappearance of the interface as a space for direct visual manipulation gives way here to voice-activated command, signaling not the fading away but the triumph of anthropomorphism. Computers join the human taxonomy, only in the form of a less socially evolved class of life, as distributed delegates. How, then, under the complete reduction of computational process to human agency, can we hope to *become* digital, as Negroponte dreams? To move outside of ourselves and form new assemblages in relation to machines?

The marketing of algorithms as graphic virtual pets—a strategy for making computational technologies more user-friendly—also evinces this reterritorialization of the digital machine by the human face. "The Norns," first released in 1996, represents this pole of facialization.[20] Produced by the company Cyberlife, "norns" are software algorithms represented by graphical interfaces in the form of virtual pets "living" on the desktop, programmed to breed, mutate and "evolve" over generations. Again human agency becomes the meeting space for interaction between user and computer by codifying a machinic process as subordinate to, but partaking in, behavior that humans can comprehend. Cyberlife elevates the computer subroutine from slave or servant status to the same ground of ethical life as the human: "CyberLife is concerned with the re-vivification of technology. Through CyberLife we are putting the soul back into lifeless machines—not the souls of slaves, but willing spirits, who actually enjoy the tasks they are set and reward themselves for being successful."[21]

Historically the movements of the soul in the human body in Western thinking have been seen to play themselves out across facial expression and structure. Patricia Magli argues that it has been the role of the animal's face to provide a comparative anatomy with the human through the disciplines of physiognomy, phrenology and, later, anthropology.[22] The animal enforces an identity for the human inasmuch as the human can be judged by its varying degrees of proximity to, or removal from, the animal's face. Facialization is a system that requires differences to be meted out in terms of deviation from a norm: the face. Rather than detect a new form of digital "life" growing on our desktops when we install "The Norns," we find instead the algorithm functioning as a code for faciality. These cyberlife forms become the new computational sets of deviations against which we measure the steadfastness of an exclusively androcentric control over and relation to technology. Additionally, the friendly and cheerful pet interface now assigned to digital technology relieves us of the ethical burden of an emerging class of machine slaves.

The rise of useability discourse in the area of Web design throughout the 1990s and its seepage into the broader domain of software interface development comprise the culmination of digital facialization. This discourse subsumes the face of computing under the control of the information-seeking user. The problem for useability gurus such as Nielsen lies in the current state of sociotechnical affairs to which we have succumbed: "humanity has lost mastery of its tools."[23] Interface design must be made to lean toward easy navigability rather than be swept away by artifice and its distraction. Indeed, the interface should obediently facilitate the movement of the user in one direction only—toward obtaining the desired information. Embedded within this position is a deep distrust of the surface altogether and its tendencies toward the decorative, the spectacular and the deceptive. Rather, one must steer a clear course through these distractions by ceaselessly invoking the centrality of the human user. As it happens, Nielsen concomitantly holds this user in poor esteem, insisting that useable interface design equals easy navigability; the figure of the user that emerges here is a dumbed-down consumer requiring repetition and bullet-point text in order to digest a Web site.

Nielsen's defense of the design-engineer's opposition to the artifice of design in fact disregards the artificiality lying at the core of the engineered, digital machine. Any signs of superfluity at the level of the interface, particularly the unsparing use of the image as navigation metaphor, should be treated with suspicion and represent a likely attempt to beguile the user.[24] We find echoes here of the debate initiated by the *philosophes* and moral philosophers such as Rousseau from the mid to late eighteenth century. During this period, the decorative excesses of late baroque visual culture were sternly denounced. The tendency to collect and display ever more bizarre objects in the *Wunderkammer*, the spectacle of opulence enacted in courtly entertainment, the lavishness of rococo architecture and the corruption of the sciences through a reliance on quackery and visual tricks became the target for a lament about the general decline of culture.[25] Useability and user-centered interface design revive the late-eighteenth-century turn away from the sumptuousness of visual culture and toward utilitarianism. The basic constitution of the human interacting with the computational machine must be information seeking; the surface/interface that the machine presents to this human must therefore be stripped of the signs of artifice. Artifice, especially visual artifice, may connote the digital as a wayward, uncontrollable entity, and therefore something to be brought to obedience. In the words of one software interface designer, "How can the program put an understandable and controllable face on technology?"[26] It is the human face that must ultimately emerge satisfied, if smiling somewhat dumbly, from this encounter.

The second set of facialization strategies lies with the attempt by interface designers to eliminate the interface as a space of differentiation between human and computer. But this does not imply a dismantling of the face system itself, even though designers such as Brenda Laurel have argued against personifying the computer at the level of the interface.[27] She insightfully analyzes the conflict within the interface, in that it involves the production of two faces—user and computer—that require constant rejoining in order to communicate. The mark of the interface should therefore be erased, particularly within immersive systems. Here the user and system can both be conceived as agents incorporated into a shared dramatic context that, she argues, operates at the level of virtual representation. Nevertheless, two interrelated problems present themselves in Laurel's disappearing of the interface that concern the type of incorporation being proposed and the level at which computer representation can be said to occur. For Laurel the computer represents a virtual system that need not refer realistically or metaphorically to any referent.[28] The representation of the user within this view must occur purely on the basis of the system's own requirements: thus the user, to interact with the system, must be "translated" into code. Thinking this through in terms of the power of facialization means that the material differences between the user and the computational system are erased. As Deleuze and Guattari propose, "When the faciality machine translates formed contents of whatever kind into a single substance of expression, it already subjugates them to the exclusive form of signifying and subjective expression."[29]

It has become common HCI parlance to desire the erasure of the interface but to nevertheless reinscribe the power of the face as a single form of expression. In this approach, differentiality can never be accommodated. The need for the interface to act as a surface for translation is apparently lessened if the human can be translated into a complex type of "informational processing unit." Both the computer system and the human can then be represented as internal to a virtual world: as information. Typically, the reduction of human to machine is achieved in two steps: the reduction of corporeality to the brain, and the reduction of the brain to a centralized or even neurologically networked computer. For example, Alan Dix joins others in *Human-Computer Interaction,* a kind of neuro-informational design manual for the construction of interactive systems, in claiming to devote an entire chapter to "the human."[30] Yet they deal solely with aspects of the brain. The brain is then discussed using computational rhetoric, dividing memory into three areas: sensory buffers, short-term memory and long-term memory. But these divisions and their descriptions make no sense outside of the structures used to analyze, build and operate the fabrications of software itself, such as scripting languages and databases. Their description of the operation of long-term memory in the human brain reads like the introduction to a manual for interactive authoring: "Structured representations such as *frames* and *scripts* organize information into data structures. *Slots* in these structures allow attribute values to be added . . . Frames and scripts can be linked together in networks to represent hierarchical structured knowledge."[31] There is nothing spectacularly new in treating the human as an information system. But here the disappearance of the human face of computing into the symbolic world of information is accomplished by a rhetoric of translation typical of digital operations. By translating the human into an informational cog in an integrated and immersive interface design, a closed and level playing field is erected. This effectively cuts the cybernetic world off from any relation to an outside—to heterogeneous series such as the flux of bodily, lived speeds.[32]

Laurel's aim in erasing the interface is far removed from this informational reductionism, as she shifts the notion of representation away from pure information and toward the way it plays out in the dramatic context of HCI. But she nevertheless participates in a facialized logic: that of the technological makeover. Believing that the visible interface maintains a distinction between the (alienated) human and the rich, representational possibilities of the simulated computer world, she draws the human agent into functioning as an "actor" within the computer's world:

> What if we were to define the action of information retrieval, not as looking for something, but examining or experiencing it? . . . These are activities in which the human agent is typically left alone on the other side of the screen to do . . . well, whatever a person does with information. Presenting information in a dramatic form—as an active encounter—provides the means for comprehending and reintegrating these lonely activities into the mimetic context.[33]

But Laurel's floundering point is embodiment. Although her emphasis on virtual worlds and their design points toward a multisensory experience that moves beyond the face-to-face encounter of traditional screen/user interface design, Laurel's virtual worlds only accommodate "the body" and not the heterogeneity typical of *embodied life*. According to her, a virtual world should be capable of maintaining engagement, an affective state that takes place when, for instance, a human agent plays computer games. But in order to maintain the internal coherence and nonreferentiality of the virtual world, the human body must be disengaged from a continuous series of differential, affective states that fluctuates between virtual and actual spaces. The simulated nature of the virtual dramaturgy for Laurel depends upon the discrete distinction between virtual affect and actual bodies: "The distinguishing characteristic of the emotions we feel in a representational context is that there is *no threat of pain or harm in the real world*."[34] For Laurel the corporeal aspect to virtual worlds amounts to the averaging of differential embodied intensities to one speed, experienced in the thrill of the chase. The heaviness and slow duration of sadness, loss or pain can play no role in the "multisensorial" Laurellian realm. Plenty of empirical evidence suggests, however, that these affective states are just as present as excitement in our interactions with digital technologies.[35] The visible signs of the interface fade in Laurel's encounter, but facialization—a mode of organizing bodies into a unified system of codification—continues.

Within design practices inspired by information theory, facialization inflects the organization of encounters between humans and computers despite the apparent erasure of the interface and the fact that resemblances to the actual face recede into over-coded renderings such as the happy Mac. In a sense, the reduction of the face to a vacuous icon evacuates the resemblance of the face to anything other than technology itself. Camilla Griggers analyzes this change in the operation of faciality as it shifts between cinema and digital media. She argues that television, as a medium of mass distribution and consumption, is a precedent to the conditions of production for digital facialization.[36] The televisual image offers up the expressive pole of faciality to a large audience, making it widely available and turning it into a commodity. At the same time, the "quality" image of the close-up cinematic face disperses as it pixellates more and more through a greater number of digital media—now we see the close-up of the face on home video, multimedia, computer games and the Internet. Griggers argues that the semiotics of information no longer requires that the *logic* of the face lines up with the *sign* of the face. Instead, we inhabit an economy of meaning in which repetition, multiple modes of distribution and the discontinuous flows of signs predominate: "The sensorimotor model based in the organic body, reproduced in continuity style realism, and promulgated by the cinematographic image, was challenged not only by the televisual image (and its switchable programming) and the video image (and its economy of mass reproduction and home distribution) but also by the digital image (and its capabilities for hypermediation and hyperprocessing) and later the interactive image."[37] For Griggers, the limit poles of informatic faciality swing between rupture from the organic site of the face itself, on the one hand, and the relentless saturation of the sexed body, over-coded by the ubiquitous pornographic face, on the other. There is no escaping the face in this regime, even if the face escapes from view or is reduced to the status of animated icon. To Griggers, faces are everywhere: surfaces, monitors watching the subject or watching the subject being watched, the interchangeable faces of porn stars, supermodels and so on. We do not dismantle the face via multiplication of the media; we only create an endless wall of faciality to bounce along. Here we are, trapped in the psychosis of the digital makeover, which denies its relation to the organic but desperately solicits the human face to "communicate," to engage, to permit expressivity. Here we are, balancing precariously between the before and after face, the human and the technologically reconstituted face. We are caught between faces: interfaciality.

Stelarc's work *Prosthetic Head* is about exactly this capture of both the human and the computer within interfacial logic (figure 17).[38] Resembling the face of the artist himself, the "prosthetic head" is an interface projection of a 3-D real-time animated head that seems to hang in mid-air, begging for a participant to start a conversation with it. The friendly face of a complex database of possible conversational starting points and responses to the human who engages it, *Prosthetic Head* extends the "conversation" we have been having with computers since the mid-twentieth century. Yet the conversational agent in this work is neither slavelike nor human in the

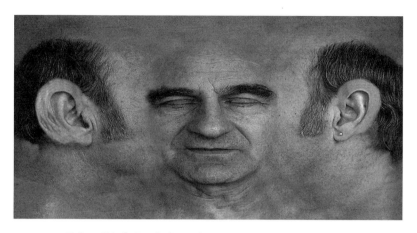

FIGURE 17. Stelarc, *Skin for Prosthetic Head* (2002).
Image by Barret Fox. Courtesy of the artist.

usual anthropomorphic sense. Trying to have a conversation with it soon reveals that it is both seductive and frustrating. Utilizing real-time speech synthesis, lip-synching and picking up nonverbal cues from individual participants, the head seems lifelike and autonomously intelligent. And yet certain questions or conversational topics initiated by the participant prompt the head to speak as if it were a member of a machine species and completely alien from human needs and desires. Ask it about the contents of its dreams, and it is likely that it will talk in a mildly erotic way about circuitry. The head appears lifelike from the standpoint of technical simulation of speech and motion, and yet the "life" about which it converses does not resemble a human mode of being.

Prosthetic Head suspends the space of conversation as a natural meeting place for the human and computer, replacing it with the interface as a surface of friction and irresolvable tension. In shaping his head as an animated prosthesis, Stelarc displaces the logic of facialization that dominates HCI design. Although *Prosthetic Head* looms large in the exhibition space, the idea that the head—and its "window," the face—can become a mere unattached appendage undercuts the centrality of mind, intelligence and even expression in a determination of humanness. As Stelarc notes, we are seduced by *Prosthetic Head* into interacting with the face of a computer, but all of those stalwarts of the human-centered conception of the self are simultaneously called into question: "This is not an illustration of a disembodied intelligence. Rather, notions of awareness, identity, agency and embodiment become problematic. Just as a physical body has been exposed as inadequate, empty and involuntary, so simultaneously the ECA [embodied conversational agent] becomes seductive with its uncanny simulation of real-time recognition and response."[39]

Interfaciality, as the logic dominating HCI, may also work seductively, but it does little to make us aware of what is at stake in "submitting" to the computer. Instead, it positions the human and the computer as two faces deterritorialized from their differing materiality, destined to either reflect or dissolve the one into the other. Interfaciality swings psychotically between two poles: the anthropomorphization of the machine on the one hand, and the technological makeover of the organic by digital technologies on the other. This logic no longer requires faciality to operate at the representational level, as it had done in the aesthetics of figurative painting and narrative cinema.[40] Perhaps this is also why Stelarc's *Prosthetic Head* is startling; it refacializes a logic that has become invisible and subsumed into the language of "user-friendly" design. There is a relative paucity of facial representation in everyday new media iconography. Hence it may appear that the power vested in the face has disintegrated, and that we have entered a period of fragmentation and hybrid subjectivity that has been identified by some artists and cultural theorists as posthuman. But I would suggest that it is through the interface as a mechanism for arranging anthropomorphic or informatic translations of human/computer relations that a continuing subjectivation to faciality is maintained. We need to radically rethink the interface in our modes of realizing our relations with the machine as the point of both contact surface and disappearance of the space of difference between humans and computers.

Interfacing with Posthuman and Programmatic Subjects
What of the attempts by artists and cultural theorists, in the light of mutant digital directions, to move beyond the human and its codification via the face and pose a post-biological life form—the posthuman? To what extent might these alternative subject positions provide an escape from interfacial subjectivation? Is the posthuman also produced under the sign of the face? Katherine Hayles has argued that variants of posthumanism have been summoned to encapsulate a range of complex developments in, and cultural responses to, biotechnologies and cybernetic sciences.[41] For her, the posthuman signals a closure in the history of a certain form of the self: the human. This form is not so much biologically limited as delimited by a liberal conception of subjectivity. She offers up a version of posthumanism beyond liberalism, in which the radical openness of embodied life would be acknowledged. Yet aside from Hayles, many iterations of the

posthuman deploy an evolutionary logic in which the prefix "post" marks human biology retroactively as a set of limited, even retarding, capacities. These iterations posit a program for moving to the next stage of our evolution so that we become retrospectively aware of these limitations of "the body" as we surrender to the more developed cybernetic machine. Although posthumanism in its aesthetic manifestations forges new territories for human/machine interaction, it may simultaneously assist the logic of neoliberalism. Targeting the machine as the new thing for bodies to become encourages info-capital investment in an increasing technical apparatus to drive us beyond the limits of corporeality.

At times the aesthetic directions of posthumanist exploration at the human-machine interface level have failed to recognize the complexity of the sociotechnical contexts in which they are inevitably embedded. In 1997, the groundbreaking Ars Electronica festival chose the interface as its theme, bringing the organic and the cybernetic into contact through the title *Flesh Factor*.[42] In his introductory catalogue essay, Gerfried Stocker remarks upon the way in which the interface had been shifting its status from an intermediary at the boundaries between the human and the machine to a sign of the collapse of human, digital code and machine boundaries: "The classic Western model of the individual as an autonomous, inwardly oriented entity is being dropped in favor of a hybrid, networked subjectivity, whereby we comprehend ourselves as dynamic interfaces in a social communications network."[43] This emphasis on the dynamism engaged by, and at, the interface provides an important shift in the late 1990s aesthetic articulation of interaction. And yet there is nevertheless a sense in which the prevailing artistic strategies for dealing with human/machine interaction at *Flesh Factor* remain enmeshed within the logic of interfaciality. The posthuman evolution of the human beyond current biological limitations is caught in the impasse between overcoming the body and needing the body as a site for a new interface with the machine. Alternatively, the assignation of a protosubjectivity we could call "programmatic" to the computational machine performs the double operation of losing the human in the machine *and* appropriating her or his expressivity for the machine's "program." These two directions are encapsulated at *Flesh Factor* in Stelarc and in Huge Harry, a performative voice synthesis program. Stelarc is the artist who has most consistently pursued the dynamism of the interface as a productive movement between computer system and human body. Inserting sensors, stimulators, chips and recording devices into the flesh of his body and connecting these to digital systems for their control, mapping, digitization and projection, Stelarc creates performances that consist of building cybernetic loops of body/information feedback that expand into patterns of increasing complexity. His work prior to *Prosthetic Head* examines the displacement of the interface from intermediary between human and computer to the site of the body within digital culture. Virtual reality systems, biotechnologies and more common devices like pacemakers have demanded an extended surface to fix themselves. In this way, human bodies have become interface "hosts" for parasitic computing technologies.

Stelarc follows the trajectory of the invasion of the body by technology, its emptying of agency, will and control as it becomes an interface for technology to redistribute and connect back into itself: "What becomes important is not merely the body's identity, but its connectivity—not its mobility or location, but its interface."[44] Although we may marvel at this breakdown of the body as a marker of discrete identity, it is remarkable how easily this notion of body as interface also acquiesces to the most rampant form of technological consumption. To return momentarily to Griggers's argument, the makeover of the body by technology in digital culture amounts to the offer of subjectivity as freedom of choice, freedom to look good, freedom to buy back the reconstituted body—ultimately, freedom to consume. Stelarc sometimes champions the aesthetic as an arena for increasing cybercultural commerce. As he states:

> THE FUNDAMENTAL FREEDOM IS FOR INDIVIDUALS TO
> DETERMINE THEIR OWN DNA DESTINY. Biological change
> becomes a matter of choice rather than chance. Evolution
> by INDIVIDUAL, FOR THE INDIVIDUAL. Medical technologies
> that monitor, map and modify the body also provide the
> means to manipulate the structure of the body. When we
> attach or implant *prosthetic devices* to prolong a person's
> life, we have also created the potential to propel post-
> evolutionary development.[45]

We are not far here from the familiar autonomous liberal subject. Postbiology, subtended by a developmental logic of evolution operating via choice, can land us back within the sphere of liberal subjectivity. Stelarc's earlier enthusiasm for alternative interfaces with the machine verges on 1990s cyberculture hype. He falls into the trap of thinking of bodies as "the body," in which only one speed—absolute velocity and/or absolute stasis—unfolds. This is revealed in his endorsement of the "electronic erasure" of embodied rhythms in order to clear the surface for technological hook-up: "perhaps what is necessary is electronic erasure with new intimate, internalized interfaces to allow for the design of a body with more adequate inputs and outputs for performance and awareness augmented by search engines."[46] This process of erasure hardly wipes the slate clean, for it takes us back to that machine of absolute emptiness: the face. Now the computer has nothing to look at, nothing to connect with—to make faces at—except itself. The body, hollowed out, a shell of its former self, becomes the flat surface for a network of cyberdevices. Stelarc's performances from the 1990s, such as *Parasite*, project a possible future for body/ machine interaction. The posthuman dimension of these experiments seems so obsessed with exhausting itself of the "limitations" of the body that it inadvertently reinstalls the interface as a kind of screen against the untidiness of embodied human life. Talking about remotely activated performance that takes place through distributed networked communications, Stelarc states:

> Given tactile and force-feedback, I would feel my touch via another person from another place as a secondary and additional sensation. Or, by feeling my chest I can also feel her breast. An intimacy through interface, an intimacy without proximity. Remember that Stimbod is not merely a sensation of touch but an actuation system. Can a body cope with experiences of extreme absence and alien action without becoming overcome by outmoded metaphysical fears and obsessions of individuality and free agency?[47]

This remote interface for intimacy is fascinating, suggesting the potential of a dynamic displacement and interchange between bodies, machines and others' bodies. Sensation is both doubled and displaced so as to sustain a new kind of affectivity that operates through relations and networks. Here we are reminded of the concept of the fold as a more productive description of the operations between bodies and new-media technologies in information aesthetics. Rather than seek the interface as a place for conjunction between different participant's bodies, Stelarc is looking for designs that conjure the differential at work in cybernetic connection: intimate and sensate relations between people are marked by intervals and distances inscribed by networked information. And yet there is considerable hesitation in Stelarc's question, testament to his doubt about the capacity of humans' bodies to be controlled by anything other than the face of a lingering anthropomorphic subjectivity.

We might consider Stelarc's performances less as attempts to transcend embodiment than as exercises that deplete the regimes through which "the body" has been culturally regulated. As such, they reflect a more general cultural exhaustion with regimes of both containment (the modern subject) *and* excess (the postmodern multiplication of subjectivities). Typically Stelarc's works in situ run to four or five hours, and he emerges from them scarred, stunned and spent.[48] It is as if the discipline of making his body act as an autonomous or voluntary agent—the liberal concepts of subjectivity—has surrendered to pure automation. There is a sense in which these performances always return us to "the body" as a kind of tabula rasa in which all energies and intensities have been worn out. But the efforts to which Stelarc's actual body goes are doubled by not simply emptying itself out but, just as importantly, maintaining a pure surface for technology—a system propelling itself toward constant update and renewal. Stelarc's invocation of the parasite is entirely apt; the fantasy of the digital body involves its existence as a mere host for the lifecycle of machines. Stelarc's performance trajectory over the past two decades in fact provides an interesting map of the shifts in rhetoric and ideas about HCI. Whereas many of his 1990s performance works oscillate between an enthusiasm for the machine and an exhaustion of the body, by the time he exhibited *Prosthetic Head* in 2003 the seductive logic of the interface itself had become the object of aesthetic interrogation.

If we compare *Prosthetic Head* with Huge Harry, a voice synthesis program developed at the MIT Speech Laboratory and used to interface with performance artist Arthur Elsenaar, we can see that *FleshFactor* encapsulated a period of aesthetic ambivalence about interfaces. Huge Harry offered audiences the other side of the interface debates—an unashamed viewpoint emanating from the machine.[49] Controlling the human "interface" of the man Elsenaar, Huge Harry presented the machine's view on the future superiority of algorithmically generated art and in this way inverted the idea of the human as controller of the computer via the interface. Instead, the human becomes a mere interface panel for communication between the computer and the audience. Harry's play for equal machine rights in the aesthetic sphere is part and parcel of Elsenaar's performative strategy of reversing relations between humans and computers. In turn, this draws attention to the dynamic nature of the interaction, freed from the presumption that the human is always in control.[50] Subjectivity is overtaken by the machine and becomes configurable, computable and ultimately programmable, and this is what is meant by my concept of "programmatic subjectivity."

Yet it seems that Huge Harry does not so much desire to take on the human but to take her place; in the performances, the machine interface literally returns to the site of the face. Elsenaar has developed a portable controller system that allows computational control of the human *facial* muscles. Thus the voice of Harry now gains a vehicle of expression via facialization, thereby facilitating communication between the hardware of computational intelligence and the "wetware" of the human audience. On the one hand, we have a possible way out of facialization. Instead of providing a screen for the emergence of subjectivity as expression, Huge Harry appears to be treating the face as a mere peel-off mask for a set of hardware and software requirements and parameters:

> Let us take a closer look at such a person. What is the closest thing they have to a C.R.T. display?
>
> Right. They have a face. Now I have observed that humans use their faces quite effectively to signal the parameter settings of their operating systems. And that they are very good at decoding the meanings of each other's faces.[51]

But as we discover, Harry has already *facialized* this mask by dividing the muscle groups to be manipulated into areas of predetermined human expression:

> First I put a slowly increasing signal on the muscles called Frontalis, or Muscles of Attention.
>
> We see that this muscle can lift the eyebrow to a considerable extent, also producing a very pronounced curvature of the eyebrow.
>
> As a side-effect of this motion, the forehead is wrinkled with curved furrows that are concentric with the curvature of the eyebrow. The contraction of this muscle indicates a person's readiness to receive new signals, and the availability of processing power and working memory for analyzing these signals.
>
> Now, I will stimulate a part of the Orbicularis Oculi that is called the Muscle of Reflection.[52]

Harry's use of the human face as a site for expression, from the muscles of attention through to those of contempt, in fact reproduces the parameters of faciality analyzed by Deleuze in his treatment of the cinematic face.[53] Indeed, Deleuze notes that the attentive face, contemplating an object in its sight, represents the reflective pole of faciality: the thinking subject ratified by the Cartesian ego and by the "science" of physiognomy from the seventeenth century onward. This face presents itself as a smooth surface that can assume any mode of expression whatsoever. Its opposite pole can be found in the ruffling of this smooth reflection by the contraction of muscles as the emotion of contempt passes across the face. Hence the face appropriated by Harry is not stripped of its subjectivation through the programming of subjectivity. The computer is already subjectified by being already facialized. The "program" does not so much erase human qualities as work with presumptions about the human (inter)face. Huge Harry preserves the domain of human expressivity in the face rather that challenging the face via its machine qualities.

Interfaciality as a mode of arranging our engagement with computers and informing our cultural theorization and aesthetic productions has continued to provide machines and humans with a face. Although the reconfiguration of faciality through interfaciality is psychotic, prefiguring the possibility of a crisis of representation, this breakdown never amounts to much. Facialized subjectivations continue to be produced. These exist within the clear boundaries of the surface/depth poles that Deleuze and Guattari suggest support the system of the face, even as they bounce erratically between them.[54] The major achievement of interfaciality is not so much in escaping the face but rather multiplying it. We increasingly find ourselves running the gamut of a slippery middle ground, bouncing back and forth between the surfaces of new technologies and those of our own skin. What we need, then, is a way to rethink this area in terms other than those offered to us by the intermediary positioning of the interface between two opponents: the human and the inhuman machine. For from this position, one side will always be required to conjoin with or eradicate the other.

Affective Mappings of Dynamic Body-Code Interfaces

So, how does one dismantle the interface? Perhaps the problem lies with the two entities between which the interface is constantly forced to negotiate. Hayles has suggested that a radical posthumanism can open up the remnants of a contained liberal subject to the heterogeneous flux of engagements with informatic flows and lived corporeality. In this section I want to examine some attempts to open digital code to an engagement with corporeality through, paradoxically, informatic renderings of bodies.

In some cases the relation of informatic coding to bodies has been reductive, producing bodies that are manageable and whose problems, if decoded, can be seemingly eradicated. This is of course the rationale behind projects such as the HGP. I want to suggest that these very same processes of mapping the body as a knowable, manageable entity can also open up the possibility of "the gap," the "unrepresentable," the disjunctive interval between "the body" and embodiment. Digital media translate continua into discontinuous code, which severs the intensive relations that inhere within the continuous properties of materialities. I want to argue that it is in the gaps between the series of corporealities and the informatic renderings of bodies that the interface can emerge as an *interfolding* of disparities or disjunction. Embodiment need no longer be situated as inadequate if we focus on the interstitial space between matter and code. Instead it might be thought of as an open and dynamic set of capacities for moving across the very gaps that open up in relation to information aesthetics. We now need to consider how artists have worked with digital media through an aesthetic of limitation rather than plenitude.

Instead of looking for the ways in which digital translation homogenizes all of the body's components into similar code we might rethink coding as differing arrangements of "lines of expression."[55] Following Guattari's reading of the "lines of expression" that operate in cinematic aesthetics— described as the parallel and intersecting lines of color, vision and sound traversing a film—we see how they function to create a complex spatialization. The complexity lies in the excess offered to the viewer of these qualitative, affective elements, because they are not reducible to predetermined representation or signification and there are always more of these elements than can be realized in any one viewing of the film. In the case of cinema, actual spatializations of these potential or virtual lines of expression are produced in relation to the architectural, geographic, historical, cultural and molecular (at the level of the body's temporal rhythms; for example, the time of day of viewing) conditions for engaging with its aesthetics. The very specificity of these conditions means that the affective elements will always exceed each viewing. Not only is making cinema an activity of aesthetic composition but *viewing* cinema, under the specific conditions in which this occurs, is likewise compositional, in that affective relations to the flow of image and sound compose the body as a *viewing* body.

Affect is not a thing or a substance; it is not reducible to or located at the level of "the body." Nor is it a mode of knowing, ordering or representing this body. It cannot be rendered through the mapping of emotional activity located at specific points in the brain, although images of PET scans attempt this by showing in vivo the brain centers involved while a subject experiences emotions such as sadness.[56] Nor can affect be represented per se in aesthetic terms. Rather, affect occurs as a process of composition that is sustained through a relation between body and expression, representation, map and knowledge. As Brian Massumi has suggested, there is a missing period between the bodily beginning of an event and its completion in an outwardly directed expression of emotion.[57] This missing period is the affective duration during which bodies sense a sensation.

If cinema's affective compositional modes operate through the logic of excess, then information aesthetics operates affectively through expressive dearth. The visualization of the body that occurs in medical and scientific imaging opens even further the indexical gap between raw biology and representation by constituting these chemical, neural processes as encoded and mapped functions of information. Paradoxically, the alterity that this introduces between *sensing* and *mapping* sensation is also capable of sustaining a particular affect: informatic affect. This is even more the case when the disjunction between images and experiences of bodily sensations is drawn further apart and then temporally brought back together in new media artworks. We saw that this disjunction between computers and bodies became the basis upon which artists such as Rokeby and Ludin constructed interfaces for HCI. New media art pieces likewise use biomedical or informatic visualizations of bodies. These aesthetic productions work primarily at the affective level yet additionally produce an affective working-through of representations of the body. They often appear to us visually in these works in the form of our shadows, outlines or silhouettes— the reductions one might expect to encounter as bodies are processed through informatics. But these outlines also comprise the spectral reminders of the unrepresentable, heterogeneous dimensions of corporeality returning through digital visualization. We find ourselves in the presence of death and decay in information aesthetics.

Detractors of informatic renderings of the body have suggested that they reduce the substance of corporeality to the status of ideal pattern alone. If we were then to argue that affect involves embodied viewing and response, then such a reduction would also render these modes of visualization affectless. Additionally, such patterns of information can only be approached through a subjectively alienating device such as the computational interface. Slavov Zizek has captured this diminution of both subject and body by contemporary bio-information, stating that "it is as if it were an inside which appears only when viewed from the outside, on the interface screen."[58]. This "inside which appears only when viewed from the outside" is exactly what we have come to expect as the digital imaging experience of the body par excellence. Whether in the form of the 3-D flythroughs of the viscera and musculature familiar to those who have experienced the

Visible Human Project, or the reconstructed walk-rounds of foetuses in ultrasounds, or the diagnostic tools of PET scans, insides are being made to appear only as views from the outside; that is to say, as instrumentalized perspectives that are accessible only through the latest imaging technology.

But it is worth remembering here that the perspective from which we are producing bodies via these imaging processes is a perspective that sustains a relation to alterity, to an outside. Neurologist Antonio Damasio draws our attention to this phenomenon when examining images of neural activity and pattern: "Neural patterns can be accessed *only in a third-person perspective. If I had a chance of looking at my own neural patterns with the help of the most advanced technologies, I would still be looking at them from a third-person perspective.*"[59] The problem Damasio wants to draw our attention to *is* the fact that these kinds of images cannot provide us with subjective (first-person) experiences of the activity of the body. In his view they provide the *objective scientific* substrate of the biological basis of emotion, feeling and mood. Here then we have an inside—an interiority in the classic psychological sense—that is quantifiable when viewed from the outside, as an effect of computer imaging. Damasio separates the experiencing self from its rendering as informatic pattern. But at the same time, this effectively cuts us off from interfacing with the biology of our bodies. Matter has become a substrate readable and accessible only in the third person, and the third person is a perspective rendered by the machine. It is only technology that can internally access "the body" as an "outside." But is this rendering of the body as technical artifact necessarily reductive? Although we have excluded the perspective of the "felt subjective body"—the personalized perspective—might there not be some way in which this rendering process touches upon an element involved in the composition of subjectivity anyway? Could we call this impersonal process of subjectivation "affectivity"?

I would argue that rendering the body as information is not in itself reductive and that such renderings do not instrumentalize matter. We can approach this body produced from the outside in a number of ways. There is the direction offered to us by Damasio, whereby medical science and its techniques of visualization shift our view of the self and its processes from being seen as fixed images to being seen as emergent phenomena of embodied processes. Yet Damasio continues to pursue a very familiar trajectory that eventually leads to a collapse of embodiment back into the service of a scientifically accessible understanding. For him it must be possible to conquer the alterity opened up by artificially produced views of the body.

The outside view of our bodies that imaging technologies provide for us replicates the same action that the conscious human self performs on the sensing self: "having a feeling is not the same as knowing a feeling, that reflection on feeling is yet another step up."[60] Feeling or sensing here becomes the "object" of experience, as the brain—acting like the process of a neurological visualization itself—creates representations of its proto-subjective states, which it then presents to itself in order to "know" them. Damasio recuperates alterity through the activity of consciousness and its reflexive modes of representation. In doing so, he replays the longstanding separations between mind and sensation, technology and body that are attributed to Cartesianism.

Alternatively, we might take visually enhanced, altered, digital bodies in a divergent direction. We might work *across* the split between sensation and the insides of bodies, on the one hand, and their representation through technical images or the internal patterning that consciousness performs, on the other. The first step would require acknowledging that rendering bodily states as informatic pattern naturally or through technological means is never a direct route to "being in and of the body." But we could say that affect slips in and "inhabits the passage" between sensing and rendering. Affect arises relationally and is produced out of the difference between being *in* the body and representing/mapping the body from the outside.[61] Affect sustains the singularity of sensing and of representing as a differential experience of embodiment, one in which alterity has a place. And in any interface between bodies and technology we will always encounter this difference. Informatic affect is a process of subjective bodily recomposition that occurs in relation to the alterity that pattern and code renderings open up for us.

Working with Damasio's exploration of "the feeling of what happens," we can move further in the direction of a processual understanding of the relation between body and digital code by focusing on composition rather than representation. Asking what it might mean to think differently about the actions of an obsessive compulsive who constantly washes his hands, Guattari suggests that we forgo a search for signification in action.[62] Instead, we can think of the making of this form of self through the sensing of sensation, "the feeling that one is in the washing of one's hands."[63] With regard to informatic renderings of body, sensation, emotion and even self, we could consider forming a similar affective relation, one expressed through the phrase "the feeling that one is in the mapping of one's self." This affectivity produced in relation to the body rendered as information is at once strangely distant or removed *and* immediately intimate. What informatic visualizations might open up for us here is not a reductive rendering of interiorities (brain, self, viscera) but a topological mapping of self as a pattern of microcompositions traversing the gaps between interiority and exteriority. The interface between body and technology is no longer locatable within the sphere of corporeality or of code. Yet it has not disappeared. It exists as an aftereffect of the dynamic encoding of bodies.

The Aesthetics of Informatic Bodies

I want to suggest that this affectivity especially emerges through new media artworks that deploy informatic and scientific mappings of the body. Here the viewer/participant is placed dynamically in the process of "feeling that they are in the mapping" of an embodied self. The aesthetic of the informatic body offers a trajectory different from the escapist version of VR, which promises either a full, complete, "lifelike" experience delivered via technology or a removal of the subject from the body altogether. Instead, work such as Dunning and Woodrow's *Einstein's Brain Project,* which I touched upon in the last chapter, uses scientific visualization and data gathered from the human body, particularly biometric data, to concentrate on creating expressive lines of connection between its various visual elements.[64] In *The Crucible* (part of *Einstein's Brain*) the interactant enters an immersive space of four rear-projected walls. The images on these walls are fed by a database that is activated when one pushes sensors arranged across the ceramic skull of a nineteenth-century phrenology model. Although the projected images change in response to the sensors, the relation of sensor activation to image call-up is randomly programmed. The illusion of user control rapidly gives way to the patterns of color, text and movement emerging and collapsing around the interactant, patterns that emerge from the bio-informatic images of bodily processes traversing the piece. The other visual effect of these projected environments is to render the interactant's body as a silhouette projected onto the walls against the changing patterns of images. Our bodies join the images of bodies surrounding us, but as "shadows" of ourselves.

Another example of these shadowy bodies haunting aesthetic treatments of scientific visualization can be found in Justine Cooper's longstanding fascination with medical imaging. In her installation and single-channel video work *RAPT I* and *RAPT II* (1998) Cooper literally gave substance to the shadowy images of the body produced by magnetic resonance imaging (MRI).[65] The installation piece uses seventy-six "slices" or MRI scans mounted individually onto Perspex and hung so as to produce an entire image sculpture of Cooper's databody (figure 18). Here scientific

FIGURE 18. Installation shot of *Rapt II* (2005) by Justine Cooper. Courtesy of the artist and Novamedia, Australia's New Media Arts Agency.

imaging techniques double Cooper's own body, yet the impression they leave is faint, ephemeral and shadowy. The shadow comes to life in her video piece, where the MRI slices seem to have a life of their own, dancing, folding and emerging from the screen space. These databodies seem distanced from actual bodies, but they are not lifeless; they both foreclose and impel visual seduction and fascination.

The distance *and* proximity of data to physical experience and embodied life is further explored in Cooper's immersive environment *Scynescape* (2000).[66] Animated sequences of images produced from scans of Cooper's membranes are visualized through an electron microscope and then projected onto a latex maze. They are accompanied by a soundscape generated interactively as participants wander through the environment. The sounds are recordings of amplified internal bodily noises that provide an aural counterpoint to the visual display and its close-up investigation of Cooper's membranous surfaces. We experience the composition through our navigation of audiovisual elements that suspends between surface and depth, external and internal, microscopic and macroscopic. Rather than the usual scenario of escape in which the user enters an imaginary, dematerialized world of information, Cooper's installation focuses the feeling of traversing and mapping embodied space back onto the participant. The participant's body must negotiate inverted sensory and proprioceptive experience as what were once internally located bodily sounds becomes an engulfing audioscape and invisible microscopic images are scaled up and projected at oversized proportions. At the same time, the structure of the installation's maze renders the presence of other participants within it as shadows projected onto its latex walls. Both the intimate clinical details of the medically rendered body and the outlines of the breathing bodies of others cohabit *Scynescape*. What one makes of bodies and how one makes one's embodied way through this information landscape literally forms a drift (*dérive*) between immersion and dispersal, intimacy and distance.

These kinds of new media artworks neither promise a direct relation to the sensorium rendered by informatic visualization nor bypass the body altogether. Rather they suggest that any future for embodiment in the landscape of information must leave space for the aesthetic processes of composition. This is not space marked by a controlling, organizing subject or cogito who looks back at its body from the outside or a technology that adopts a similar position of knowingly representing the body. This space is instead inflected by the shadow and absence of the self, as the bodily silhouettes of participants are projected onto the topology of biological visualization. This shadowy figure is the mark of the death of the subject as knowable, manageable or reducible to a recognizable pattern of information. We might also think of it as an outline yet to be filled in, an unknown territory that requires an active and affective negotiation with the world before it can become a body we "know." Or we might like to leave this outline mysteriously blank, as a mark of its opening onto the outside, to a future that may always have to wait to be filled in.

The use of the silhouette in new media art has other, less accidental deployments as well. In Myron Krueger's *VideoPlace* (which began its development in 1974) participants' bodies were captured by video and projected onto a facing surface where, in colored silhouette form, they shadowed the action of the bodies in actual space. Participants "used" these silhouettes to interact with digital objects in the screen space. *VideoPlace* was an important forerunner for the aesthetics of informatic bodies because it underscored the doubling of the body's materiality by means of data visualization. This doubling raises a number of disjunctions, including that of physical and virtual space and their apparent synchronization through the technical construct of real time and the differential between onscreen navigation dependent upon vision and the movement, in physical space, of the proprioceptive body. Documentation of participants negotiating *VideoPlace* reveals a kind of awkward choreography in the actual movement of the interactant flailing around in physical space, which is then integrated into a smooth interaction between the shadow avatar and its digital object partners in the screen space of the installation.

This stitching of the silhouette of the participant into the video action in Krueger's work uncannily signals a coming of age for special-effects digital cinema, in which the actor or actress interacts with absent objects and subjects against a blue screen and is digitally composited into the action and time of the film through post-production techniques. Although Krueger initially worked with the silhouette because of technical problems in rendering interactive real time video, the absence here of a photorealistic depiction of the participant also signals the emergence of an interesting problem in the production of informatic bodies. Whereas bluescreen capture matches the actor with a background or some synthetic characters in an attempt to reconstruct a seamless visual experience, the silhouetted avatar mitigates against complete visual identification or the "stitching" between physical and digital bodies. Instead the silhouette in *VideoPlace* operates as a mark of the visual failure of the technology to perfectly double the physical body by flattening and compressing volume and depth, and in the partiality of movement it enacts. Although *VideoPlace*'s silhouette representation allows a certain amount of bodily orientation in the virtual screen space for the participant, it does not produce an exact visual match. Accordingly, the actual body of the participant must learn to conduct itself as a body of information rather than as a representation of a body. In fact, I want to suggest that the silhouette in *VideoPlace* marks an absence in visualized informatic bodies and hence their concomitant reliance upon the proprioceptive capacities of the actual body in physical space. The relative clumsiness of the physical body performing in *VideoPlace* can then be understood as the perceptual and motor-sensory effort required to proprioceptively renegotiate an experiential gap between actual and informatic bodies. The physical body of interactants in immersive new media environments is not a clumsy body, lacking navigational skills. It is a body working overtime and over two spaces, producing in gesture the very differential that is the interval between information and the physical world.

A number of theorists have argued for the importance of proprioception as a kind of sixth sense that enables the body to orient itself through its habitual movement in space. Habit here can be thought of as the recurrent patterns that form as the body's sensorimotor system generates microscopic transitions while negotiating time and space in the world.[67] One of the effects of the digital doubling of bodies through the accidental or intentional projection of participants' silhouettes is to foreground the habitual movement of bodies so that it becomes strange rather than automatic. The dominant trajectory in interactive and virtual environments has moved in the direction of a correspondence between actual bodies and their shadows and a disappearance of the interface. Yet we should also consider aesthetic experiments that have focused upon an estrangement between the physical space of the body and the informatic space of the silhouette. One such investigation can be found in the work of artist Rafael Lorenzo-Hemmer, who shifts attention completely away from the actual bodies of participants and toward the active and dynamic contribution made by the shadow itself. In his architectural and Internet installation *Re: Positioning Fear* (1997) the shadow of the interactant, captured through light sources that tracked his or her movement, was projected onto the wall of the *Landeszeughaus*, a historical military arsenal in Graz, Austria.[68] More than simply a scaled-up double of the actual body, the interactant's shadow became the interface itself, creating an area of darkness on the wall against which projected conversational texts became visible. Drawn from Internet relay chat sessions in which remote participants discussed fear in relation to technology, biology, geography and politics, among other arenas, the chat text had to be actively decoded and materialized by the Graz audience. The relation of the participant's movement to the light sources surrounding the arsenal's forecourt allowed a shadow to be cast onto the wall, which was scaled up to the proportions of the building itself. The shadow cast was much more than interface as a contact surface between preexisting entities; it became an active field of relations that required negotiation between body, building and imaging technologies. Lorenzo-Hemmer calls this negotiated field "relational architecture" and underscores the way in which the shadow moves beyond being a body-double and plays a *constitutive* role in the production of "tele-absence": "'Tele-absence' is defined as the technological acknowledgement of the impossibility of self transmission. Tele-absence is a celebration of where and when the body is not. The shadow is not an avatar, an agent, nor an alias of the participant's body, it is projected darkness, a play of geometries, a disembodied bodypart."[69] *Re: Positioning Fear* conjoins with the effects produced by the shadows of participants in the immersive environments of Cooper and Dunning and Woodrow. Informatic bodies fail to match up with the desire to transmit or produce contained and manageable subjectivities such as the human face. But nor do they offer a conception of technology that *disposes* of the embodied capacities of the human being. Although Lorenzo-Hemmer engages the immaterial propensities of informatics, as is highlighted by the shadow interface of *Re: Positioning Fear,* his work is located at the very core of contemporary affect and experience. By emphasizing a differential interplay between personal and architectural scale, the amplificatory qualities of doubling in digital environments and the location of fear in the interstices between the shadow of history, and the remoteness of the present and the anticipation of the future, he shifts the experience away from the interface as a thing in itself. It becomes a kind of quality that emerges in the experience of these relations in information spaces. As Massumi has suggested, the alliance of experimental art and architecture in Lorenzo-Hemmer's work changes the trajectory of informatic technologies away from the visual matching of a given body with its given informatic representation: "Technologies that can be twisted away from addressing preesisting forms and functions toward operating directly as *technologies of emergent experience*."[70] For Lorenzo-Hemmer, relational architecture creates "situations," not interfaces, between the urban, technological environment and humans, in which new or strange relations and behavior become possible. He is concerned with the qualitative changes that information aesthetics can bring to the active and reactive relations between humans and the spaces they inhabit.

Digital media involve a translation of the continuity of embodied experience into a discontinuous code, severing the indistinct foldings of intensive corporeality. In the history of interface design, interfaciality has tried to screen out the qualitative differences between the informatic and the embodied registers by attempting to humanize the computer, has attempted, in short, to erase computational and human differences. But it can only do so by pretending that the engagement between humans and digital technologies occurs primarily at the communicative and cognitive levels. The concomitant effect of locating the interface relation there is to rule out the possibility of code engaging embodied experience through the body's incorporeal dimensions. The undervaluing of "the body" as a brute and inert force emerges as a secondary consequence of interfaciality and produces a desire to assimilate the human to the machine and lose the qualitative difference of the space between, the inter-face, altogether. Digital technologies organized by this system of interfacialization reconstitute these relations supplementarily as discrete relations between binary integers. The interface will always suffer a loss of face if it is situated here, as a translator between human and machine, body and information, analog and digital. These are all modalities, rather than things, and do not combine smoothly to create forms of belonging with each other. Yet it is in those gaps between corporeality and information that the interface as a dissonant folding, an *interfolding*, emerges. Instead of situating bodies as inadequate, we might look at ways in which embodiment can be conceived of as open and dynamic, operating and traversing these gaps; not a property that "I" have but something I produce, that is produced, in relation to other bodies and machines. Increasingly, it is these emergent and qualitative dimensions of human embodiment that will feature in our engagements with the digital, especially if we are concerned with globally sustainable relations to technologies.

The digital camera allows a proximity to material, to skin, to the surface of paint that excels the eye's trained ability to sort and recognize. Skin pores become alien matter folding in billows, blunt bags trimmed with iridescent grease, pinked mudflats. Hair meets paint slabbed on like cold marge.   — MATHEW FULLER[1]

There are Mexicans in cyberspace, and Poles, Nigerians, Turks and Italians, in the same way as there are Mexicans, Poles, Nigerians, Turks and Italians in New York City. These are nobody's Others and that is reality as I understand it.   — OLU OGUIBE[2]

5 digitality
an ethico-aesthetic paradigm for information

The Digital, the Ethical and the Aesthetic

Where and how to locate a digital aesthetic? In a sense the question, reaching us from the already faded past of the early 1990s, is no longer of value for theorists and practitioners of electronic, new media and digital arts. Indicative of the lag and catch-up that culture, cultural practice and the theorization of that practice play with each other, the digital has since located itself ubiquitously, if one is privileged enough to take advantage of the globalization of computing technologies. The niche carved out by art festivals such as ISEA (International Society for the Electronic Arts) and Ars Electronica, or the curatorial attention given to digital work in shows such as *010101*, *Net_Condition* and the Whitney's *Bitstreams* already seems out of step with a more general acceptance of digital technology as a mode of living the everyday, albeit, again, only for those with the means.[3] During the early 1990s, when both computing networks in the commercial and academic worlds and a range of relatively new art forms such as CD-ROMs and terminal-based interactive installation exploded into the art world, the self-conscious announcement of a genre and medium of artwork called "digital" had some strategic, and aesthetic, substance to it. But as Mitchell Whitelaw has argued, the range of practices to come under the umbrella of digital art is now so diverse, and the digital as a category itself so mundane, that the art is done a disservice by being grouped in such a way.[4] Furthermore, one of the main problems for articulating a digital aesthetic is that mutability seems immanent to computation. It is impossible to gain any classical aesthetic or contemplative distance from an object that is so constantly updating and transforming itself. We quickly realize, then, that reflective aesthetics will not stand us in good stead in this shifting terrain.

Yet even Kantian aesthetics gives us the possibility of a mutable perception, in that it poses the existence of other modes of living apart from ours and hence the possibility of the transformation of our own. Sean Cubitt argues that although this classical aesthetics reduces the act of contemplating different possibilities for life to the individual psyche, any ethical imperative for aesthetics today must be rethought via the social dimension.[5] The globalization of computing technologies has brought about a transformation in which the individual accesses the terminal in solitude but our social and political relations are increasingly ones of mutual dependence. I have been arguing throughout this book that aesthetics can be more productively thought of through a set of nascent baroque antecedents than through classical ones. Aesthetics as a baroque event is emergent rather than disciplinary and is articulated through a focus upon differential modes of perception and sensation. What is clear in the contemporary moment, as Cubitt suggests, is that we cannot psychologize the organization of these modes; they develop in tandem with and in turn impinge upon specific social and technical arrangements. Moreover, aesthetics in contemporary culture cannot rise above and remain undisturbed by the machine, for the machine is more intimately than ever an arranger of our perceptual apparatus. Equally, the aesthetics of technologically inflected, augmented and managed modes of perception is also about relations to others in the socius, to the ways in which these relations are themselves reorganized by the globalization of technologies and the concomitant responsibilities summoned by these rearrangements. In this chapter, I will suggest that the discussion of embodied engagement with information culture we have pursued so far be expanded to allow for a contemporary ethical "imperative" to be engaged. In seeking to articulate an embodied, digital aesthetic we are also forced to think ubiquitously and to engage with the bodies of others, both proximate and remote. To be engaged is not the same as to be connected. Engagement is an active and ongoing confrontation with others, whereas connection, as Steven Shaviro has suggested, is to the network and away from sociality.[6]

Yet as Olu Oguibe has argued, it will not do to bring predetermined conceptions of others' bodies to a discussion of the digital: networked information creates its own specific form of othering along a divide between those who are and are not connected to new technologies.[7] The everyday experience of network users may well be that global connectivity ignores the construction of identities based upon geographical place and cultural history. But connectivity as a glossy image of globalized computing has, to an extent, elided differential social relations among nations themselves and within their regions, cities and suburbs that materially facilitate or mitigate against actual connection: "Connectivity, the transport of disembodied information, outstrips the more robust portability of the book, but demands a material infrastructure which only connects a minority of the world's people."[8] If we conceive of the digital as itself differential, qualifying not just "the body" but *bodies* throughout the socius, we must likewise look at the effect of this qualification upon the processual inventiveness of aesthetics and its propulsion toward new affective experiences. This qualification takes place in an ethical, or rather, as Deleuze suggests, *ethological* dimension.[9] This dimension concerns the ways in which bodies affect and are affected by others' bodies, and in turn the ways in which these affective relations make possible the production of certain kinds of sociability. Hence *being connected* is a form of sociability in which access to the speed of information (itself not absolute but differentiated economically, institutionally, technically and geographically) affectively strengthens the digital "haves" while affectively weakening the digital "have nots." This ethological dimension is not a qualification that occurs after the process of aesthetic creation, determining social responsibility toward others in a secondary manner. Rather it is about what kind of engagement with others does or does not occur, is or is not enabled, within the processes of production. The ethico-aesthetic dimension of digital culture asks us to consider the extent to which the politics of connectivity foregrounds, cuts short or enables our capacity to engage with others and their differences in the interfaces, environments and artifacts produced. But it also asks us to make or create differently so that engagement with differences and others might be actualized in, rather than ceded to, the political economy of connectivity.

In this chapter, a digital aesthetics bound by formalism or medium specificity fades. Instead, I will be looking for signs of "digitality," which I discern in the broader social phenomenon in which an ethico-aesthetic paradigm for digital production has begun to emerge. This may be at odds with the usual technique for surveying digital art forms or seeking out the shared characteristics of virtuality, interactivity or dematerialization that some have claimed belong to a digital aesthetic.[10] Although I will be concerned with art that, broadly speaking, is produced by and runs as a result of digital technologies, the pieces themselves are formally and materially disparate. The work considered throughout this chapter commands our attention because it materializes out of the ethico-aesthetic field specific to the production of digital art: the global relationship of bodies to each other, irregularly arranged by the differential speeds and durations of new media technologies. This approach to information aesthetics does not prevent the investigation of a specific digital art form or technology. Andrew Murphie has suggested that a digital audio aesthetic emerges from digital music technologies that are significantly different in their technicity from what he calls the "target-message-impact" trajectory of the technologies of office software and email packages.[11] He considers the way in which the openness to augmentation and reconfiguration in the software and hardware of digital music indicates the technologies' internalization of a subjective mode of musical operation that is forever in process. It is the playing, mixing and engineering DJ who provides a processual subject node at the differential core of digital audio—a subjectivity quite different from the standardized formation of the "end-user" of software. The DJ instead encourages experimentation and creation. Here the technology and the music not only produce new affective experiences but open onto and allow the formation of new nonstandardized subjectivities. Their propensity is toward an engagement with others and toward engaging a relation to alterity—to becoming different. It is possible to deploy an ethico-aesthetic paradigm in the examination of specific digital forms such as digital music by focusing on the extent to which these forms enable new subjectivations and produce protosocialities.

Defining new media art via the medium has landed high-tech digital artwork and artists in a paradoxical political and cultural position. On the one hand, it has secured a place for such art within a trajectory that demands constant technological upgrading to be considered "state of the art."[12] As a result, artwork that uses "new technologies" seems to belong to the future or to deliver to gasping audiences a glimpse of the full promise that these technologies will deliver at some later date. Roy Ascott, for example, has been at the forefront of this position on digital art, arguing that the computer is not simply a tool but an entirely new medium ushering in a novel visual language and producing new conditions for making and receiving the digitally produced artwork.[13] Within the art historical domain, delineation according to the *medium* of artistic realization stands squarely within the tradition of modernism. As Clement Greenberg argued in his essay "Modernist Painting," what was unique to a particular art coincided with what was unique about the medium it deployed.[14] Modernism is, above all, a mode of calling attention to the conditions and limitations of a medium in order to produce from these something positively different out of the nature of the medium itself. The concentration on technology per se, whether it features as part of the content, the development of a kind of digital style or the emphasis on computational processes, thus draws the "cutting-edge" digital artwork back within the modernist tradition. It is also possible to trace an aesthetic relation from electronic modernism, particularly through the interactive work of people such as Robert Rauschenberg and Billy Kluver and the Art and Technology Movement, to more contemporary high-tech digital art.[15] Although writers such as Frank Popper and Cynthia Goodman tried to promote digital art during the late 1980s and early 1990s as a new aesthetic based upon the technological nature of the medium, this now feels like an attempt to legitimate the digital with a genealogy by entrenching it within acceptable art history traditions.[16]

Peter Lunenfeld has wittily described the way in which digital aesthetics owes much to the performative demands that information culture requires of its technology, with the acute emphasis on a product's ability to function flawlessly on command.[17] This "demo-or-die" aesthetic, he suggests, has taken hold of the entire field of digital cultural production, from the software developer to the new media artist. It is an aesthetic that imbues digital culture with a performativity directed toward demonstrating—either at the trade fair or in the interactive installation—that the technology works seamlessly regardless of contingencies of time, place and end user. Yet I want to argue that this is not the only digital aesthetic possible. There are movements afoot that indicate a critical and productive relation to the old "demo-or-die" hype surrounding new media. Aesthetically these coalesce around vectors that flee away from technical and cultural standardization and travel instead toward the invention of alternative digitalities. These vectors are propensities, leaving their traces in artistic experimentation and affirming the proximity *but not collapse* of bodies and digital technologies to each other; underscoring the lag rather than the correlation of information and globalization; and offering to move us toward distributed, networked experiences of time. Each of these vectors is a force greater than the specific instance of the artwork, yet the aesthetics of the art I will consider here gives power to the affective dimension at work in these forces, shifting us toward new subjectivations and different relations to others. This is art that opens up alternative constructions and deployments of the digital, art that gives shape to *digitality* as a virtual ecology of bodies, technologies and socialities.

Proxomities

Graham Harwood's Internet art piece *Uncomfortable Proximity* will act as a starting point for the discussion about proximity.[18] Harwood's site acts as a mirror to the official Web site for the Tate Gallery in London and in fact was commissioned by Tate Online. Navigating through the official site allows access to his version of the same site, which, when activated from its hyperlink, opens as a new window in the browser on top of or next to the official one. This is Harwood's first step in playing with proximity through the technique of mirroring that is itself part of Web design and the display of sites in online environments. Mirroring sites is an online ploy commonly used to breach copyright, divert Internet traffic and circumvent the censorship of banned material such as pornography. A mirrored site may simply reproduce a particular site at another server location or it may partially mirror the site in order to subvert, hack or intervene into this site. Typical of the activities of the online and offline collective Mongrel, to which Harwood belongs, his mirroring fits within the hacking tradition, where the mirrored site no longer reflects an original but works to inflect and subvert it.[19]

Perhaps what allows this strategy to remain startling and to produce its uncomfortable affect is the proximity of Harwood's mirror, sitting as it does on the same desktop as the public Web face of the Tate. It is not a hacking strategy per se that allows the politics and aesthetics of this digital work to unfold; after all, mimicry as ironic comment or subversion is a well-trodden path within postmodern aesthetics. *Uncomfortable Proximity* instead unleashes momentary flashes of astonishment, discomfort and squeamishness by mobilizing the capacities of digital technologies to forge extreme juxtapositions, unbearable proximities and unspeakable intimacies. The proximity Harwood's site offers to the Tate disturbs the comfortable and bland proximities that information search and retrieval invariably serves up. The notion that the networked computer files away the world in a methodical manner or provides a neutral window onto it are shattered as we begin to feel that online networks might instead be nodes for siphoning, blocking and redistributing information spaces. For Harwood, information becomes a repoliticized space in which we collide with the material differences wrought by proximate worlds. As Mathew Fuller has argued, *Uncomfortable Proximity* opens up the history and politics of the visual that the Tate has had a hand in constructing by contributing to an exclusive, class-based canon of British art history.[20] The public and institutional spaces of gallery and museum are often seamless with their representation in online space, as almost all large arts institutions use Web sites to reproduce or disseminate their "collections." *Uncomfortable Proximity* acts to break up the homogenization of actual and online spaces by diverting the museal space and history back through its heterogeneous origins. Harwood's work seizes upon the desire for a seamless proximity between online and offline representations of the museum and breaks it open in order to uncover the differential voices that comprise the history of institutionalized collecting: "Despite the architecture, it must be understood that museums are not monolithic. They are riven with interdepartmental factions and disciplinary approaches, bids for new angles on which careers can be made. At the same time, for artists they act as a megaphone which can be grabbed, through which public thought can be taken on a detour."[21] *Uncomfortable Proximity* uses digital snapshots of the Tate's British masters, Turner, Gainsborough, Hogarth, that are designed not to disseminate the perfect copy but to show up the dirty texture of low-resolution digital imaging. Using the techniques that make up the stock of digital manipulation—cut, copy, paste—Harwood creates roughly hewn portraits carved from the masters, juxtaposing these with images of his own body, of family and friends, close-ups of skin infections, and the visceral, dredged landscape of the muddy Thames river adjoining the actual site of Tate Modern.

Digital imaging manipulation is devoted to seamless construction, yet Harwood instead points crudely to artifice. Other kinds of links can enter the composited image space: links to the excluded, the minor, the disenfranchised and those obliterated from public and institutional histories.[22] Joined together by the flattened screen space of the computer monitor, Harwood's bodies briefly occupy a spatiotemporal equivalence with the canon of British painting. The material and technical conditions for the production and reception of online terminal-based work involve compression, in which images lose spatial information and may gain noise. These conditions, which disregard the content of the image and treat all signals equally, comprise the plane across which Harwood redistributes things that are held apart through the social divide of class relations. These re-alignments pass into the sensations experienced when engaging with a work such as *Uncomfortable Proximity,* sensations encountered when bodies press too closely together for comfort:

> The archive becomes a space of subjective involvement
> and invention, of fantasy, as much as a location for critique.
> Life stories feed into history, feed into aesthetics. And this is
> surely where Harwood is aiming. To produce an open diffi-
> culty in the representation of the Tate to effect a thorough-
> going conflict with its procedures and modes of operation
> and representation. But also to weave that difficulty into a
> process of his own self-composition as a member of a class
> that has been scrubbed from the walls of the Museum, is to
> provide the foundations for opening things up still further.[23]

Proximity allows Harwood to develop a digital aesthetic beyond the technical specificities of the medium and challenges the medium's status as simply the neutral bearer of information. Developing the digital in prox-imity to organic and embodied life and interweaving these images with the material conditions of official and unofficial histories, Harwood deploys the digital as a process for recomposition.[24] Although digital art cannot claim compositional superiority over other forms of aesthetic creation, it does allow for particular modes of composition that create zones through which the organic and the informatic can become approximate to each other. Digital artists are able to produce flashes of wonder, shock, incredu-lity and squeamishness by laying out both corporeality and the informatic across a plane of artificiality where both then appear as productions, in-ventions or chicanery. Harwood's piece gets close to the viewer through its digitality; it uses techniques at the core of digital image manipulation yet exaggerates these so that they are unsutured (figure 19). Their rough, im-mediate and poor quality provides the stuff of a different aesthetics, an aes-thetics that connects to life itself as a process of composing/compositing the self. Harwood indicates that the digital is not a technology that easily or seamlessly facilitates this process but rather one that lays open the very wounds and edges that form the interface of proximities. The borders be-tween the scabs and the Turner fragments, the hair follicles of his sister and the brushstrokes of an oil painting, the polluted mud of the river and the aura of the masterpiece, are digital scars of corporeal events. They mark Harwood's own memories of walking the Tate, consuming the art but never feeling proximate to its world. They follow instead the proximity

FIGURE 19. "Hogarth, My Mum 1700–2000," from the website *Uncomfortable Proximity* (2000) by Graham Harwood. Courtesy of the artist.

to something with which digital spaces can bring us into contact: a sense of the heterogeneous worlds of others' lives.

There are also decompositions that the digital makes of other media, such as photography, that we might be tempted to argue amount to the loss of materiality in the artwork. But we are quickly moving into a different regime of the digital image, which no longer requires a relentless comparison to the analogue image. Digital modes of image production are no less kinaesthetic simply because they are negotiated through coded terrain. They do, however, constitute a deterritorialization of the bodily movements often thought to mark the surface or material of art practice. As Deleuze suggests, codification envelops the hand's movements completely within its internal switching relations: "Once again, these basic units or elementary visual forms [i.e., digital code] are indeed aesthetic and not mathematic, inasmuch as they have completely internalized the manual movement that produces them."[25] *Uncomfortable Proximity* reminds us of this switching by making the eyes pass uncomfortably across the pixels.

Harwood's rough tears at the borders of his images, the jamming of visual incongruities to form conflicting proximities that recall the corporeal memory of feeling "out of place," and the slapdash realignment of fragments jostling for screen space constitute a form of digital visuality that is intensively kinaesthetic.

Rather than producing an exact science of feelings or resulting in a judgement of taste, digital aesthetics would at best be approximate. Digital media are quite capable of registering affectively; we underestimate our corporeal capacities if we suggest that the speed and geographical fragmentation wrought by these media lead to dematerialization, indifference or desensitization. But we also need to be wary of the claims made for digital media's abilities to capture a more authentic or fuller sensorium because of its proximity to "the real." Approximation as a differential qualifier of the proximate gives us new ways to configure digital aesthetics. First, it captures the sense in which the theorizing of contemporary artwork like new media art often lags behind the work itself because the technologies are always temporary and constantly remaking themselves. Second, approximation qualifies the thrill of the new gained in those flashes and the hankering after speed that has surrounded the making and consumption of technological art. The experience of new media artwork is marked by the broader cultural claims to the fast, efficient and high-bandwidth delivery of information that the integration of computing into day-to-day life has brought to millennial culture. Where new media art experiments with poor proximity to the "real" it often seems, comparatively, to be lacking in something. An open platform of aesthetic approximation undermines the exacting tyranny of remaining up to date with the latest technical standards. Most importantly, approximation gives us a way of looking at what I am suggesting is one of the most important conditions and issues running through new media art, the problem of proximity itself.[26]

Proximity can become a way to elaborate not just the relation of corporeality to technology but to how others become proximate to digital technologies. It offers a means of fleshing out information aesthetics that must take into account the reliance on information culture, hence jettisoning the new media artist into the spheres of the ethical and political. This is not to say that all digital artists voice these concerns or are willing to engage with these issues. But for those who do, digitality becomes partial and approximate to the conditions of living in digital times. It is possible to argue, then, for a digital aesthetics that is not reduced to the material specifications of the medium but develops its own particular concerns in relation to the differentially embodied experiences of contemporary life. Approxi-

mation is about paring down the expectations that the digital, and in particular digital art, has been burdened with: delivering the real; promising
freedom, authenticity or utopia. But it is also about nearness to underrep-
resented experiences and organizations of the visual—the potential for
digital media to throw up new affinities and compounds. The harsh qualities of low-resolution, low-bandwidth experimentation with digital imaging pose an alternative aesthetics to the slick photorealism of mainstream
computer graphics. Here proximity brings us into contact with the diverse
grit of the world, just as it lets go of its claims for realistic representation.

My sense of these aesthetic possibilities comes from the way in which
digitality provides sets of lived circumstances in which our senses are en-
croached upon, engaged and felt differently. Living life in relation to digital
computation is about the emergence of a spatiality and duration in which
relative speeds and differential relations are foregrounded in our corporeal
negotiation of the world. New media art offers us specific and unique in-
sights into the rearrangements of "blocks of sensation."[27] In exploring the
possibilities of machine perception—the alien *r*epresentation of the digital
image, the different speeds of engagement demanded from interactant and
producer, the differential speeds of information itself, where instantaneity
is coupled with interminable arrests, crashes and system failures—we can
begin to see the aesthesia of the digital operate. Digital aesthesia provides a
set of conditions for machine perception. But in the new media artwork itself the intensive speeds of embodied interaction and engagement also
enter the fray. The relations of movement that make up the speed of a particular body, machine or human, also allow it to be affected by and affect
other bodies. As Katherine Hayles has argued, the materiality of embodiment has a particular way of receiving and generating meaning that gives
it a vector of movement that may have the potential to alter *but is not equivalent* to the vectors of digital information.[28] Embodiment carries the sense
of personal and cultural history lingering in the fibers of corporeal memory. These histories themselves distribute different kinds of speeds within
and across the differences of humans' bodies, making them resistant, slow,
malleable, adaptable, heavy and light. Artists are using the opportunity of
the differential relation that corporeal experience brings to the informatic
universe to explore the conflicting proximities of body and machine.

Linda Dement's CD-ROM *In My Gash* (1999) moves us along these vec-
toral tensions.[29] Conceptually the work addresses issues of bodily memory
and scarring, probing the wound as an interface for an embodied visual
and mnemonic storehouse. With its slang references to the cultural degra-
dation of femininity, Dement's three-dimensional animated renderings of

gashes seemingly offer representations of the mysterious leap from the physical to the psychical, from the outside to the inside, from the beautiful to the grotesque that straddle the classical understanding of both relations to machines and relations of sexual difference. But this is no naïve or essentialist intervention with the promise of direct passage to the senses via new media. For even as we are urged to enter each of the four "gash" locations of the interface, we penetrate yet another media space. Dement's "gashes" house fragments that gain their memorial qualities by recycling genres such as the home video, the pornographic snapshot and the extreme close-up (figure 20). These are not just corporeal memories but screen memories of new media's relation to its own media lineage. The visual qualities of these fragments utilize moody and intense studio lighting to indicate continuity with Dement's photomedia practice in which she composes brightly lit but grotesquely composed photographic stills. The relation to the rhythms of other media and/or art practices constitutes part of the piece's affectivity.

In My Gash is cognizant of the space-time of the computer monitor and its flickering, conditions which make it difficult to hold the viewer's rapt gaze. Although these conditions for new media perception often lead to a

she is driven

FIGURE 20. Screenshot from *In My Gash* CD-ROM (1999) by Linda Dement. Courtesy of the artist.

hysterical aesthetics of information oversaturation, Dement uses the opulence of her prior photographic practice to slow down this informatic propensity. Rather than abandon photography, she allows the screen space of multimedia to reassemble her visual practices and preoccupations. Dement's work has consistently valued a rich, visual style garnered from her early days as a studio-based photomedia artist. *In My Gash* allows the fullness of her imagery to unfold slowly in relation to the user's actions, revealing layers and screens of lacerated bodily organs, destroyed petals, discarded syringes and torn limbs to appear and fade across the field of vision. Subsequently the manic desire to point and click that informed so much early interactivity gives way here to an engagement with the piece as multimediated. This tends to provide a slower tempo for engagement; iterations do not follow the speed of cyclical repetition but move in terms of the decomposition and recomposition of images. At other points filmic fragments tear at the fabric of the synthetic 3-D computer image, as if the prehistories of computation's engagements with other media were capable of bearing down upon the imaged body and wounding it. What Dement realizes here is the redeployment of photographic and filmic *découpage* as the dream and memory space for digital media. The aesthetic experience for the interactant, a responsive shiver to the dilating and contracting of Dement's digital wounds, is simultaneously a digital mediation of other media experience.

The zones of proximity digitality can call up for us in contemporary life include the digital's relations to other media forms, such as the photographic and the cinematic, and to institutions such as the gallery, museum and archive, in which art and media are housed and displayed. They also include our relations to others in the world and thus implicate the production of digital aesthetics within a wider context of ethics. As a result of both of these foregoing sets of relations, digitality as an aesthesia is produced in differentially proximate relations to corporeal experience. The digital always introduces elements of the hypermediated—for example, media histories—and of the incorporeal—for instance, the world of machine perception. Yet the aesthetic experiences these intersecting vectors conjure can be uncomfortable in their proximity, in the case of Harwood's work, or galvanic, in a work like Dement's *In My Gash*.

Lags

Digital technologies are providing a platform for broader social processes of self-composition. This is not to argue that they provide some renewed possibility for self-representation, that they are inherently libertarian or that access to them will provide for a more open political process. Artists such as Keith Piper demonstrate that the global reaches of cyberspace are principally organized through the synergy of corporate and military surveillance technologies. These regulate the spaces and times through which bodies pass, such as the massive channeling of immigrant workers in and out of collapsed nation states and borders of virtual territories such as the "new European state." In his 1992 interactive installation *Tagging the Other,* Piper foregrounds the production of an "other" through technologies of surveillance that in turn forms an outside to the fictional white state of the European Union. This "other" has been composed by technologically monitoring the bodies, lives and movements of Southeast Asian, West Indian and African migrants who have been forced to locate and relocate themselves in the wake of reconfigurations of technology, sociality and economy under the aegis of the information age:

> The new technologies that are being implemented to fix and survey the "un-European other" in the faltering consolidation of this "new European state" form the basis of *Tagging the Other.* Central to the piece are the framing and fixing of the black European, under a high-tech gaze—a gaze that seeks to classify and codify the individual within an arena where the logical constraints of race, ethnicity, nationality and culture are unchanging, and delineated in a discourse of exclusion.[30]

Piper offers us an addendum to the disembodiment debate in digital aesthetics by calling attention to the limits of composing fluid subjectivities that have permeated the rhetoric of new media. In other words, one disembodied avatar's gender, race or class appropriation is another person's lived and dislocated embodiment.

The seeming lack of bodily markers in cyberspatial relations was initially taken as hopeful for a digital politics of tolerance, as in Sherry Turkle's exploration of online sociability: "We do not feel compelled to rank or judge the elements of our multiplicity. We do not feel compelled to exclude what does not fit."[31] But artists such as Harwood and Piper remind us that this rhetoric belongs to only one time and space of subjective composition. It is here that aesthetics opens onto ethics, the sphere of embodied relations and actions toward others. In composing the self, we also compose relations to others, relations that are not mutable in the way information culture might promote them to be. In Sean Cubitt's words, there is a "radical disjuncture between the new media and the new geopolitics."[32] Constructions of self within new media have revolved, as Maria Fernandez suggests, around the extent to which the individual can create or control identity.[33] This form of hyperindividuation places the self once more at the center of a world: claiming a stake in virtual real estate, controlling the production of virtual game worlds, customizing browsers as easily as consumer preferences and feeding into a universalist, albeit flowing and mobilizing, informatics.

Cubitt, Fernandez and Piper have all brought a postcolonialist perspective to bear upon digital aesthetics, insisting on the relation between digital art and the global economic and social polarizations brought about by the more general deployment of digital technologies. Connectivity, for example, cannot just be thought of as an experience produced by interactive artwork; it enables the larger flow of information only through networks delivering to and utilized by a small percentage of people.[34] Within the sphere of new media art this translates to unevenness in access to technology and also to specific kinds of new media art forms requiring computational power. Fernandez makes the salient point that the place where electronic art and the postcolonial impulse have met lies with forms such as digital photomedia and video, already regarded as the "older" practices of new media.[35] There are several lags surfacing here: the lag in access to self-composition within new media, the lag between the promise of global technological diffusion and the geopolitical reality of limited technological access, and the lag between "cutting-edge" digital art and the critically reflexive practices of technologically outmoded new media art.

I want to argue that the lag itself has become an important aesthetic strategy in underscoring and negotiating these glaring disjunctions. The lag has become a mode of differentiating within the homogenizing forces of global digital culture and of foregrounding the way in which "othering" is organized by forces that implicitly or explicitly privilege standardization. There have been a number of newer transcultural voices that affirm the digital reality of proliferating differences in a way that does not reproduce the naïve rhetoric of the global village. In the artists' statement accompanying the installation *location n* (2002) by New Delhi's raqs media collective, we hear an existential description for a multitude of people working within the global "knowledge" economy, from call center telephonist through to frazzled lecturer: "We are now everywhere and always in a state of jet lag, catching up with ourselves and with others, slightly short of breath, slightly short of time. With the soft insidious ticking away of panic in our heads, in time with accelerated heartbeats and the speedening [*sic*] of our everyday lives, our daily bio-rhythms . . . get muddled as our faces find themselves lit by the light of millions of networked screens."[36]

The installation *location n* is a video-, object- and computer-based installation that questions the production of global or standardized corporate time at the expense of other times—the corporeal time of biorhythms, reflective times, the labor time underpinning and invisibly incorporated into the information technology (IT) economy. Substituting the ticking away of numeric units on displayed clock faces with epithets for our current affective experiences of time, *location n* suggests that global temporalities are neither perfectly calibrated nor clearly demarcated (figure 21). Reminiscent of those clocks that hang over airport bars, travel agent's desks and now globally franchised nightclubs, promising both the simultaneity of a world that never sleeps and the glimpse of others elsewhere sleeping, the faces here gather together the differentiality of duration that evades measurement: "So that when it is five minutes to Panic in San Paulo, it could be two minutes to Epiphany (in another time zone) say in New Delhi."[37] Interspersed with the clocks is a circle of computer terminals on which the video image of an expressionless human face travels from terminal to terminal, as if dragging itself from port to port in a circumnavigation of the electronic globe. And yet in spite of the familiar exhaustion the terminal face signals, works such as *location n,* alongside a number of pieces emerging from the Indian new

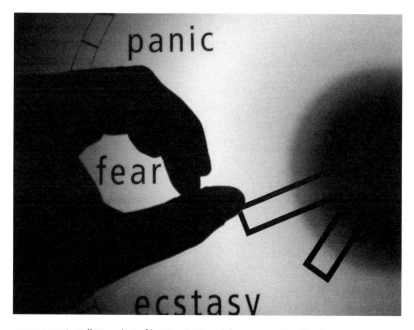

FIGURE 21. Installation shot of *location 'n'* (2002) by raqs media collective. Courtesy of the artists.

media art scenes, do not replicate or simply oppose the global standardization of experience. Instead they take media time as the subject of their work
and open it up to contestation by conceiving of speed as differentially constituted rather than absolutely given. In spite of the encroaching experience
of a 24/7 work cycle through the networked flow of services, finance and
knowledge, works such as *location n* emphatically refuse the synchronization of that experience as they gesture toward a situated experience of time
zones. If someone is panicking in New Delhi, others are affectively located
elsewhere in London, desiring, guilty, fearful and so on.

We cannot comprehend the temporal gestures of such a work without
recourse to *both* the claims for standardization made by critics and propo-
nents of globalization *and* the inflection produced by active, cultural transformations and contestations of these standards. It is important, then, to locate *location n* itself, not within the nation or even place "India" or even as
manifestation of an aesthetic captured by the nomenclature of "postcolonial new media art." To do either would be to presume the operation of an
aesthetic grounded only in a politics of identity, manifesting some essential
quality or basis of otherness. Rather we need to consider these works within
the context of a socio-technical-ethical assemblage of relations. These relations draw attention to the specific time-zone relation the Indian IT economy holds to globally networked information flows. Moreover, they trace
the asynchronous development of electronic cultures within India. These,
Ravi Sundaram has argued, work via a model of recycling, producing an alternative experience of the now or modernity, one that is outside of na-
tional/state regulation and irreducible to Western, global sensibilities.[38]

We also need to consider the cultural work done by groups and organizations such as raqs media collective and the Sarai New Media Initiative in
producing an alternatively positioned public domain for aesthetic work
through the deployment of these very same global new media technologies. This three-way dynamic at once situates the new media artwork coming out of Delhi and Mumbai and catapults it into the global arena, making time—ontological, durational, historical times—an arena of conflict
and contestation. These differential interventions into the possibility of
other speeds for electronic life provide us with a resource for what Arjun
Apppardurai has called "self-imagining as an everyday social project."[39]
Here self-composition is not a process of the individuated self but one
through which many bodies form affinities and compounds together, out
of which more complex bodies, such as proto-socialities, might grow.

As media theorist Geert Lovink has argued, corporate attempts to standardize an emerging public domain such as the Internet have not simply

been imposed through the technical development of infrastructural and software protocols.[40] Lovink has criticized the branding of a universally synchronized "Internet time" by the Swiss corporation Swatch in 1998. Internet time was launched on October 23 and was set to 000 beats at midnight in Biel, Switzerland, where Swatch headquarters is located. It became available both as a feature of new Swatch watches themselves and as a downloadable and linkable piece of software for websites.[41] Measured in "dot.beats," Swatch launched Internet time in the presence of Nicholas Negroponte, then director of MIT's prestigious Media Lab and a figure synonymous with the promised salvation invested in late-twentieth-century digital culture. At the launch it was stated, if somewhat confusedly, that "Internet time is absolute time for everybody. Now is now and the same time for all people and places. Later is the same subsequent period for everybody. The numbers are the same for all. Internet time is not geopolitical. It is global."[42] Lovink has suggested that this technique of standardization amounted to tangible evidence of the emerging standard of value underpinning networked society: the creeping corporatization of time through the imposition of a twenty-four-hour working day.

And yet any global analysis of the IT industry's networked infrastructure supporting the exchange of informational services will quickly reveal that large sectors rely precisely upon differences in time zones to sustain productivity. Indeed, the time difference between business days in India and the United States (between seven and twelve hours) has, in effect, allowed the growth of a cyber-elite of Indian programmers and developers as well as a pool of support-service cheap labor (such as the many women who staff the call centers spreading across New Delhi, Calcutta and Mumbai) to attend to the continuing business of the American IT economy while its corporations sleep. The managing director of a software start-up company in Bangalore states: "You're working when your customer is sleeping. To that extent, if he gives you a problem during his working hours you solve it and send it back to him by the time he starts working."[43] The time difference, or "lag," between India and America has allowed the center of the IT universe to be maintained in Silicon Valley. One way of understanding the effects of lag, then, is to suggest that the outsourcing of software skills, so as to reap the benefits of cheaper labor, maintains a colonial relation of dependency for India upon America. The Indian IT sector was staffed by Indian programmers and IT managers who had graduated from the elite Indian Technology Colleges and cut their teeth on round-the-clock computational problem solving. Yet, as Sundaram suggests, by pointing to either this participation of India in global IT culture or by remarking upon the dependency this relation has reproduced, one instills a position that privileges Americanization and the labor of only a section of the IT economy: the cyber-elites.[44] Sundaram has another story to tell concerning the rise of an alternative and everyday electronic culture within urban Indian centers, this one revolving around the growth of Public Communication Offices in the 1980s. These were run by people who taught themselves information and computer literacy. They often passed this literacy on to the customers who used their word-processing, fax and photocopying services. This culture is entwined with an alternative IT economy, where the illegal trade in recycled electronic goods, pirated media and software flourishes in the streets and markets around sites such as Nehru Place in New Delhi.[45]

It is into this electro-streetscape that we need to insert the cultural work of a media arts group such as raqs media collective; it also provides us with a useful crossroads for thinking about the actual and virtual relations that intersect in the work of Mumbai artist Shilpa Gupta. Raqs is a collective of media practitioners that formed in 1991 and works across digital art practice, filmmaking, photography, critical media theory and curation. Based in New Delhi, its members helped to instigate Sarai, a program and actual space of interdisciplinary research and practice around media, city space and urban culture. Raqs took part in the exhibition *Documenta 11* (2002) and used an Internet element in their work as part of the exhibition's broader political and aesthetic strategies.[46] "Opus," or Open Platform for Unlimited Signification, is an online environment for presenting content and a workspace that allows for collaboration, modification and the republication of others' content. It follows the principles and practices of free software or open source digital communities: the source (code) and the content presented including video, image, sound and text, is free to use, edit and redistribute. "Opus" could therefore be seen as part of the broader, indeed global, open source movement that has developed in the wake of operating systems such as Linux and the work of critical Internet theorists and writers, such as Laurence Lessig, who argue for a digital public domain based upon access by "the commons" to free and non-copyrighted software.[47]

But "Opus" is connected quite specifically, in its content and in its navigational pathways, to the urban spaces of New Delhi and to the practices of recycling and pirating that challenge the regulation of space in the street. These connect raqs not to any time and any space but to the reach of a zone between digital space and everyday urban space, a zone we might diffusely locate at point "n": the zone of an alternative, electronic modernity. As Sundaram suggests in a different context, it is through recycling and adaptation, coincidentally the fundamental techniques of an open software developer's practice, that the absolute speed of one modernity is inflected by the differential speeds of located cultural transformation: "this is a constantly shifting universe of adaptation to available tools of speed . . . in a third world country such as India, where both the given-ness of access to the net and the purchase of processing power do not exist in simultaneity. They have to be created, partly by developing new techniques, and partly through breaking the laws of global electronic capital."[48] Raqs's "creative commons" project exists in relation to the broader Sarai initiatives to circulate free software in a culture that, they suggest, regulates the production of knowledge through hierarchy and inequity. "Opus" as a public domain generates excessive lags, recycling and reusing code standards and file formats, and mediating digital space itself through the registers of urban differences in Indian life.

The lag has itself become a device in new media, and more specifically Internet art, that is used to address the flux of temporalities that lurk within media time's aura of smooth seamlessness. In Shilpa Gupta's 2001 work *sentiment-express*, created as part of the Tate Modern's *Century City Progam*, an indeterminate lag inserts itself between the actual worlds of Mumbai, the international postal system and the labor of transcription, on the one hand, and the digital realm of virtual sentiment, net connectivity and data translation, on the other.[49] *Sentiment-express* invites you, with all of the luminescent colours of World Wide Web seduction at its disposal, to speak an unrestrained missive into the microphone, which is translated, using voice-to-text synthesis software, into a text file (figure 22).

Thus far we remain comfortably within the zone of data and of formal analyses of new media, which argue that the numerical translation of any data, including voice, via digitization produces a transcoding of culture, permitting any of its formats to be manipulated and programmable.[50] This data world of translated modules and infinitely variable combinations turns out to be the familiar world of online consumption, in which users enter information into fields and pick from pull-down menus in order to customize their desires. This point is reinforced by an option in *sentiment-express* allowing the user to save time by sending a one-model-tweaked-for-all, easy-to-write love letter.

But the first lags begin to express themselves in Gupta's work as she introduces a heterogeneity of times, in which the hurried world of online consumption, supported by the speed of interconnectivity, gives way to the choices made at each page-click, upon which this seamless world of consumption rests. Here we are faced with the ethical choice of consuming someone else's labor time in some other offshore yet real location. The user is reminded of the effect of choosing various pull-down options by having this choice implicated in the exploitation of others' labor time. The screen reads "choose one: I have been busy yes and I would like to express myself now; I want to tap into labour from Mumbai because it is cheap; I want to tap into labour because there are many well-educated jobless people there; I want someone to don phoney identities at work." Furthermore, Gupta commits the ultimate interface transgression by introducing a photo identity for the very nameless workers of the IT economy who will be transcribing (rather than translating) the final love letter package into material form. And yet, like all Internet scams, one feels both hopeful and doubtful that this identity is authentic. As Gupta says:

> It's a take-off on the back-office nature of the IT market in India. You have call centres or transcription businesses where doctors in the US will dictate something on a dicta-phone and note patient history or something, and overnight it will land up in Bombay. So you have lots of people sitting in droves and droves with headphones and transcribing it and sending it back . . . Instead of mundane information like patient history, you have personal information like love letters. It's as personal as you can get. Also there is an option where the users can choose the transcribers, but I give ficti-tious information about them. I'll raise their identity but not expose them.[51]

Lucky enough to speak my desires into the voice-to-text translation program at the *sentiment-express* site, I wrote to a lover who eventually received a hand-written letter on cheap, scented Indian paper, shipped through the anti-quated and nonstandardized international surface postal system. Arriving in a mailbox in Sydney four long forgotten months after the fact, it came as a tangible reminder of our disconnected and uneven relations to the place, work and time of unknown others throughout the world. Gupta's small but fulfilled promise of material delivery against all odds in an age that promises to deliver so much yet rarely comes up with the goods aesthetically straddles the collapse of the "dot.com" economy, which partly failed because it was un-able to synchronize its virtual and actual delivery watches. In the lag between data and delivery times, we are made only too aware of the laboring bodies of others whose sweat supports the flows of information exchange.

The promise of Internet time, and indeed cyberspace, has been to wrap the globe in a frictionless and undifferentiated mesh of connectivity in which now is always now and later only begins if we set the time and date

to say how much you care

choose one
choose one
I have been busy, yes, and I would like to express myself now
I want to tap into labour from Mumbai because it is cheap
I want to tap into labour from Mumbai because there are many
well-educated jobless people there
I want someone to don phoney identities at work

to say how much you care

FIGURE 22. Screenshot of *sentiment-express* (2001) by Shilpa Gupta. Courtesy of the artist.

to media contractions such as 24/7 or 9/11. But the mutability of a public domain produced through the transactions of informatic codes allows for changing and renegotiating its very temporal and spatial coordinates. That their regulation and deregulation can both be seen to derive from techniques of standardization positions digital art practices that undermine, parody and forcibly differentiate the smooth flows of global speed along a meridian of new vectors and keeps them open to contestation.

Distributed Aesthetics

During my discussion in chapter 3 of the possibilities implicit in digital productions of virtual duration, I suggested that virtual reality and computer gaming offer experiences of nonlinear temporalities where time is compressed, layered and multimodal rather than disappearing or monotonously stretched into an eternal present. I want to turn to this conception of digital temporality again in order to trace the final vector I suggest is unfolding for global information aesthetics, a vector that perhaps signals its most radical shift yet. In all modes of digital media production we are witnessing the move from regimes of spatialization to those of temporalization: media are no longer sent from one location and received in another but diffusely distributed and qualitatively changed by the differentials that guide that distribution. These differentials may include (but are not limited to) the larger flows of global capital that I have, in the last section, suggested carve up and reallocate relations and access to the information economy. Just as important are the new forms and communities of networked information and sociality that set in motion, contract and divert data so that it becomes a collective and individuated product, transactions that, not coincidentally, are all supported by the social and technical infrastructure of online interactions and telecommunications such as blogging, text messaging and "mashed-up pop."[52] These might all be considered experiments in distributed aesthetics. What is crucial and holds tremendous potential for the production of alternative digitalities is the extent to which a distributed aesthetics simultaneously engages new experiences perceptually and socially. That is to say, we are in the midst of a shift to aesthetic regimes that rely upon temporalities rather than spatialities while they are being supported by emergent, networked socialities. This means these new aesthetic experiences are not simply produced or consumed in isolation but result directly from collective, social exchange. There is no guarantee that this exchange will be equitable, but the potential is there for acknowledging the outcomes of these aesthetic directions as the collective result of socially networked exchanges. At the same time, these collectivities remain differentiated by contact with the localized experience of others.

In Deleuze's analysis of the shift from an aesthetic cinematic regime governed by the movement-image (classical cinema) to one in which the time-image (modern cinema) is crucial, he prefigures the ways in which information images will have new effects upon the flow of images in time, cutting into, sliding over and producing an "incessant stream of images."[53] Moreover, he remarks upon the loss of a system of space that externally orients the image:

> The new images no longer have any outside (out-of-field), any
> more than they are internalized in a whole: rather they have a
> right side and a reverse, reversible and non-superimposable,
> like a power to turn back on themselves. They are the object
> of a perceptual reorganization, in which a new image can
> arise from any point whatever of the preceding image. The
> organization of space here loses its privileged directions,
> and first of all the privilege of the vertical which the position
> of the screen still displays, in favour of an omni-directional
> space which constantly varies its angles and co-ordinates,
> to exchange the vertical and the horizontal.[54]

This sense of space as everywhere yet nowhere has provided an analytic and speculative theme in the exploration of cyberspace generally and virtual environments specifically. But it is not so much how omnidirectionality affects and transforms a phenomenological experience of space that concerns me here; rather it is the way in which a dynamic between sequential and nonsequential variation (chronological and nonlinear time) begins to function as a set of temporal coordinates for digital aesthetic production. This is particularly prevalent in the case of the digital image, and even more so as it increasingly becomes the digitized *moving* image in motion graphics, animation, interactivity and immersive environments. If we turn to a specific case of the digital moving image encapsulated in the widely used Flash software package we can chart this more general shift from a located, spatialized aesthetics to a distributed, temporal aesthetics. The widespread use of Flash software has culminated in a particular style for the digital image, a kind of flattening of the image's plane and depth. The dispersal of both the software and its identifiable aesthetic is made possible by the program's technical specifications and by the circulation of animations, interfaces and designs among online art, design, fashion and music communities.[55]

Significantly, in a majority of the analyses of the digital image to date, bitmapped graphics have formed the default layer for an understanding of how new forms of digital visual culture might operate. Bitmapped graphics fix the data describing the location and value of the pixels in an image to a grid of a particular size. Digital images comprised of pixels are thus imbricated with and depend upon a form of spatiality external to and independent of them: the Cartesian coordinate system. Flash, as well as many generative graphics now used in digital illustration, design and even 3-D animation programs, works with vector graphics. The spatial information in the image (which places it at a precise location on the screen) is now generated intrinsically as points calculated by the variable and continuing relations between lines and curves. The description accompanying the Flash 5 program's online "Help" section on "Vector Graphics" summarizes the change:

> The image of a leaf is described by points through which lines pass, creating the shape of the leaf's outline. The color of the leaf is determined by the color of the outline and the color of the area enclosed by the outline. When you edit a vector graphic, you modify the properties of the lines and curves that describe its shape. You can move, resize, reshape, and change the color of a vector graphic without changing the quality of its appearance.

Moreover, in Flash's moving images (whether in edit or playback modes), movement itself is not a function of the actual *spatial* relation between image instants across time, as it is in analog animation. Nor is it generated by the changing value of pixel information in relation to a grid, as it is in bitmapped animation. Instead, movement results from the deformations and transformations that the image information undergoes in *time*.

The networked environment in which Flash operates fleshes out earlier experiments in the 1990s with the topology of the image and its form in digital aesthetics, some of which I examined in detail in chapter 1 while discussing the place of folding within contemporary architecture. The use of Flash as an online design tool shifts the very status of the digital interface; it becomes less a spatial environment for navigation and habitation than a series of movements through and across unfolding surfaces. Some of the more abstract and experimental Flash web interfaces, such as design firm Yugop's site, draw attention to this new topological organization of the image by providing a user experience in which the cursor's movement "draws" across the monitor's surface varied series of undulating and deforming shapes and outlines that change in time yet retain image quality.[56] Here we have the image generating a topological terrain that has pre-programmed parameters but is unpredictable and responds to the vicissitudes of user movement. Although this has resonances with minimalist and abstract aesthetics, the fundamental difference between modernist and Flash aesthetics lies in Flash's abandonment of an obsession with predetermined spatial configuration, particularly with the space enclosed or excluded by the image.[57] Information aesthetics moves into a regime in which temporality conjoins image planes. Visually flattened space, such as we find in Japanese and post-animé art and design, *The Simpsons* and *South Park*, and the tracing of vector outlines and color to substitute for photographic depth of field in advertising campaigns, prefigures the compression and eventual disposal of externally referenced volumetric space within the overall aesthetic regime of the digital image. It is as if images can no longer be located as distinct sets of coordinates upon a grid providing them with place and context in a system. They are now laid out on a plane, to be organized principally by directions and speeds in time: backwards, forwards, fast, and slow.

Of course, the actual conditions in which most Flash animation eventually operates—the networked distribution of packaged information across nonstandardized connections—mean that the delimitations of location effectively matter and operate to impinge upon and qualify the intrinsic unfolding of visual information. But location itself within informatic, networked socialities comes to be measured in terms of the effects of differential speeds, as I argued earlier. Again, it is time that becomes the key factor: the time it takes for information to download, the connection speed of terminal to network, the routing time of information (dependent upon a variety of technical and social factors from Internet infrastructure through to censorship avoidance), the flows and blockages of network traffic, and so forth.

Online interfaces that play with the temporal dimension of digital visual culture stretch, layer and compress the image so that it comes to resemble an experimental sound piece. This is hardly surprising if we take into account my hypothesis about the transformation of image space into image time in information aesthetics. Sound, after all, is the medium of temporality par excellence. One of the appealing features of Flash for artists and designers has been its relatively high-quality compression codec for digital sound. This has allowed artists to produce sophisticated sonic dimensions for their Web interfaces without major sacrifices to download speed. As a scripting application, Flash also allows for sound to be triggered asynchronously from the image, often as a result of user-activated events such as a mouse-click or rollover. The sonic dimension further inflects the informatic image by forcing it to work through rhythm and variation rather than spatiality and representation.

In Simon Bigg's *Great Wall of China,* different rhythms animate the movement of visual information and work to disturb the conception of user control that mouse-driven events often bring to digital interfaces.[58] The Web aspect of Biggs's work, from 1995–96, predates the Flash environment. But the visual and textual display is produced through programming that uses executed algorithms to draw interactively on the end-user's terminal in real time. The piece deals both formally and semantically with the generation of, and the relation between, human linguistic comprehension and incomprehensible machine languages. The visual aesthetics of *Great Wall of China* provide an ongoing interface in which human and machine rhythms and systems intersect to produce the multiple surfaces of elision and contact. The screen is divided by Chinese characters: on one side sits a dissolving and layered set of visually filtered architectural images that are activated to run at different speeds through rollover hotspots in the text directly beneath them. The closer a user moves into this text with the cursor, the faster words within the text and the layers within the images change, becoming increasingly incomprehensible. At the edge of the event horizon for the piece, the user can just make sense of the information. Alongside this whirl of animation, the other side of the screen remains motionless. Yet one's visual attention hardly partakes of the stillness. As soon as the cursor moves to the static area, the space frantically transforms into a torrent of graphic textual information that changes in relation to both randomly programmed and event-driven movement. But the changes are too rapid and random to make sense of the text; instead, it becomes a visual plane shot through, fragmented and intersected by slices of rhythm coming at it from angles that roll up from, yet also seem perpendicular to, the screen space. Only by carefully tracing the cursor slowly over the Chinese characters that divide the screen can one slow the textual flows to the pace of comprehension. Biggs produced the piece as a "language machine . . . capable of creating an endless stream of ever evolving and changing texts."[59] At the time of its production, the Web delivery of digital images was still tied to bitmapped graphics. In order to compact the visual space and highlight the varying and converging speeds of sense and nonsense generation, Biggs produced a piece that dispensed with the bitmapped image altogether, thereby subjecting visual production entirely to the times of the computational machine: "One way to achieve this degree of compactness was to not use images. Everything you see is created during runtime using the available drawing and typography tools on your own computer. When you download a component of the *Great Wall of China* all you are downloading is a program."[60] In *Great Wall of China* image space is lost as the text sheds its information content; the different locations of sending and receiving communication are no longer important in connecting and disconnecting from the aesthetics of the image. Instead, everything becomes pure movement, pure transmission, as communication and meaning surrender to processual and affective flows.

More recently, the expansive temporal environment that Flash aesthetics produces in its compression and intensification of information has allowed potential forms of online cinematic space to emerge. Interestingly, these have been signaled not through a rich visual language but through the minimal graphics of Flash design in combination with layered and textured sonic environments. Mark Amerika's *FILMTEXT 2.0* (2002) is one such experiment in distributed informatic cinema. In collaboration with Flash animator John Vega and sound design by Twine, the online and offline versions of the piece compress digital forms such as gaming, Web design, digital writing and digital music into ambient information that is sculpted and textured through layers of sound that are triggered by the user. Rather than information being at the behest of user control or responding in a meaning-laden way to user events, the soundscapes that emerge suspend the user at any given moment in time within *FILMTEXT*

2.0's nonlinear game environment. Small sound sequences merge to produce richly textured sonic environments that expand one moment of the "game" into an exploration of a time in which nothing much happens at all apart from the game's elusive atmosphere. *FILMTEXT 2.0* shares a relationship with the rapidly transforming virtual worlds of multi-user online role-playing games (MORPGs) such as Everquest and CounterStrike.[61] But whereas the emphasis in these games remains with shooting and strategy, Amerika's piece provides a kind of vacated and goalless digitalscape in which one is both set adrift and made buoyant by the currents of information rhythm and flow.

Amerika builds sequences of meaning through a mélange of cultural commentary, fragments of scripting syntax appropriated from Action Script (Flash's scripting language) and literary texts. These sequences spew forth across the screen and move the sense of the piece along in fits, starts, stutters and cycles. Completed cycles of text sequences initiate the user to new levels of the "game." To pass through the game play, then, one must submit oneself to the clutches of the text's writing spaces, which offer neither promise nor denial of comprehension or communication, nor indeed any conception of where a particular sentence or segment of information may be heading. Differentiated rhythms compete for the user's attention and participation, making the experience of playing *FILMTEXT 2.0* both lingering and propulsive.

Digital work like this offers us an insight into the very status of our aesthetics and ethics in global information cultures, a crossroads where we can choose to hang around and soak up the rhythmic atmosphere or move the playing field itself so that it expands and contracts to accommodate heterogeneous directions. These kinds of flattened and compressed spaces that distribute information and its users through flows, accumulations and dispersals offer us encounters with disparate, nonstandardized and as yet unassimilated elements across informatic and embodied universes. It will be up to artists, designers, technicians and new media activists of all shapes and sizes to create these with an eye for not simply new perceptual experiences but the production of new forms of social, political and ethical relationships.

postscript emerging tendencies in embodied information aesthetics

In an extraordinary new media work, *Loops,* the collaborative team of Paul Kaiser, Shelley Eshkar, Merce Cunningham and Marc Downie created an abstract motion portrait of the dancer drawn from a changing database of information captured through motion sensors placed on Cunningham's hands.[1] As he performs a series of varying loop gestures, Cunningham's artistry—embedded in his fingers' joints and muscles—is translated into a set of mutable information coordinates and stored in a database. Recalling Moholy-Nagy's black-and-white cinematic studies in light and movement, the trails of quixotic points and lines comprising this portrait transcribe the relationship between staccato and fluid rhythm that animates the agile separation of the dancer's physical limbs. In an interview, Kaiser and Eshkar discuss the potential of new visualization technologies for the continual manipulation and tweaking of data into patterned flows.[2] These processes allow the production of an entirely different kind of portrait an image of the self or body no longer based upon appearance but instead expressed through motion and across time. And yet, in this instance, the artists themselves remain unaware of the broader implications of such modes of aesthetic production. Kaiser reinscribes such forms of visualization in terms that have plagued and stultified new media art: he refers to this kind of portrait as "disembodied."

But from the point of view of the audience, in whom abstraction can indeed produce sensate responses (as was likewise the case with various strands of modernist abstraction), the informatic portrait could not be more *em*bodied. The internal discreteness *and* connectivity of the dancer's muscular-skeletal system, trained and refined through years of choreographic experience and experiment, is traditionally presented as a total and externalized form in the spectacle of dance. But in *Loops* we gain visual access to the intensive deformations and twists of contracted and protracted bodily movements that animate the energy of dance. The fact that these now appear to us in a visually pared-down form—as monochromatic lines unfolding and transforming through time—foregrounds the temporal and *topological* propensities of information visualization. What we are "seeing," then, is a doubling and amplification by data of intensive bodily activity. It may well be that we can no longer call these kind of images portraiture, based as this tradition has been on the face as the seat of self-expression and identity. Perhaps the database portrait gives us a different interface between human action—dancing—and computer processes that include motion capture, database storage and dynamic recall. This interface no longer relies upon facialization but upon an intensively folding embodiment into the informatic world. We could welcome portraits such as these that open corporeality up, extending it toward the flows and temporality of information's incorporeal spacetime.

The challenge for new media art and theory in both making and thinking with digital technologies is to move beyond the twin premises of disembodiment and extension in space that continue to qualify both information and corporeality. The informatic visualizations or sonic renderings of bodies we see in a work like *Loops,* and increasingly in scientific and medical renderings of the body, transpose fixed forms of corporeal experience. But this transposition does not simply turn material experience into dematerialized data; rather, it challenges the categories and perceptual habits we have historically acquired for thinking about and "imaging" both the corporeal and the abstract. In their interview about the making of *Loops*, Kaiser and Eshkar refer to both the body work carried out by Cunningham and the digital work by programmer Downie of producing the visual database as "performances." This hints at the level of aesthetic, sensory engagement—rather than disembodied manipulation—that is required to work data into a graphic, cultural artefact, even if it is acknowledged solely at the stage of artistic production. Equally, watching *Loops* asks us to change how we think about bodies. Like all technologies associated with our sensorium, it requires us to undertake a labor of perception.[3] Informatic bodies no longer summon the immediate presence of corporeal existence, which can be affirmed through habitual codes and conventions of visual representation. They disclose a body's potential for becoming different, for transmutation. Information does not simply represent a body or corporeal experience; it renders the emergent properties and capacities of bodies as mutable states that are variable (and delimited) within certain parameters. In *Loops*, sensation and affect transpire in the relation between the abstract topological traces of virtual movement that we see and the personalized narration of time and memory that we hear in Cunningham's voiceover from his diary. This is not simply data stored in an impersonal memory bank to be arranged into code by a machine. Instead we are offered a kind of choreography of machine programming and bodily movement, unfolding iterative yet situated instances of motion, image and sound and conveying to us the abstract tendencies toward which a body extends itself.

For new media art, two key vectors for *embodied* information aesthetics have opened up in the divergent and convergent relations that information and corporeality now plot in tandem. A number of artists and designers are increasingly aware of the potential of new media for providing intensive sensate engagement via abstract forms and displays of data. We can discern here one trend of experimenting with sensory modes of engagement that have been displaced from a visual economy concerned with extensive and fixed space. Corporeal experience is now relocated within a mesh of intersections between shifting patterns, maps and forces of digital information. Actual bodies are virtually catapulted into these interstices of enmeshed information: the bodily movement of dancers and actors captured by motion sensors; the corporeal performance of the tweaking programmer; the engagement of the audience and interactants' sensory and proprioceptive capacities in situating and rearranging the database.

In the TGarden Sensor Lab, a responsive media environment for developing and evolving new media performance, new conceptions about both body and information emerge through an interactive exploration of their respective topologies.[4] Entering the TGarden environment with costumes that are wearable computers, participants engage with both media and each other via gesture, movement and dance. Video and sound are "brushed," caressed and coaxed into pattern through the air and across the walls and floor of the space as the "players" discover how their movements trigger them. In turn, these media are programmed to work as a sophisticated system, developing a dynamic response to the particular topology of bodily gesture performed within the space. The software-media system is therefore also operating in topological mode, updating, deforming and transforming the production of an immersive aesthetic experience according to the positions and performances of the bodies in its space over time. These kinds of environments create delicate and complex articulations between body and media that are infinitely richer than the goal of adding the body back into the disembodied realm of information, which we saw develop as a strategy for "embodying" earlier VR spaces in chapter 3. In TGarden both embodiment and information emerge as differential aggregates of the other:

> There are no users in the TGarden, nor tasks to be solved.
> The space is not there to be navigated or searched but rather
> to hang out and dance in. The movement of players' bodies is
> used by the TGarden's nervous system (hardware and soft-
> ware network) to shape visual, aural and tactile media. The
> gestures—that are not so different from everyday gestures
> such as touching, brushing along other bodies, dancing,
> stretching and falling—are an impetus for the generative
> processes in TGarden. Ultimately, the virtuosity of the play-
> ers should grow through the interaction with the TGarden
> system, and allow them to actualize their imagination.[5]

Importantly, the design of TGarden is both social and non-navigational; it returns information to the possibility of relationships inflected by affect. But this is not affect realized through purely individualized instances of participation in technology. New media, as I have argued throughout this book, have consistently provided us with modes for engaging sensory and affective elements. Often, though, we have been promised or presented with only the immediacy of sensation, accessed through a solitary user's response to a terminal. A number of new media artists, such as Simon Penny and his reworking of the CAVE environment in *Traces*, or the projects of the immersive environment design team Metraform that are designed for group interaction in virtual semi-immersive environments, are pursuing an engagement with information aesthetics that is embodied and aware of emerging social relations among users.[6] Works such as these provide us with an alternative direction for digital culture and make us consider what technologically mediated interactions between people yield for the ways in which both our bodies and our sense of others can cohabit the space of information. These kinds of social experiments in responsive media environments indicate that new media artists are beginning to shift their attention to the relationship between information aesthetics and ethics. As I suggested in chapter 5 we are moving into a period of new media production in which not only the body has returned with a vengeance: *bodies* have multiplied exponentially, and the question of their differentiated connections in information culture is assuming a critical status.

Moving in almost the opposite direction and experimenting with the broader scientific, ethical and cultural deployment of information technologies, other artists have quite literally been interpolated back into "the body" through their aesthetic exploration of biology. "Bioart" is developing into a practice concerned with technically manipulating life for the purposes of producing cultural objects, processes and concepts or critically examining the use of biotechnologies in society at large.[7] It may well be that bioart develops into an entire aesthetic field of its own. It is certainly distinguished by its tendency to incorporate technically manipulated living matter into its aesthetic processes and outcomes. As an emerging field, genre or movement, then, it is difficult to say whether bioartists are engaged with new media aesthetics and concerns or with a more general arena of contemporary art practice that has been termed "art-science" collaboration.[8] Nevertheless, what is important about bioart is that it takes as a condition of its investigations the now inextricable imbrication of biology with information and information technologies. Hence we might, for the most part, consider it to be a tendency that has arisen from information aesthetics. In its direct insertion of manipulated, technologically maintained and digitally arranged organisms into artistic settings, bioart returns us to a startling yet mediated confrontation with living matter. It makes us viscerally aware of the current sociopolitical contexts through which information is actualized and reacquires "a body."

In the biotech laboratory matter is routinely dismembered into its cellular and genetic components for utilitarian purposes: the production of biometric information-gathering techniques for the security, insurance and military industries and services; the understanding and application of medical and pharmaceutical therapies; the growth of the agricultural sector. Although there has been critical discussion of the social and ethical implications of biotechnologies, much of this critique rests upon an "androcentric" assumption that there is or should be a sphere of life untarnished by association with technology and artifice.[9] This domain is often assumed to be coterminous with aesthetic, cognitive and ethical human activity and endeavor. Bioart inserts itself between the utilitarian ethos of the biotech industry and the reassertion of a privileging of human life over other species and the strict separation of the natural and the artificial. In an approach that redeploys a media arts perspective that used mass media in a self-reflexive way and a common new media strategy that insists upon the technical as the material, form and content of its aesthetics, bioartists have familiarized themselves with standard techniques used in the biotech industry. These technologies then reappear in the artworks but with results that are far removed from a utilitarian or androcentric ethos: Heath Bunting's *Superweed* yields a seed genetically modified to resist the weedkillers used by agricultural corporations like Monsanto; the Tissue Culture and Art (TCA) Project's various semi-living sculptures of worry dolls, victimless meat and unattached human organs require "killing off" by the artists and audience at the end of each exhibition period; Adam Zaretsky's installations place humans, rats, bacteria and a host of organisms in close contact with each other.[10]

Instead, by viewing, visiting or interacting with bioart we are to arrive at the conclusion that life is not simply a force that inhabits the organism but a network coextensive with information gathering, retrieving, storage, manipulation and management techniques. And yet at the same time this networked formation manifests as living things that demand care and response and ask us to acknowledge their specificity. It is impossible to peer into the incubator that houses a semiliving sculpture such as TCA and Stelarc's *Extra Ear 1/4 Scale* and not sense that technically initiated and manipulated life is similarly as fragile and unique as any other living matter. Bioart implicates and engages both its practioners and its audiences in the ethical dimension of information aesthetics. Bioartists are tactically positioned to quite literally produce and investigate an important aspect of the material conditions of information culture. If biology has become an informatic network, to recontexualize its materialization in ethico-aesthetic terms produces an excess of matter and a redundancy for information management in the apparently seamless flows of biocapital. Both in terms of the biotechnical artefacts they produce and the standard biotech processes they deploy in their art making, bioartists have the opportunity to exceed the normative regulation of life and its ordering into an "information society."

In this book I have been concerned with producing a radically different conceptual and aesthetic genealogy for information aesthetics, one that acknowledges new media's relation to materiality. Materializing new media culture means insisting upon an analysis of its artefacts that takes into account the ongoing engagement of information and new technologies with embodiment. New media artists have found new ways of producing these engagements, ranging from the development of haptic and gestural interfaces to a constructive acknowledgment of the impact that corporeal movement and material and environmental circumstances have had in producing new media art and culture. Information aesthetics, then, has emerged in the reconfiguration of relations between body, materiality and computer. At the levels of image and interface, artists, designers and architects using new media have consistently considered the impact of bodies and material life on these technologies, as I suggested in my analysis of folding in architecture, of new renderings of data bodies and of artists' redesign of human-computer interfaces. The aesthetics of information culture is concerned with modes of sensory engagement in which distributed spaces and temporal variation play crucial roles. In engaging with and visualizing bodies and in responding to material parameters, new media simultaneously change our understanding of and relationships with our own bodies. No longer can we consider "the body" an antinomy of code; its incorporeal capacities are simultaneously amplified and divided from its physicality as we come to think of digital embodiment as a process of living in information culture: the labor of folding corporeality and code across its many differentiated instantiations.

I have been equally concerned with the political consequences of continuing to sustain a disembodied analysis of new media technologies and culture. To argue, as have various posthumanist, populist and theoretical analyses, that digital machines will supercede, make obsolete or dispose of time, space and embodied life has direct implications for the valuing of material differences in contemporary culture. An argument for disembodiment, whether celebratory or critical, is an argument that denies the importance of differences. Hence we are left with a view of contemporary digital machines as responsible for producing an even field of global culture. Many "body" theorists have sought to locate the impact of materiality upon culture in bodies and their lived existence per se and consequently give the body a determining or essentialist role. But "digital embodiment" is an unstable and uneven condition produced out of the differential impact of bodies and technologies as they globally impinge upon one another in widely varying circumstances. Material differences make themselves felt by being produced rather than by inhering to substances. These differences do not only transpire at the microlevel, when individual bodies engage with digital codes to produce new and different sensations and affects. They are likewise experienced at the level of social, collective and cultural organization, as information flows globally through and across non-standardized conditions of distribution, transmission and reception. Under global conditions, time and place have enormous impact upon the speeds and rhythms at which informatic code and living bodies interact. It is not that bodies, time and space have disappeared from digital culture, but the experience of them has shifted to the arenas of technological speeds, lived intensities and information flows. This emerging digital culture, globally circulating and locally experienced, places humans in differential relations with bodies everywhere. It is the movements, modulations and transformations peculiar to global digital culture that make the political and ethical relations we form (or deny) with other bodies so important.

Information culture depends upon distinction and variation. Yet digital distinction is synaptic rather than oppositional or exclusionary. It attempts to sustain connections across its variations and lags. The logic of the differential or of the fold, I have suggested, has its genesis in European early modern thought. This comes to us directly through the proto-aesthetics of Leibniz but can also be seen to permeate the natural sciences and even inflect Descartes's work on the passions. The baroque's emphasis on the continuity and variability between the organic and the artificial, the senses and thought, the arts and the sciences, has provided us with a paradigm for understanding the ambivalent directions of connectivity and disconnection currently permeating information aesthetics. Forces of both convergence and divergence are of equal importance in shaping the directions and outcomes of new media technologies and the artefacts they produce. And perhaps the forces interacting with these technologies, and carrying the greatest tendency toward divergence, emanate from human bodies. Bodies reconfigure digital culture through rhythms of variation driven by place, habit, history, circumstance and accident. They are the chaos and interruption with which the machine cannot dispense, a set of expansive forces that challenge the pace, interaction and relations we have and are capable of sustaining with informatic media.

We might superficially surmise that the two vectors emerging from current practices and debate within information aesthetics—the one toward abstraction as a means for engaging intensive corporeal experience, the other toward an investigation of biology as a materialization of information—seem to offer quite divergent approaches and opportunities for new media art. And yet their shared concern with the social and cultural specificities of living and breathing informatic bodies and with the processes of embodying information also tells us that contemporary art has never been more critically engaged with the formation, regulation and renewal of sense and perception.

NOTES

Punctuation following Web URLs is for grammatical sense; it should not be entered into the Web browser.

Introduction (pp. 1–24)

1. David Rokeby, artist's statement for *Very Nervous System* (2000), http://homepage.mac.com/davidrokeby/vns.html.

2. Manuel de Landa, *A Thousand Years of Nonlinear History* (New York: Swerve Editions, 1997), 273.

3. "Grids, Guys and Gals: Are You Oppressed by the Cartesian Coordinate System?" Chair: G. Garvey, panelists: B. Laurel, R. Tow, J. Staveley, A. R. Stone. *Computer Graphics Proceedings, SIGGRAPH '95 Conference Proceedings, August 6–11, 1995*, ed. R. Cook (New York: ACM SIGGRAPH Publication, 1995): 503.

4. Ibid., 504.

5. Bukatman's argument is more complex than this perspective, and I am borrowing from the sense in which "terminal" connotes both a relation to computing terminals and a friction/subsumption anxiety to describe the human/machine dilemma in late-twentieth-century accounts of subjectivity. As Bukatman shows, fantasies of technological penetration and merging in which subjectivity is reduced to the machine often result in providing the subject with a sense of greater power or control, hence enforcing the notion of the autonomous subject. See Scott Bukatman, *Terminal Identity* (Durham, N.C.: Duke University Press, 1993), 301–20.

6. Ulrike Gabriel, interview in the film *Artists in Cyberculture (Third International Symposium of Electronic Arts)*, dir. Johnathon Cohen, Ronin Films, Sydney, 1993.

7. An example of this kind of analysis can be found in David Antin's article "Video: The Distinctive Features of the Medium," in *Videoculture: A Critical Investigation* (New York: Visual Studies Workshop Press, 1986), 147–66.

8. I consider two examples in detail that use the *Wunderkammer* to structure online spaces in the "Revealing Things" prototype interface for the Smithsonian Institution's online initiative *Smithsonian Without Walls*, http://www.si.edu/revealingthings/, and in the initiative of Australian Museums Online to create a searchable database of national museums' collections using the interface metaphor of a cabinet of wonder. For a discussion of this, see Sarah Kernderdine, "Inside the Meta-Center: A Wonder Cabinet," http://amol.org.au/about_amol/wonder_cabinet.asp. Both of these online spaces are discussed in detail in chapter 2.

9. Barbara M. Stafford, *Good Looking: Essays on the Virtue of Images* (Cambridge, Mass.: MIT Press, 1996), 31–34.

10. Deleuze's reading of Leibniz's work through the concept of the fold is multilayered and deserves to be taken on its own terms. My particular interest is in Deleuze's reading of the baroque perspective on matter and bodies, and so I have

chosen to elaborate on this aspect only. My reading of the Deleuzian fold is taken from the following sources: Gilles Deleuze, *Foucault*, tr. and ed. Steven Hand (Minneapolis: University of Minnesota Press, 1988); *The Fold*, tr. Tom Conley (Minneapolis: University of Minnesota Press, 1993); and "A Portrait of Foucault" and "On Leibniz" in *Negotiations: 1972–1990*, tr. Martin Joughin (New York: Columbia University Press, 1995), 102–18, 156–62.

11. Deleuze, *The Fold*, 6.

12. For example, René Descartes, whose work is often viewed as the antithesis of Leibniz's, was particularly interested in the organic folding of the structure of the brain. See *The Philosophical Writings of Descartes*, vol. 3, tr. J. Cottingham, R. Stroothoff and D. Murdoch (Cambridge: Cambridge University Press, 1985), 143–44. This is explored in more detail in chapter 2.

13. Deleuze, *The Fold*, 10, 131, 137.

14. For an account of the important studies carried out during the 1980s on the roles played by cell spatialization, differentiation and genetic pathways in embryonic morphogenesis, see Evelyn Fox Keller, *Making Sense of Life* (Cambridge, Mass.: Harvard University Press, 2002), 110–12, 185–90. For a critical account of the role of genes and chromosomes as structures, determinants and pathways in the organism, see Steven Rose, *Lifelines: Biology, Freedom and Determinism* (London: Allen Lane, 1997), 98–135.

15. See Gilles Deleuze, *Nietzsche and Philosophy*, tr. Hugh Tomlinson (New York: Columbia University Press, 1983), 2–4.

16. See, for example, the anthology *Resisting the Virtual Life: The Culture and Politics of Information*, edited by James Brook and Ian. A. Boal (San Francisco: City Lights, 1995). In particular, the article by Ian Boal places the information age as the social, political and economic heir of the processes of modernization that began with the scientific revolution. See "A Flow of Monsters: Luddism and Virtual Technologies," 3–15.

17. See Kevin Kelly, *Out of Control: The New Biology of Machines* (London: Fourth Estate, 1994), 36–47; Lee M. Silver, *Remaking Eden: Cloning and Beyond in a Brave New World* (London: Weidenfield and Nicolson, 1998), 227–39.

18. For a detailed account of these projects, see Kevin Warwick, *I, Cyborg* (London: Century, 2002).

19. De Landa, *A Thousand Years of Nonlinear History*, 274.

20. Gilles Deleuze and Felix Guattari, *A Thousand Plateaus*, tr. Brian Massumi (London: Athlone Press, 1988), 142–46; Manuel de Landa, "Meshworks, Hierarchies and Interfaces," in *The Virtual Dimension: Architecture, Representation and Crash Culture*, edited by Jonathon Beckman (New York: Princeton Architectural Press, 1998), 279–85; Keith Ansell Pearson, *Viroid Life* (New York: Routledge, 1997), 124–34.

21. Felix Guattari, *Chaosmosis: An Ethico-Aesthetic Paradigm* (Sydney: Power Publications, 1995), 36.

22. Gilles Deleuze and Felix Guattari, "In Flux," in Felix Guattari, *Chaosophy* (New York: Semiotexte, 1995), 98.

23. Ansell Pearson, *Viroid Life*, 145.

24. I am here leaning on the distinction made by the mathematician René Thom between the ability to predict and describe local models of form and the

inability of global morphologies to grow directly from this construction. Thom's work on complexity mathematics, particularly his notion of the catastrophe set as a model to explain sudden discontinuities and changes in local forms that lead to global morphogeneses, lies at the heart of Deleuze and Guattari's conception of rhizomatic connection and change. I believe this also informs Deleuze's notion of the gaps that inflect and produce folded space. See René Thom, *Structural Stability and Morphogenesis: An Outline of a General Theory of Models*, tr. D. H. Fowler (Reading, Mass.: W. A. Benjamin, Inc., 1975), 7–11.

25. See Marshall McLuhan, *Understanding Media* (New York: Signet, 1966), 63–67.

26. Manuel Castells, *The Rise of the Network Society*, vol.1 (Oxford: Blackwell, 2000), 442ff.

27. Elements of the project have been realized; a tissue-engineered nonfunctional sculpture of the ear has been grown and was exhibited in Slovenia and Australia in 2003–4. For a detailed description of this work, see Stelarc's website, http://www.stelarc.va.com.au/quarterear/index.html, and the Tissue Culture and Art Project's website, http://www.tca.uwa.edu.au/extra/extra_ear.html.

28. N. Katherine Hayles, *How We Became Posthuman: Virtual Bodies in Cybernetics, Literature and Informatics* (Chicago: University of Chicago Press, 1999), 19.

29. Deleuze and Guattari, *A Thousand Plateaus*, 167–91.

30. Lev Manovich, "Database as Symbolic Form," 1998, http://www.manovich.net/.

Chapter 1. Sampling and Folding (pp. 25–54)

1. John von Neumann, "The General and Logical Theory of Automata," in *Collected Works*, vol. 5, edited by A. H. Taub (Oxford: Pergamon Press, 1963), 293.

2. Gottfried W. F. Leibniz, "The Monadology," in *The Monadology and Other Philosophical Writings*, translated by Robert Latta (London: Oxford University Press, 1951), paragraph 71, 258.

3. For further information see the Australian Museum's Thylacine website, http://www.austmus.gov.au/thylacine/. The museum announced in 2005 that it was discontinuing this project.

4. Mike Archer quoted in the *Sun Herald*, Sydney, May 29, 2002: 5, and the *Courier Mail*, Brisbane, May 29, 2002: 3.

5. Haraway argues that the cyborg represents a confusion of machine/organism boundaries. Yet it is precisely a visual representation of this unassimilated confusion that has popularly become associated with the cyborg. This is particularly true of the liquid terminator or T-1000, Arnold Schwarzenegger's nemesis, played by Robert Patrick in *Terminator 2* (dir. James Cameron, Carolco Pictures, 1991). Many images of circuitry encroaching upon or into human flesh circulated in the 1990s through the cyberpunk genre in magazines such as the now-defunct *Mondo 2000*. See also Donna Haraway, *Symians, Cyborgs and Women: The Reinvention of Nature* (London: Free Association Books, 1991), 157–69.

6. A detailed account of the spectacle of the seventeenth-century automaton can be found in Zara Hanafi, *The Monster in the Machine* (Durham, N.C.: Duke University Press, 2000), 54ff.

7. Ian Wilmut, Keith Campbell and Colin Tudge, *The Second Creation* (London: Headline, 2000), 239–40.

8. In positing the difference between the "analogy principle" and "the digital principle," mathematician John von Neumann favored the use of the binary system as the basis for digital notation. Although von Neumann indicated that the binary notation was arbitrary rather than essential, the development of a system that proceeded through discrete on/off switching mechanisms has become synonymous with the structure of the digital. Von Neumann himself remarked that the digital principle could simply be understood as the representation of numbers through aggregates of digits, in effect enabling summed combinations to stand in for larger quantities. See "The General and Logical Theory of Automata," 294–95.

9. William J. T. Mitchell, *The Reconfigured Eye* (Cambridge, Mass.: MIT Press, 1994).

10. See Silver, *Remaking Eden*, 199–203. Silver constructs a future scenario in which the genetic profiles of embryos could appear as both biological data *and* images of a virtual child. This would allow parents to select their children on the basis of both potential disease development and aesthetics.

11. For documentation on this project, see Natalie Jeremijenko, *OneTree*, http://www.onetrees.org/.

12. Natalie Jeremijenko, "A Response to the *Paradise Now* Exhibition: How to Understand Genetic Information—and Why?" panel discussion in response to *Paradise Now: Picturing the Genetic Revolution*, an exhibition at Exit Art, New York, September 9–October 28, 2000.

13. For an accessible account of the development of differential and integral calculus, see Richard Mankeiwicz, *The Story of Mathematics* (London: Cassell, 2000), 100–131. There is some historical dispute as to whether Leibniz or Isaac Newton invented calculus. They were clearly working on similar problems.

14. Deleuze, *Foucault*, 131.

15. I am not suggesting that these are technically or contextually the same. Indeed, the appearance of similarity quickly disappears when one considers the extent to which the context of mediated images produces different meanings for them. There are also issues of resolution and compression that mark and transform the digital information of an image within different media. But this is the point: variation can be produced in repetition.

16. Deleuze is ambivalent about *digital* coding, seeing its wider application through information science as part of a society of control. But he also refers to the forces of silicon with which we create contemporary folds. Silicon, of course, is the matter of the digital, but its force lies precisely in its ability to conduct at enormous speeds and in infinitely small spaces such as microprocessors. These forces form the folding of digital code. The following two articles of Deleuze need to be read together in order to realize that this ambivalence lies at the heart of an analysis of contemporary control societies: "A Portrait of Foucault," and "Postscript on Control Societies," in Deleuze, *Negotiations: 1972–1990*, 102–18, 177–82.

17. This argument draws upon a rethinking of the notion of the genetic made by Daniel Smith in "'A Life of Pure Immanence': Deleuze's 'Critique and Clinique' Project," in Gilles Deleuze, *Essays Critical and Clinical*, translated by Daniel W. Smith and Michael A. Greco (Minneapolis: University of Minnesota Press, 1998), xxiv.

18. Deleuze and Guattari, *A Thousand Plateaus*, 146.

19. On this model, simulations of complex systems are generated or emerge from the interactions of local, relatively simple components, such as genetic algorithms, which specify at the level of code a number of event parameters. The local events these components set off interact, and from this interaction complex behaviors and systems can emerge. For an example of this mode of theorizing, see O. E. Holland and C. R. Melhuish, "Getting the Most from the Least: Lessons for the Nanoscale from Mininimal Mobile Agents," in *Artificial Life V: Proceedings of the Fifth International Workshop on the Synthesis and Simulation of Living Systems*, edited by Christopher Langton and Katsunori Shimohara (Cambridge, Mass.: MIT Press, 1997), 60–66.

20. Deleuze and Guattari, *A Thousand Plateaus*, 145.

21. Ibid., 142.

22. Deleuze, "Postscript on Control Societies," 180.

23. James Watson quoted in an interview and excerpted from the transcripts of "Winding Your Way through DNA," a symposium at the University of California, San Francisco, in 1992; http://www.accessexcellence.org/RC/CC/watson.html.

24. The term the "networked society" is coined by Castells in *The Rise of the Network Society*. Castells's analysis is a complex sociological approach to the understanding of late-twentieth-century urbanization and globalization. Although he accords information technologies a central role in these phenomena, his concept of the "networked society" is not confined to their effects. My use of the term here is intended only to indicate the shift from computationally managed information to distributed and mobile information. I am of course interested in the ways in which this shift enables and is enabled by changing social and political relations.

25. The list *.microsound* has a Web site that links to its archive and to various biographies and audio tracks by artists. See http://www.microsound.org/.

26. Kim Cascone, "The Aesthetics of Failure: 'Post-Digital' Tendencies in Contemporary Computer Music," *Computer Music Journal* 24:4 (winter 2000): 13.

27. Von Neumann, "The General and Logical Theory of Automata," 293.

28. The *Parasites* CD was released in 2001 on the Anechoic label. The reworking of the *Parasites* samples took place from December 2001 to February 2002, and the results can be downloaded from the Web site for the project, http://www.microsound.org/parasites/.

29. Deleuze, *The Fold*, 29–31.

30. Anthony van Leeuwenhoek, "The First Observations on 'Little Animals' (Protozoa and Bacteria) in Waters," in *Antony Van Leeuwenhoek and His "Little Animals,"* edited and translated by Charles Dobell (New York: John Bale, Sons and Danielson, Ltd., 1932), 109–66.

31. In the text accompanying Hooke's drawings, he quite clearly states that a true rendition of microscopic objects could only be captured by drafting from many perspectives and then handing over the rough sketches to a skilled artist who could draw a composite of the many views. Robert Hooke cited in Lisa Jardine, *Ingenious Pursuits* (London: Little, Brown and Company, 1999), 99–102.

32. Leibniz, "The Monadology," *The Monadology and Other Philosophical Writings*, paragraph 57, 248.

33. Ibid., paragraph 71–72, 258–59.

34. Gottfried W. F. Leibniz, "Considerations on the Principles of Life, and on Plastic Natures; By the Author of the System of Pre-Established Harmony," in *Leibniz: Selections*, edited by Philip P. Weiner (New York: Charles Scribner's Sons, 1951), 198.

35. Deleuze refers to the way he works on concepts as a form of artisanship; the fold is useful only insofar as it allows one to follow the movement of matter in a productive way. Deleuze, "On Leibniz," 156–71.

36. Deleuze and Guattari describe a plateau in the following way: "a continuous self-vibrating region of intensities whose development avoids any orientation towards a culmination point or external end." *A Thousand Plateaus*, 22.

37. I am using de Landa rather loosely here. In fact, he characterizes a virtuality as a trajectory within a system that displays a global regularity across the system's potential actualizations, which, in relation to its other virtualities, might lead to the production of one specific actualization of the system. Manuel de Landa, *Intensive Science and Virtual Philosophy* (London: Continuum, 2002), 17.

38. Jeffrey Barnouw, "The Beginnings of 'Aesthetics' and the Leibnizian Concept of Sensation," in *Eighteenth-Century Aesthetics and the Reconstruction of Art*, edited by Paul Mattick Jr. (Cambridge: Cambridge University Press, 1993), 52–95.

39. See Gottfried W. F. Leibniz, *Discourse on Metaphysics*, translated by G. W. Montgomery (La Salle, Ill.: Open Court Publishing, 1962), paragraph 33, 56–57.

40. Deleuze and Guattari, *A Thousand Plateaus*, 361–62.

41. Christine Buci-Glucksmann, *Baroque Reason: The Aesthetics of Modernity*, translated by Patrick Camiller (London: Sage, 1994), 134.

42. Ibid., 66–70.

43. For example, Barbara Maria Stafford takes this up by contrasting the development of physiognomic knowledge and illustrative techniques as part of enlightenment scientific knowledge with the more corporeally situated pathognomy. The latter dealt with the body as a surface of flowing affective signs and could therefore be more appropriately viewed as part of late baroque or rococo style: "Physiognomics was 'Neoclassical' and male in its linguistic and single-minded will to impose sequence and logic on experiential confusion. Pathognomics, however was 'Rococo' and female in its tolerance of optical indirection and refusal to subjugate baffling inconsistencies." Barbara M. Stafford, *Body Criticism: Imaging the Unseen in Enlightenment Art and Medicine* (Cambridge, Mass.: MIT Press, 1993), 127–28.

44. For Buci-Glucksmann this occurs in the baroque proper but also in the mid- to late nineteenth century, particularly in the writings of Baudelaire, and again in the response of the avant-garde to early-twentieth-century modernity.

45. Heinrich Wölfflin, *Renaissance and Baroque*, 1888, translated by Kathrin Simon (Ithaca, N.Y.: Cornell University Press, 1992), 16.

46. Ibid., 62.

47. Ibid., 40.

48. Leibniz, "On Substance as Active Force Rather Than Mere Extension," in *Leibniz: Selections*, 158 (my emphasis).

49. This point is made in a slightly different way in Robert Latta's introduction to Leibniz, *The Monadology and Other Philosophical Writings*, 28.

50. Gottfried W. F. Leibniz, *Theodicy: Essays on the Goodness of God, the Freedom of Man and the Origin of Evil* (London: Routledge and Kegan Paul, 1951).

51. Deleuze, *The Fold*, 81–82.

52. José A. Maravall, *The Culture of the Baroque: Analysis of a Historical Structure*, translated by Terry Cochran (Minneapolis: University of Minnesota Press, 1986), 53.

53. The most unsophisticated version of this argument is run via the reductionist postevolutionary arguments of Kevin Kelly. He argues, on the one hand, for the superiority of parallel processing, of which supercomputers and the neural "wetware" of the brain are capable, and, on the other, for the inability of consciousness, as a serial processor, to keep speed with this supercomputational power. The problem is that Kelly misses the entire argument about complexity that regards consciousness as emergent behavior resulting not simply from the firing of neurons along networks but from the kinaesthetic and proprioceptive interactions of bodies and the contextual meaning that these actions provide for these bodies. See Kelly, *Out of Control: The New Biology of Machines*, 437–41.

54. See, for example, Alluquere Rosanne Stone, "Will the Real Body Please Stand Up? Boundary Stories about Virtual Cultures," in *Cyberspace: First Steps*, edited by Michael Benedikt (Cambridge, Mass.: MIT Press, 1994), 81–118; Simon Penny, "Virtual Reality as the Completion of the Enlightenment Project," in *Culture on the Brink: Ideologies of Technology*, edited by Gretchen Bender and Timothy Druckrey (Seattle: Bay Press, 1994), 231–48.

55. *Dust Theories* is released on the Cycling '74 label.

56. For further information on MAX/MSP see the Web site http://www .cycling74.com/products/maxmsp.html.

57. Kim Cascone quoted in "An Interview with Kim Cascone," conducted by Ben Neville, 2004, http://www.cycling74.com/community/cascone.html.

58. See, for example, Mark Seltzer, "Wound Culture: Trauma in the Pathological Public Sphere," *October* 80 (1997): 3–27.

59. See the issue of *Architectural Design Profile* devoted to exploring these concepts: *Folding in Architecture*, edited by Greg Lynn, *Architectural Design Profile* 103 (1993).

60. This is perhaps best characterized theoretically in the work of Mark Wigley in *The Architecture of Deconstruction: Derrida's Haunt* (Cambridge, Mass.: MIT Press, 1993). It is concretized in the buildings and designs of Robert Venturi and the earlier work of Frank Gehry and Rem Koolhaus.

61. Brian Massumi, "Sensing the Virtual, Building the Insensible," in *Hypersurface Architecture*, special issue, *Architectural Design Profile* 133 (1998): 16.

62. For a simple discussion of the nineteenth-century development of topology as a new kind of geometry, see Mankeiwicz, *The Story of Mathematics*, 126–32.

63. Marcus Novak, "Liquid Architecture in Cyberspace," in *Cyberspace: First Steps*, 225–54.

64. Greg Lynn uses the term "blob" not only to describe the forms produced through the use of "meta-ball" three-dimensional modeling software but also to suggest how designers may start to give form to new ideas about complexity that have swept through not only design and architecture but also the physical and life sciences. See Greg Lynn, "Blobs," in *Folds, Bodies and Blobs: Collected Essays* (Brussels: La Lettre Volée, 1998), 157–68.

65. Brian Massumi, "Sensing the Virtual, Building the Insensible," 17–19; Steven Perrella, "Hypersurface Theory: Architecture><Culture," *Architectural Design Profile* (1998) 133: 6–7.

66. See Bernard Cache, *Earth Moves: The Furnishing of Territories*, edited by Michael Speaks, translated by Anne Boyman (Cambridge, Mass.: MIT Press, 1995), 88.

67. Ibid., 38–41.

Chapter 2. Natural History and Digital History (pp. 55–85)

1. John Evelyn, *The Diary of John Evelyn*, 1641, edited by Esmond S. de Beer, vol. 2 (Oxford: Clarendon Press, 1955), 53–54.

2. Bruno Latour, *We Have Never Been Modern*, translated by Catherine Porter (Cambridge, Mass.: Harvard University Press, 1993), 2.

3. One could cite a range of sources that encompass the notion of digital technologies within the adjective of the new. Two places to start might be Timothy Druckrey's introduction to *Culture on the Brink: Ideologies of Technology*, 7–11, and Newt Gingrich's many speeches on computers and information technologies. Gingrich's take is that the "information revolution" is only just starting and that we therefore are not in the middle of change but only surrounded by the newness of it all. See, for example, Newt Gingrich, "Thirty Years Forward, Thirty Years Back," *Opinion* (September 26, 2000), http://www.newt.org/index.php?src=news&prid=116&category=Opinion.

4. Pierre Lévy has argued that a foundational history for digital technology is a problematic enterprise. Although the 1947 date indicates the construction of the EDSAC (Electronic Delay Storage Automatic Computer) by Maurice Wilkes, the relation of this machine to prior models was one of appropriation, delay and capture. The history of technology does not rest upon a specific invention but rather upon how computational machines interface with commercial concerns and concurrent and prior scientific concepts and technical practices. See Pierre Lévy, "The Invention of the Computer," in *A History of Scientific Thought: Elements of a History of Science*, edited by Michel Serres (Oxford: Blackwell, 1995), 636–63.

5. Guattari, *Chaosmosis*, 45–49.

6. Some contemporary accounts elucidate the rise of natural history in Europe during the sixteenth century through recourse to a revival of the study of the ancients' texts on the natural world. See Joy Kenseth, "A World of Wonders in One Closet Shut," in *The Age of the Marvelous*, edited by Joy Kenseth (Hanover, N.H.: Hood Museum of Art, Dartmouth College, 1991), 84.

7. See, for example, Andreas Huyssen, *Twilight Memories: Marking Time in a Culture of Amnesia* (New York: Routledge, 1995), 23–35.

8. The prototype is still online at http://www.si.edu/revealingthings/.

9. Ibid.

10. For further information about Thinkmap software, see http://www.thinkmap.com.

11. From "Thinkmap FAQ," http://www.thinkmap.com/faq.jsp#12.

12. George Legrady, *Pockets Full of Memories*, Pompidou Center, Paris, April 18–September 3, 2001. An archive of this project can be found at *Pockets Full of Memories*, http://www.pocketsfullofmemories.net.

13. Legrady, *Pockets Full of Memories*, http://217.206.88.230/pfom_lang.html.

14. Paul Levinson, *The Soft Edge* (New York: Routledge, 1997), 1.

15. Although Norbert Wiener is generally deemed to be the cybernetician responsible for spreading this notion of information across a broad field of disciplines with the publication of his *Cybernetics or Control and Communication in the Animal and the Machine* in 1948, the idea that information could provide a generalized theory for all modes of communication had already permeated electrical engineering, neurological research, sociology and genetics. See *Cybernetics or Control and Communication in the Animal and the Machine* (Cambridge, Mass.: MIT Press, 1991). Lily Kay charts the progress of the extraction of information as pure signal from its embeddedness in materiality prior to and following the popularization of Wiener's ideas: Lily E. Kay, "Cybernetics, Information, Life: The Emergence of Scriptural Representations of Heredity," *Configurations* 5:1 (1997): 23–91.

16. Levinson, *The Soft Edge*, 2.

17. Ibid., 1.

18. Levinson's account of evolution should not be taken as typical of the enormous amount of considered work being done on evolution within current natural history and biology circles. Rather, I see him as representative of the crude kind of biologizing that takes place within digital debates. For an example of an interactionist account of evolution and the part of genetic code within it, see Rose, *Lifelines: Biology, Freedom, Determinism*, 113–21. In particular, Rose illustrates how the notion of "a gene for," in the sense of an instruction to perform, no longer fits even for determining physical characteristics. Rather, there are differences in the biochemical pathways that lead to the production of characteristics, notably the presence or absence of particular enzymes that catalyze chemical reactions. The gene that allows for the production of the presence or absence of an enzyme is significant, but no more so than the entire pathway that leads to the eventual synthesis producing the characteristic.

19. This is Friedrich Nietzsche's phrase. See *On the Genealogy of Morals*, translated by Walter Kaufman and R. J. Hollingdale (New York: Vintage Books, 1969); section 6, 20.

20. Michel Foucault, "Nietzsche, Genealogy, History," in *Language, Counter-Memory, Practice*, edited by Donald F. Bouchard (Ithaca, N.Y.: Cornell University Press, 1977), 148.

21. The hypothesis that the brain is like a computer, in that it stores and processes data using a centralized system of executing commands, forms the basis of much work done to simulate human thinking in digital machines. See Hans Moravec, *Mind Children* (Cambridge, Mass.: Harvard University Press, 1988). Although artificial life research begins in diametric opposition to this model with its theses of bottom-up rules leading to complex behaviors emerging from the interaction of relatively simple actions, it nevertheless partakes in a similar anthropomorphism. This occurs by conceiving of the activity of biological life from the point of view of a formalized system (complexity mathematics) rather than from the viewpoint of an activity immanent to biology itself. Alastair Welchman argues that this is precisely the gesture of a "royal" science—that of mapping complex dynamic systems onto those of a formalized logic—that once again leaves matter bereft of its own capabilities. See Alastair Welchman, "Machinic Thinking," in *Deleuze and Philosophy: The Difference Engineer*, edited by Keith Ansell Pearson (New York: Routledge, 1997), 225. There have, of course, also been attempts to understand the

biological as a complex dynamic system in its own terms: see Francesco J. Varela, *Principles of Biological Autonomy* (New York: North Holland Press, 1979), and Rose, *Lifelines: Biology, Freedom, Determinism*..

22. Hayles, *How We Became Posthuman*, 196.

23. Ibid., 197.

24. Conversely, in its pure mathematical sense, information cannot be conceived of outside of its relation to noise, that quantity of interference implicit in the transmission of signal through media. The possibility of separating out something that exists as completely pure data, then, is inconceivable within the very definition of information, that is, a signal *transmitted* from one point to another. See Claude Shannon and Warren Weaver, "The Mathematical Theory of Communication," *The Bell Laboratory Technical Journal* 27 (July 1948): 379–423.

25. Hayles, *How We Became Posthuman*, 207.

26. This clip was initially released with the single "All Is Full of Love" in 1999, but it has also been exhibited within an arts context as part of a video projection of three consecutive pieces by Chris Cunningham at the Plateau of Humanity, *49th Venice Biennale*, Venice, 2001.

27. Daniel W. Smith, "Deleuze's Theory of Sensation: Overcoming the Kantian Duality," in *Deleuze: A Critical Reader*, edited by Paul Patton (Oxford: Blackwell, 1996), 32.

28. See, for example, Peter Bentley, *Digital Biology: How Nature Is Transforming Our Technology* (London: Headline, 2001), 6–8.

29. I borrow this phrase from de Landa's *A Thousand Years of Nonlinear History*, 15. Like Deleuze's fold, it suggests the possibility of historical connections and developments between "states" or events in history that do not follow linear pathways but are nevertheless conceptually, locally and contingently dependent upon each other.

30. See Lorraine Daston and Katherine Park, *Wonders and the Order of Nature* (New York: Zone Books, 1998), 260–96; Kenseth, "A World of Wonders in One Closet Shut," 82–84; Kate Whitaker, "The Culture of Curiosity," in *Cultures of Natural History*, edited by Nicholas Jardine, James A. Secord and Emma C. Spary (Cambridge: Cambridge University Press, 1996), 75–84.

31. John Sutton, *Philosophy and Memory Traces: Descartes to Connectionism* (Cambridge: Cambridge University Press, 1998), 23–24.

32. Although I concur with Foucault's view that natural history as it developed in the eighteenth century only allowed for species interminglings in the available gaps between strictly classified types, I would suggest that other kinds of relations to "the natural" and to materiality developed alongside stratified scientific systems, and that these relations made inroads into classical systems. For a discussion of the classical *episteme*, see Michel Foucault, *The Order of Things: An Archaeology of the Human Sciences* (New York: Vintage Books, 1970), 150–57.

33. See Frances Yates, *The Art of Memory* (New York: Routledge and Kegan Paul, 1996), 358. On the other hand, Paolo Rossi has argued that early modern science sees a decisive break with the alchemical tradition of renaissance arts and sciences. See Paolo Rossi, "Universal Languages, Classifications and Nomenclatures in the Seventeenth Century," *History and Philosophy of the Life Sciences* 6:2 (1984): 119–31. Thus Descartes, Bacon and Leibniz, for example, cannot be seen as just part of the

ars memoria tradition in another guise; the emphasis on method is, for Rossi, an indication of a radical shift. I would suggest that both of these arguments be incorporated into a view of the seventeenth century that sees it as a shifting field of emerging and retreating sciences rather than as the end or beginning of an era.

34. The *Dissertatio de arte combinatoria* is not translated into English. It can be found in Gottfried W. Leibniz, *Gothofridi Guillemi Leibnitii opera omnia*, vol. 2, edited by Louis, Dutens, Genevae (Hildesheim: Georg Olms,1989). I have relied upon Yates's analysis of the mnemonic tables here.

35. Yates, *The Art of Memory*, 368–73.

36. Although tracing the influences of instrumentalist science in digital technology is an important and critical project, it seems to me that this critique does not go far enough. It tends to make the importance of this proclivity in science monumental, leaving the digital as a foreclosed arena. It is precipitous to make digital culture carry either the weight of history or the shock of the new when it operates as a set of forces manifesting their own materiality, affects and modes of cultural operation. My point would be that we should not bestow upon it a lineage from which it may be difficult to escape. Nevertheless, for an excellent exposition of the viewpoint that aspects of digital technology constitute the apex of the Enlightenment project, see Penny, "Virtual Reality as the Completion of the Enlightenment Project."

37. To list only a few: Robert Hubert, *A Catalogue of Many Natural Rarities*, London, 1664; Nathanial Crouch, *The Surprising Miracles of Nature and Art*, London, 1685; and Charles Hitch, *The British Apollo*, London, 1740.

38. René Descartes, *The Passions of the Soul*, 1649, can be found in *The Philosophical Writings of Descartes*, vol. 1; Thomas Hobbes, *The Leviathan*, 1660 (London: Penguin Books, 1968); Baruch de Spinoza, *The Ethics*, in 1677, translated by Andrew Boyle (London: Dent, 1989).

39. For an example of a neurological critique, see Antonio R. Damasio, *Descartes' Error: Emotion, Reason and the Human Brain* (New York: G. P. Putnum's Sons, 1994), 245–52; for a feminist example, see Elizabeth Grosz, *Volatile Bodies: Toward a Corporeal Feminism* (Sydney: Allen and Unwin, 1994), 6–10.

40. See, for example, Stone, "Virtual Systems," 618–20.

41. Descartes, *The Passions of the Soul*, 353–56.

42. Thomas Hobbes, for example, saw curiosity as a distinguishing passion because it resided in humans alone as "lust of the mind." Likewise, curiosity, for him, had a longer duration than passions that aroused carnal pleasures because it excited the mind to further knowledge. See *Leviathan*, 124.

43. For a general discussion of the role of passions in the seventeenth century, see Susan James, *Passion and Action: The Emotions in Seventeenth-Century Philosophy* (Oxford: Clarendon Press, 1997), 1–25.

44. Descartes, *The Passions of the Soul*, 339ff.

45. Ibid., 353.

46. Ibid.

47. Ibid., 356.

48. James, *Passion and Action*, 187.

49. Descartes, *The Passions of the Soul*, 349.

50. Timothy J. Reiss, "Denying the Body? Memory and the Dilemmas of History in Descartes," *Journal of the History of Ideas* 57: 4 (October 1996): 587–606.

51. Descartes, *The Philosophical Writings of Descartes*, vol. 3, 143–44.

52. Hans-Olaf Bostrom makes the point that much of baroque visual and leisure culture was designed to trick and astonish its viewers and participants; for example, the use of surprise water jets in palace parks that would saturate those who strayed close, or wire insects placed inside nut kernels. See Hans-Olaf Bostrom, "Philipp Hainhofer and Gustavus Adolphus's *Kunstschrank* in Uppsala," in *The Origins of Museums*, edited by Oliver Impey and Arthur MacGregor (Oxford: Clarendon Press, 1985), 97.

53. Descartes, *The Passions of the Soul*, 371–72.

54. See Whitaker, "The Culture of Curiosity," 75. This view contradicts historians who argue that the *Wunderkammer* provide the basis for the steady systematizing of the natural world that began with the advent of early modern science. See, Elizabeth Schulz, "Notes on the History of Collecting and Museums in the Light of Selected Literature of the 16th and 17th centuries," *Journal of the History of Collections* 2:2, (1990), 205–18. It seems to me that this argument draws a naïve distinction between order and chaos that is not sensitive to the singularity of discussions about reason during the seventeenth century. Rather than seeing the order of the *Wunderkammer* emerge through the actual practices of collecting, it retroactively imposes an eighteenth-century notion of the system onto these collections.

55. Olaus Worm, *Museum Wormianum Seu Historia Rerum Rarariorum*, Amsterdam, 1655, frontispiece; Ferrante Imperato, *Historia Naturalae*, Venice, 1672, frontispiece.

56. Barbara M. Stafford, *Artful Science: Enlightenment Entertainment and the Eclipse of Visual Education* (Cambridge, Mass.: MIT Press, 1994), 220–40.

57. James Petiver, *Opera Historiam Naturalem Spectantia or Gazophylacium*, vol. 1, London, 1764 (no pagination available).

58. Ibid., table xlv.

59. Crouch, *The Surprising Miracles of Nature and Art*, London, 186–87.

60. Stephen Greenblat argues that though wondrous visual aggregates were also caught up with issues of power and status, a certain kind of aesthetic response, a resonance between looking, feeling and knowing, took shape through the viewing of cabinets of wonder. See "Resonance and Wonder," in *Exhibiting Cultures: The Poetics and Politics of Museum Display*, edited by Ivan Karp and Steven D. Lavine (Washington, D.C.: Smithsonian Institution Press, 1991), 50–51.

61. This cabinet was established around 1665 in Leiden and progressively added to until the 1730s. Part of it was bought by Peter the Great and shipped to Leningrad in the 1720s. Very little remains of Ruysch's collection; some individual specimens can be found in the *Kunstkammer* in the Winter Palace in St. Petersberg, and some at the Museum of Anatomy at the University of Leiden. Of the dioramas for which he was notorious, only illustrations remain, in his *Thesaurus Anatomicus Primus* (Amsterdam: Joannem Wolters, 1701).

62. Descriptions of the Anatomy Theater can be found in the writings of seventeenth-century itinerant diarist John Evelyn. See *The Diary of John Evelyn*, 53–54.

63. Robert James, *A Medicinal Dictionary*, entry under "Anatomy," vol. 1 (London, 1740), no pagination available.

64. The method of discovering the network of capillaries, veins and arteries in an organism by injecting the vessels shortly after death with a wax-based substance

was known in medical circles for at least a century afterward as the "Ruyschian art." See F. J. Cole, "The History of Anatomical Injections," in *Studies in the History and Method of Science*, vol. 2, edited by Charles Singer (London: Oxford University Press, 1921), 303.

65. See particularly the frontispiece and table 1 from Ruysch, *Thesaurus Anatomicus Primus*, frontispiece and 64–65.

66. This description of Ruysch's specimen is quoted in A. M. Luyendijk-Elshoust, "Death Enlightened: A Study of Frederick Ruysch," *Jama* 212:1 (April 6, 1970), 124. It is not clear who is being quoted.

67. Helmet Lueckenhausen, "Wonder and Despite: Craft and Design in Museum History," in *Craft and Contemporary Theory*, edited by Sue Rowley (Sydney: Allen and Unwin, 1997), 36.

68. The counterpoint to my argument can be found in William J. T. Mitchell, "Antitectonics: The Poetics of Virtuality," in *The Virtual Dimension: Architecture, Representation and Crash Culture*, edited by John Beckman (New York: Princeton Architectural Press, 1998), 212.

69. Alphonse d'Alembert, "Preliminary Discourse," *The Encyclopedia: Selections*, translated and edited by Steven J. Gendzier (New York: Harper Torchbooks, 1967), 36.

70. See Denis Diderot, "Encyclopedia," in *The Encyclopedia: Selections*, 91–92.

71. Hugh M. Davidson, "The Problem of Scientific Order Versus Alphabetical Order in the *Encyclopédie*," *Studies in Eighteenth Century Culture* 2 (1972): 44.

72. See John Lough, *The Encyclopédie* (Geneva: Slatkine Reprints, 1989), 81–94. See also Oscar Kenshur, *Open Form and the Shape of Ideas: Literary Structures as Representations of Philosophical Concepts* (London: Associated University Press, 1986), 121–23.

73. The piece is a permanent installation but is also connected to a web interface that dynamically updates the information. See George Legrady, "*Making Visible the Invisible*: Seattle Public Library Project," http://www.mat.ucsb.edu/~g.legrady/glWeb/Projects/spl/spl/index.php.

74. Sarah Kernderdine, "Inside the Meta-Center: A Wonder Cabinet," http://amol.org.au/about_amol/part3.asp.

75. Ibid., http://amol.org.au/about_amol/part1.asp.

76. See, for example, Colin Beardon and Suzette Worden, "The Virtual Curator: Multimedia Technologies and the Roles of Museums," in *Contextual Multimedia and Interpretation*, edited by Edward Barrett and Marie Redmond (Cambridge, Mass.: MIT Press, 1995), 74. Kernderdine quotes from this text in her paper.

77. See K. Neimanis and E. Geber, "Come and Get It to Seek and You Shall Find: Transition from a Central Resource to Information Meta Center," in *Proceedings of Museums and the Web*, 1998; also see the Consortium for the Computer Interchange of Information, http://www.cimi.org/history.html. This site is no longer active and was "frozen" in 2003.

78. For a comprehensive account of the way in which search engines work and organize their results in online spaces, see Pankaj Kamthan, "Searching the Web," 1999, http://tech.irt.org/articles/js167/index.htm.

79. See http://128.111.69.4/~jevbratt/1_to_1/index_ng.html. My thanks go to Lisa Jevbratt for her help in navigating me through this project. Other artists have explicitly used the metaphor of the *Wunderkammer* in their digital projects,

including Shiralee Saul's "Wunderkammer: The Museum on the Digital Shoreline," http://www.labyrinth.net.au/~saul/wunder/wunder2.html; Shelly Jackson, *My Body—A Wunderkammer,* http://www.altx.com/thebody/; and my own site, "wundernet," http://wundernet.cofa.unsw.edu.au.

80. See http://128.111.69.4/~jevbratt/1_to_1/description.html.

81. Ibid.

Chapter 3. Virtuality (pp. 86–116)

1. Howard Rheingold, *Virtual Reality* (New York: Summit Books, 1991), 15–16.

2. Felix Guattari, *Chaosmosis,* 91.

3. For documentation of this installation, see Catherine Richards's website for *The Virtual Body* at http://www.catherinerichards.ca/artwork/virtual_statement.html.

4. Catherine Richards, "*Virtual Body* 1993—Artist Statement," http://www.catherinerichards.ca/artwork/virtual_statement.html.

5. Ibid.

6. This phrase is the title of the anthology edited by John Beckman, *The Virtual Dimension: Architecture, Representation and Crash Culture* (New York: Princeton Architectural Press, 1998).

7. The sense in which one becomes an operator not of the computer software that enables virtual systems to run but for the hardware of the machinery to locate itself becomes apparent when reading a text such as Howard Rheingold's *Virtual Reality.* Rheingold is constantly fitting himself into elaborate systems that constrain his perception and sensations to the physical and technical requirements of reproducing real-time, interactive, 3-D graphics, sound and haptic feedback.

8. Rheingold, *Virtual Reality,* 19–20; 45–46; 99–100; 378–91.

9. Stone, "Virtual Systems," 609.

10. There is a variety of papers and texts written as a response to VR technophilia. Among those I have relied upon to inform the arguments of this chapter are Simon Penny, "Virtual Reality as the Completion of the Enlightenment Project"; N. Katherine Hayles, "Embodied Virtuality: Or How to Put Bodies Back into the Picture," in *Immersed in Technology,* edited by Marianne A. Moser and David MacLeod (Cambridge, Mass.: MIT Press, 1996), 1–28; Frances Dyson, "'Space,' 'Being' and Other Fictions in the Domain of the Virtual," in *The Virtual Dimension.*

11. Pierre Lévy, *Becoming Virtual: Reality in the Digital Age,* translated by Robert Bononno (New York: Plenum Trade, 1998), 171.

12. Ibid., 25.

13. Janet H. Murray, *Hamlet on the Holodeck: The Future of Narrative in Cyberspace* (Cambridge, Mass.: MIT Press, 1997), 108.

14. See the comments made by Brian Massumi concerning the inadequacy of ways to conceive of affect in "The Autonomy of Affect," in *Deleuze: A Critical Reader,* 221.

15. Brian Massumi, "Line Parable for the Virtual (On the Superiority of the Analog)," in *The Virtual Dimension,* 307.

16. *Walking with Dinosaurs,* BBC Television series, directed and produced by Tim Haines and Jasper James, 1999.

17. This comment was made during a public online chat session Knox conducted at http:www.community.new.com.au/chat. The site is no longer accessible.

18. Peter Lunenfeld, *Snap to Grid: A User's Guide to Digital Arts, Media, and Cultures* (Cambridge, Mass.: MIT Press, 2000), 96–97.

19. Rheingold, *Virtual Reality,* 102.

20. For further information about time multiplexing in the design of VR systems, see Mark Bolas, Ian McDowall and Dan Corr, "New Research and Explorations into Multi-User Immersive Display Systems," *IEEE Computer Graphics and Applications* (January–February 2004): 18–21.

21. Lev Manovich, "The Aesthetics of Virtual Worlds: Report from Los Angeles," 1995, http://www.manovich.net/.

22. Gilles Deleuze, *Bergsonism,* translated by Hugh Tomlinson and Barbara Habberjam (New York: Zone Books, 1991), 51–72; and Gilles Deleuze, *Cinema 2: The Time-Image,* translated by Hugh Tomlinson and Robert Galeta (London: Athlone Press, 1989), 98–125.

23. Deleuze, *Cinema 2: The Time-Image,* 99.

24. Steven Rose, *The Making of Memory* (New York: Bantam Books, 1992), 90–91.

25. Ibid., 91.

26. Murray, *Hamlet on the Holodeck,* 79–80.

27. Martin Dodge and Rob Kitchin, *Mapping Cyberspace* (New York: Routledge, 2001), 65.

28. See Paul Edwards, *The Closed World: Computers and the Politics of Discourse in Cold War America* (Cambridge, Mass.: MIT Press, 1996), especially 113–45.

29. See the MapBlast! site, http://www.mapblast.com/ (iqttpn45soucv145fp4wjlbo)/Home.aspx.

30. See Dodge and Kitchin, *Mapping Cyberspace,* 56.

31. See Thomas F. McDonough, "Situationist Space," *October* 67 (winter 1994): 58–77, and "Henri LeFebvre on the Situationist International," interview conducted and translated by Kristen Ross, *October* 79, (winter 1997): 69–83.

32. See the documentation of this project at http://irational.org/borderxing/home.html.

33. See http://irational.org/cgi-bin/border/clients/list.pl.

34. See the short artists' statement by Alan Dunning and Paul Woodrow on "Dérive," http://www.ucalgary.ca/~einbrain/derive.htm.

35. Ibid.

36. Alan Dunning and Paul Woodrow, "*Einstein's Brain* Essay," http://www.ucalgary.ca/~einbrain/EBessay.htm.

37. Scott Fisher, "Virtual Environments: Personal Simulations and Telepresence," in *Virtual Reality: Theory, Practice and Promise,* edited by Sandra K. Hesel and Judith Paris Roth (London: Meckler, 1991), 105–6.

38. The first public display of the CAVE project was at the Ars Electronica Center in 1996, where the installation was opened to show artistic and scientific projects. It is an ongoing installation. For further information, see the Ars Electronica site, http://www.aec.at/en/index.asp. This contains a dynamic search engine through which information about the CAVE projects can be accessed.

39. Michael Heim, "The Design of Virtual Reality," in *Cyberspace, Cyberbodies,*

Cyberpunk: Cultures of Technological Embodiment, edited by Mike Featherstone and Roger Burrows (London: Sage Publications, 1996), 72.

40. Char Davies, "Changing Space: Virtuality as an Arena of Embodied Being," *The Virtual Dimension*, 144–54.

41. Martin Heidegger, "The Question Concerning Technology," in *The Question Concerning Technology and Other Essays* (New York: Harper Torchbooks, 1977), 22–24.

42. I am here referring to the Heideggerian notion of "way" as the mode in which *technē*, deriving from the ancient Greek notion of technique in contrast to the modern, instrumentalist conception of technology, is capable of providing Being with a "way" to properly reveal itself. See Martin Heidegger, "The Turning," in *The Question Concerning Technology and Other Essays*, 36–49.

43. Guattari, *Chaosmosis*, 45–49.

44. Ibid., 92.

45. Massumi, "Line Parable for the Virtual," 306.

46. Hayles, *How We Became Posthuman*, 27.

47. Ibid., 13–14. Emphasis in original.

48. See, for example, Gilles Deleuze and Felix Guattari, "Balance Sheet for Desiring Machines," in Guattari, *Chaosophy*, 143.

49. Brian Massumi, "The Autonomy of Affect," *Deleuze: A Critical Reader*, 224.

50. Davies's own writing on her VR projects tends to represent these as re-embodiments of the technology rather than as producing new affective experiences for bodies within the digital domain. See Char Davies, "Ephémère: Landscape, Earth, Body, and Time in Immersive Virtual Space," in *Reframing Consciousness*, edited by Roy Ascott (Exeter, England: Intellect Books, 1999), 196–201.

51. Dyson, "'Space,' 'Being' and other Fictions in the Domain of the Virtual," 28.

Chapter 4. Interfaciality (pp. 117–49)

1. Brenda Laurel, introduction to *The Art of Human-Computer Interface Design*, edited by Brenda Laurel (Reading, Mass.: Addison-Wesley Publishing, 1990), xii.

2. Donald A. Norman, "Why Interfaces Don't Work," in *The Art of Human-Computer Interface Design*, 216.

3. Laurel argues that the "performative" aspect of behavior plays a mediating role in our relations to digital culture in her *Computers as Theater* (Reading, Mass.: Addison-Wesley Publishing, 1993). She worked during the early 1980s in a research capacity at the Atari Systems research laboratory and then in the late 1980s in the Apple Human Interface Group. She also collaborated with Rachel Strickland to produce the VR piece *Placeholder*, in 1993.

4. *Very Nervous System* developed from an initial piece titled *Body Language* that was first exhibited at the Justina M. Barnicke Gallery at the University of Toronto. It was awarded the prestigious Prix Ars Electronica Award of Distinction for Interactive Art in 1991.

5. David Rokeby, "Installations: *Very Nervous System* (1986–90)," 2000, http://homepage.mac.com/davidrokeby/vns.html.

6. An Internet record of the *Memory Flesh 2.0* performances and some statements concerning the work can be found at Diane Ludin, "*Memory Flesh 2.0: A Micro Media Record*," 2004, http://www.turbulence.org/Works/ludin/index.htm.

7. A bend sensor is a peripheral sensor device made up of tiny patches of carbon that change their resistance values as the sensor bends from convex to concave shapes. It is now often used in conjunction with the software MAX/MSP to create a "patch" (a small subroutine program) that allows analog information to be converted to digital data and used to control and affect other digital signals.

8. Diane Ludin, private email correspondence with the author, 2005.

9. This group includes such individuals as Alan Kay, who during his time at Xerox Parc conceived of the laptop personal computer (his Dynabook) and was responsible for developing "user-friendly" design features such as icons and windows for Xerox Parc, Atari and Apple; Nicolas Negroponte, who founded the MIT media laboratory in 1985; Scott Fisher, who worked at NASA-Ames developing flight simulators and wearable VR suits and helmets; and Ted Nelson, who has held development and research positions at Xerox Parc and Autodesk and is responsible for coining the word and conceptual apparatus of "hypertext."

10. See, for example, Donald A. Norman, *The Psychology of Everyday Things* (New York: Basic Books, 1988).

11. See Jakob Nielsen, *Designing Web Useability: The Practice of Simplicity* (Indianapolis: New Riders, 2000).

12. I am relying here on the conception of faciality deployed by Deleuze and Guattari in *A Thousand Plateaus*, 168–79.

13. See, for example, Steven Johnson, *Interface Culture: How New Technology Transforms the Way We Create and Communicate* (San Francisco: Harperedge, 1997), 40–51.

14. Deleuze and Guattari, *A Thousand Plateaus*, 179.

15. This argument is made by Slavoj Zizek in "Of Cells and Selves," in *The Zizek Reader*, edited by Elizabeth Wright and Edmund Leo Wright (Oxford: Blackwell, 1999), 304–20.

16. See, for example, Alan Kay, "User Interface: A Personal View," in *The Art of Human-Computer Interface Design*, 191–207; and Norman, "Why Interfaces Don't Work," 209–19.

17. Ted Nelson gives this as an example of the uselessness of metaphorics in interface design. See Ted H. Nelson, "The Right Way to Think about Software Design" in *The Art of Human-Computer Interface Design*, 237.

18. T. D. Erickson, "Working with Interface Metaphors," in *The Art of Human-Computer Interface Design*, 73.

19. Nicholas Negroponte, *Being Digital* (Great Britain: Hodder and Stoughton, 1995), 149–52.

20. See the Cyberlife Web site, http://www.cyberlife.co.uk/. Since I originally researched this chapter, the *Cyberlife* Web site has been updated, and the text quoted here as accompanying the "welcome" page is no longer available. But the entire site now provides testimony to the notion of "weblife." Although now somewhat less serious than the site's original ethical concerns, the notion of life can be detected through the various spaces assigned to the creatures on the site. For example, there is a "community" updating users on the history, ecology and communal life of the "norn" community, and there is a medical center that allows access to support software for running the creatures. In this area, one may find help on the "genetic splicing machine," for example. The growth, so to speak,

of the software and Web site have spawned the virtual life of these algorithmic creatures.

21. Ibid.

22. See Patricia Magli, "The Face and the Soul," in *Fragments for a History of the Human Body*, edited by Michel Feher with Ramona Naddaff and Nadia Tazi, vol. 2 (New York: Zone Books, 1989), 86–127.

23. Nielsen, *Designing Web Useability*, 389.

24. See Nielsen's tips for useable homepage design on his Web site, http://www.useit.com/about/nographics.html.

25. See, for example, Jean-Jacques Rousseau, "A Discourse on the Moral Effects of the Arts and the Sciences," in *The Social Contract and Discourses*, 1750 (London: Dent, 1973), 3–29.

26. Alan Cooper, *About Face: The Essentials of User Interface Design* (Foster City, Cal.: IDG Books, 1995), 20.

27. Laurel, *Computers as Theater*, 143.

28. Ibid., 132.

29. Deleuze and Guattari, *A Thousand Plateaus*, 179–80.

30. Alan Dix, Janet E. Finlay, Gregory D. Abowd, Russell Beale, *Human-Computer Interaction*, New York: Prentice Hall, 1993, 9–48.

31. Ibid., 30.

32. Recent work on evolutionary hardware has suggested that the materiality of silicon in fact comprises a heterogeneous element in computational systems. Rather than being the impassive surface onto which circuitry is written, the physical qualities or intensities of the silicon itself produce, in relation to other components, the operational conditions of a system. This research, which uses genetic algorithms to "evolve" software circuits operating on silicon chips, points to the beginnings of a machinic view of the digital. It focuses on the dynamic, virtual relations of the technology rather than a top-down design process that enshrines a hierarchical and closed approach to system design. It also suggests that there is a material specificity to silicon that is not neatly translatable into a digital logic. When attempting to understand how certain circuits "evolved," researchers noted that signal processing on the chips actually occurred by analog means and that the circuits probably deployed the capacitive properties of the physical silicon itself. This research is being carried out at the Centre for Computational Neuroscience and Robotics at the University of Sussex, England. In particular, see a number of papers by Adrian Thompson that are available to download from http://www.cogs.susx.ac.uk/users/adrianth/ade.html. My thanks to Mitchell Whitelaw for bringing this material to my attention.

33. Laurel, *Computers as Theater*, 140.

34. Ibid., 114.

35. See, for example, Carol Parker, *The Joy of Cybersex* (Kew, Vic., Aus.: Mandarin, 1997). This is an experiential account of one woman's "addiction" to online chatting and virtual worlds. Her affective states run the gamut of pleasure, anxiety, loss and disappointment. Although perhaps Laurel's argument would distinguish between action and addiction in the virtual realm, her design principles do not seem to tally with embodied digital life as it is produced through our encounters with new media technologies.

36. Camille Griggers, *Becoming Woman* (Minneapolis: University of Minnesota Press, 1997), 29.

37. Ibid.

38. *Prosthetic Head* was made in 2003 and was shown at *New Territories*, International Festival of Live Arts, Glasgow, February 3–March 15, 2003, and *Transfigure*, Australian Center for the Moving Image, Melbourne, December 8, 2003–May 9, 2004, among others. Stelarc's work is some of the most widely documented and theorized digital/cybernetic art. Many of his performances are documented at his Web site, http://www.stelarc.va.com.au. For secondary commentary see, for example, Brian Massumi, "Stelarc: The Evolutionary Alchemy of Reason," in *The Virtual Dimension*, 304–21.

39. Stelarc, *Prosthetic Head*, 2003, http://www.stelarc.va.com.au/prosthetichead/index.html.

40. For an analysis of faciality in painting see Gilles Deleuze, *Francis Bacon: The Logic of Sensation*, translated by Daniel W. Smith (London: Continuum, 2003), 20–21, 28; and for cinema, see Gilles Deleuze, *Cinema 1: The Movement Image*, translated by Hugh Tomlinson and Barbara Habberjam (Minneapolis: University of Minnesota Press, 1997), 87–88.

41. Hayles, *How We Became Posthuman*, 247.

42. Running for fifteen years and held annually in Linz, Ars Electronica is probably the largest forum for the convergence and staging of contemporary electronic art. A full history of the festival and online access to its documentation can be found at http://www.aec.at/en/index.asp.

43. Gerfried Stocker, "*FleshFactor*," http://www.aec.at/en/archiv_files/19971/E1997_014.pdf. This text is available as a pdf file.

44. Stelarc, "Parasite Visions: Alternate, Intimate and Involuntary Experiences," http://www.aec.at/en/archiv_files/19971/E1997_148.pdf. This text is available as a pdf file.

45. Stelarc, "From Psycho to Cyber Strategies: Prosthetics, Robotics and Remote Existence," *Canadian Theatre Review* 86 (Spring 1996): 19.

46. Ibid.

47. Ibid.

48. Peter Lunenfeld makes a similar comment about Stelarc's online performances in *Snap to Grid*, 22.

49. See Huge Harry, "On the Mechanism of Human Facial Expression as a Medium for Interactive Art," http://www.aec.at/en/archiv_files/19971/E1997_110.pdf. This text is available as a pdf file.

50. Ibid.

51. Ibid.

52. Ibid.

53. See Deleuze, *Cinema 1: The Movement Image*, 88.

54. Deleuze and Guattari, *A Thousand Plateaus*, 170; Deleuze, *Cinema 1: The Movement Image*, 87–101.

55. Felix Guattari, "On Machines," *Journal of Philosophy and the Visual Arts* 6 (1995): 8–12.

56. The neurologist Antonio Damasio has worked to develop physical correlates for emotional states that he claims map their location in the brain's

substrate. See *The Feeling of What Happens* (London: Harcourt Brace & Company, 1999), 58.

57. Massumi, "The Autonomy of Affect," 222–23.

58. Zizek, "Of Cells and Selves," 303.

59. Damasio, *The Feeling of What Happens*, 318.

60. Ibid., 283.

61. The phrase is borrowed from Brian Massumi in "Too-Blue: Color-Patch for an Expanded Empiricism," *Cultural Studies* 14:2 (2000): 185.

62. Guattari, "On Machines," 11.

63. Ibid.

64. See the *Einstein's Brain Project* Web site, http://www.ucalgary.ca/~einbrain/.

65. Both of these works were exhibited in the group show *Probe: Explorations into Australian Computational Space*, shown at the Australian Embassy in Beijing, October 15–24, 1999. *RAPT II* was also exhibited at the Visual Arts Gallery at the University of Alabama, January 7–February 4, 2005.

66. For further information about this work see Justine Cooper's Web site, http://justinecooper.com/scyn_synopsis.html.

67. For a discussion of the primacy of proprioceptive habit in embodiment, see Brian Massumi, "Strange Horizon: Buildings, Biograms and Body Topologic," in *Parables for the Virtual: Movement, Affect and Sensation* (Durham, N.C.: Duke University Press, 2002), 177–207; for a discussion of the role of the sensorimotor system in producing proprioceptive embodied action, see Francesco Varela, "The Re-enchantment of the Concrete," in *Incorporations*, 320–38.

68. For full details of this installation, see Raphael Lorenzo-Hemmer, "*Re: Positioning Fear:* Relational Architecture 3," http://rhizome.org/artbase/2398/fear/.

69. Ibid.

70. Massumi, "Strange Horizon," 192. Emphasis in original.

Chapter 5. Digitality (pp. 150–77)

1. Mathew Fuller, "Breach the Pieces," http://www.tate.org.uk/webart/mat2.htm.

2. Olu Oguibe, "An Interview with Olu Oguibe," Massimiliano Gioni, interviewer, *Third Text* 47 (summer 1999): 55.

3. *010101*, curated by Benjamin Weil and held in 2001 at the San Francisco Museum of Modern Art, was the first major exhibition of Internet art to be held at a mainstream contemporary gallery. See an overview of the exhibition at http://www.sfmoma.org/exhibitions/exhib_detail.asp?id=2. *Net_Condition* was organized as a collaborative project by the ICC in Tokyo and ZKM in Karlsruhe in 1999 and was an early showcase for the work of artists working between gallery and online spaces. *Net_Condition* dealt specifically with online art, a then-emerging genre within the digital. The projects exhibited are available online at http://www.zkm.de/netCondition.root/netcondition/start/language/default. *Bitstreams* was a survey show of artists working with digital technologies held at the Whitney Museum of Art, March 22–June 10, 2001. See the *Bitstreams* Web site at http://www.whitney.org/bitstreams.

4. Mitchell Whitelaw, "The End of New Media Art?" *Working the Screen 2000*, special issue, *Realtime* 38 (August–September 2000): 7. The same point was made

at the end of the 1980s, when the nomenclature of "computer art" became drab. See Richard Wright, "The Image in Art and 'Computer Art,'" *Leonardo, Computer Art in Context*, supplementary issue (1989): 49–53.

5. Sean Cubitt, *Digital Aesthetics* (London: Sage, 1998): ix–x.

6. See Steven Shaviro, *Connected, or What It Means to Live in the Network Society* (Minneapolis: University of Minnesota Press, 2003), especially 28–31.

7. Olu Oguibe, "Connectivity and the Fate of the Unconnected," *Social Identities* 5:3 (1999): 240–41.

8. Cubitt, *Digital Aesthetics*, 14.

9. See Gilles Deleuze, "Ethology: Spinoza and Us," in *Incorporations*, edited by Jonathon Crary and Sandford Kwinter (New York: Zone Books, 1992), 625–33.

10. See, for example, Frank Popper, *The Art of the Electronic Age* (London: Thames and Hudson, 1993), 86–87.

11. Andrew Murphie, "Electronicas: Differential Media and Proliferating, Transient Worlds," in *Long Paper Proceedings from the Fifth International Digital Arts and Culture Conference* (Melbourne: RMIT Publications, 2003), 152.

12. R. L. Rutsky has made a sustained argument for the fetishism that surrounds the notion of "state of the art" in relation to technology in the way that artists, designers, theorists, entrepreneurs, publicists and advertisers all deploy this term. See *High Techne: Art and Technology from the Machine Aesthetic to the Posthuman* (Minneapolis: University of Minnesota Press, 1999).

13. See, for example, Roy Ascott, "On Networking," *Leonardo* 21:3 (1988): 231–32.

14. Clement Greenberg, "Modernist Painting," *Art and Literature* 4 (spring 1965): 193–201.

15. A strong argument for the relation between current communications art and the Art and Technology Movement is made by Marga Bijvoet in "How Intimate Can Art and Technology Really Be? A Survey of the Art and Technology Movement of the Sixties," in *Culture, Technology and Creativity in the Late Twentieth Century*, edited by Philip Hayward (London: J. Libbey, 1994), 15–37.

16. See Popper, *The Art of the Electronic Age*, and Cynthia Goodman, *Digital Visions: Computers and Art* (New York: Harry N. Abrams, Inc., 1987).

17. Lunenfeld, *Snap to Grid*, 13–26.

18. See Harwood, *Uncomfortable Proximity* (2000), http://www.tate.org.uk/netart/mongrel/home/default.htm.

19. For further examples of Mongrel's use of hacking to subvert the design and assumption of neutrality in online design, see their text for the project *Natural Selection*, http://www.mongrel.org.uk/. This project "hijacked" the source code of an online search engine and used it to display results for searches that made the user aware of an entire network of black affirmative and anti-racist Web sites.

20. See Fuller, "Breach the Pieces."

21. Ibid. It is this breaking up of space, achieved by producing relations between the virtual and the concrete, the digital and the actual, that occurs so often in digital art, making it resonate with the early spaces of museum collection that I discussed in my second chapter, on the *Wunderkammer* and the seventeenth-century passions of wonder and curiosity.

22. Harwood, *Uncomfortable Proximity*.

23. Fuller, "Breach the Pieces."

24. For Deleuze and Guattari, composition *is* the work done by art: "Composition, composition is the sole definition of art. Composition is aesthetic, and what is not composed is not a work of art." *What Is Philosophy?* 191.

25. See Deleuze, *Francis Bacon*, 112.

26. My discussion of this notion of proximity was spurred on by conversations held with Mitchell Whitelaw. I am grateful for his sense of provocation and for his intellectual and conversational generosity.

27. This is Deleuze and Guattari's description of the grouping of sensations into affective moments that occurs in aesthetic experience. See Deleuze and Guattari, *What Is Philosophy?* 173–74.

28. N. Katherine Hayles, "Virtual Bodies and Flickering Signifiers," in *Electronic Culture: Technology and Visual Representation*, edited by Timothy Druckrey (New York: Aperture Foundation, 1996), 262–63.

29. Linda Dement, *In My Gash*, CD-ROM, produced in association with the Australian Film Commission, 1999.

30. Keith Piper, "Tagging the Other," in *Iterations: The New Image*, edited by Timothy Druckrey (Cambridge, Mass.: International Centre of Photography and MIT Press, 1993), 120–21.

31. Sherry Turkle, *Life on the Screen: Identity in the Age of the Internet* (London: Phoenix, 1997), 262.

32. Sean Cubitt, "Orbus Tertius," *Third Text* 47 (summer 1999): 3.

33. Maria Fernandez, "Postcolonial Media Theory," *Third Text* 47 (summer 1999): 14.

34. Ibid.

35. Ibid., 15.

36. This statement was given to me by Geert Lovink. A similar one can be found at the *Emoção Art.ficial Exhibition* Web site, http://www.itaucultural.org.br/index.cfm?cd_pagina=1415.

37. Ibid.

38. Ravi Sundaram, "Recycling Modernity: Pirate Electronic Cultures in India," *Third Text* 47 (summer, 1999): 59–67.

39. Arjun Appardurai, *Modernity at Large* (Minneapolis: University of Minnesota Press, 1997), 4.

40. Geert Lovink, *Dark Fiber* (Cambridge, Mass.: MIT Press, 2002), 142–59.

41. See the Swatch Web site for a description of and promotional material surrounding "Internet time," http://www.swatch.com/fs_index.php?haupt=collections&unter=.

42. Ibid.

43. Srikan Reddy, managing director of Sonata Software, a Bangelore start-up company, interviewed for "Nerds 2.0.1: A Brief History of the Internet," in *Wiring the World*, parts 5 and 6, directed by Stephen Segaller, 1998.

44. Sundaram, "Recycling Modernity," 59–60.

45. Ibid., 63.

46. See the "Opus" site at http://www.opuscommons.net.

47. See Lawrence Lessig, 'May the Source Be with You," 2001, http://www.wired.com/wired/archive/9.12/lessig.html.

48. Sundaram, "Recycling Modernity," 62.

49. The *sentiment-express* site is unfortunately no longer running. There is an

installation shot of the exhibition at the "Waste" site, where it was also shown as part of the exhibition *Experimenta* in 2001 at the Victorian Center for the Arts in Melbourne, http://www.experimenta.org/trash/archive/gallery/ts0008i.html.

50. Manovich, *The Language of New Media*, 20–46.

51. This quote is taken from an interview with Shilpa Gupta for part of the Tate Modern's *Century City: Art and Culture in the Modern Metropolis* exhibition in 2001. The actual site is no longer accessible at http://www.bbc.co.uk/arts/tate/century_city/bombay/shilpa.shtml.

52. "Blogging" is a contraction of "Web logging," the individual and/or collective activity of publishing straight to a publicly accessible Web site. Blogging usually takes the form of a set of daily entries in which participants share observations of life lived online and offline, direct each other to other Web sites of interest and sometimes share files. For more information about blogging, see the site by IT firm *Caslon Analytics*, http://www.caslon.com.au/weblogprofile.htm. "Mashed-up pop," sometimes known as "booty pop," involves the mixing of incongruous commercial pop, dance, hip-hop and r'n'b songs together using freely available and Internet-distributed music software. The resultant mixes are then often distributed through peer-to-peer software or attached to blogs and recirculated for other users to play and remix. See, for example, http://www.boombox.net/.

53. Deleuze, *Cinema 2: The Time-Image*, 267.

54. Ibid., 265.

55. For an analysis of various trends in Flash aesthetics, see Curt Cloninger, *Fresh Styles for Web Designers: Eye Candy from the Underground* (Indianapolis: New Riders, 2001). For an analysis of the relation between Flash aesthetics and other forms of digital and media culture, see my "Compression and the Intensification of Information in Flash Animation," in *Long Paper Proceedings of the 5th International Conference on Digital Arts and Culture* (Melbourne: RMIT Publications, 2003), 142–50.

56. See the Yugop site, http://surface.yugop.com.

57. Brian Massumi has noted this important difference between computational and modernist space, despite the former's historical and aesthetic debt to the latter: "The computer becomes a tool of indeterminacy. Abstract spaces are no longer neutral screens for imaging what has already been seen in the mind's eye. They must be actively designed to integrate a measure of indeterminacy. As a consequence, the space of abstraction itself becomes active, no longer merely prefiguring." Brian Massumi, "Sensing the Virtual, Building the Insensible," *Architectural Digest Profile* 68:5/6 (May–June 1998): 16–25.

58. See Simon Biggs, *The Great Wall of China*, http://www.greatwall.org.uk.

59. See Biggs's introduction to his piece, http://hosted.simonbiggs.easynet.co.uk/wall/greatwall.htm.

60. Ibid.

61. For Everquest see http://eqlive.station.sony.com/. For CounterStrike see http://www.counter-strike.net/.

Postscript (pp. 178–86)

1. *Loops* was initially created for the MIT Media Lab's exhibition *ID/entity: Portraits in the Twenty-first Century*, which was shown at The Kitchen in New York City in 2001.

2. The interview appears as part of the DVD documentary of the show *ID/entity:*

Portraits in the Twenty-first Century, produced by Kathy Brew and Roberto Guerra in 2003.

3. Lev Manovich uses this phrase to talk about the way in which media technologies ask us to carry out certain kinds of visual work. See Lev Manovich, "The Labor of Perception," http://www.manovich.net/TEXT/labor.html.

4. The TGarden environment was developed at the Topological Media Laboratory, part of the Graphics, Visualization and Useability Center at the Georgia Institute of Technology in Atlanta, under the directorship of Sha Xin Wei. For information about the project, see http://www.gvu.gatech.edu/people/sha.xinwei/topologicalmedia/tgarden/index.html. The overall TGarden project, however, is collaborative and operates between the institute and two other artist organizations, FoAM in Brussels and sponge in San Francisco. For further information about FoAM, see http://fo.am/tgarden/, and for sponge, see http://sponge.org.

5. "TGarden," text appearing on the FoAM Web site, http://fo.am/tgarden/.

6. The work *Traces* was developed between 1998 and 1999 by Simon Penny in collaboration with Jeffrey Smith and Andre Bernhardt. It was first shown in a CAVE environment at Ars Electronica, Linz, Austria, September 4–9, 1999. For a detailed technical explanation of the work, see Simon Penny, Jeffrey Smith and Andre Bernhardt, "*Traces:* Wireless Full Body Tracking in the CAVE," http://www.ace.uci.edu/penny/texts/traces/. Two works by Metraform, *Symbiosis* and *Exstasis,* involve group interactions in semi-immersive virtual environments and were produced at the Royal Institute of Technology in Melbourne. *Symbiosis* was exhibited as part of the *Next Wave* Festival in Melbourne, May 17–26, 2002. *Exstasis* was shown as part of the *Fifth International Digital Arts and Culture* conference, May 12–19, 2003, in Melbourne.

7. I draw upon the definition of bioart put forward by artists Oron Catts and Ionat Zurr in "Growing Semi-Living Sculptures: The Tissue Culture and Art Project," *Leonardo* 35:4 (2002): 365–70.

8. For an introduction to contemporary collaboration between the visual arts and science, see Sarah Ede, ed., *Strange and Charmed: Science and the Contemporary Visual Arts* (London: The Calouste Gulbenkian Foundation, 2000).

9. For example, see Jeremy Rifkin, *The Biotech Century* (London: Phoenix, 1998), 216–26.

10. Heath Bunting's *Superweed* kit is available to buy online through http://www.irational.org/cta/superweed/ and has been exhibited in a number of exhibitions, including *Art of the Biotech Age,* Adelaide Festival of the Arts, Experimental Art Foundation, Adelaide, Australia, February 27 –March 14, 2004. The Tissue Culture and Art Project artists have been working with tissue culture and other forms of bioart, including organic robotics, since 1998. *The Tissue Culture and Art(ificial) Womb 2000* featured the first living-tissue engineered structures to be presented as art in a gallery context. This was shown at the Ars Electronica Festival, September 2–7, 2000. Adam Zaretsky has staged a number of installations and experiments with humans and other species in which he mediates their relations through the techniques and discourses of the life sciences. One of these, the *Workhorse Zoo* installation, was enacted by Julia Reodica and Adam Zaretsky as a part of *Unmediated Vision,* an exhibition curated by Stacy Switzer at the Salina Art Center, Salina, Kansas, January 26–March 24, 2002.

BIBLIOGRAPHY

Primary Sources

Chambers, Ephraim. "The Preface." *Cyclopaedia*, vol. 1. Scotland, 1728.

Crouch, Nathanial. *The Surprising Miracles of Nature and Art*. London, 1685.

Evelyn, John. *The Diary of John Evelyn*. 1641. Ed. Esmond S. de Beer. Vol. 2. Oxford: Clarendon Press, 1955.

Grew, Nemiah. *Musaeum Regalis Societatis; or, A Catalogue & Description of the Natural and Artificial Rarities Belonging to the Royal Society and Preserved at Gresham College*. London: W. Rawlins, 1681.

Hitch, Charles. *The British Apollo*. London, 1740.

Hubert, Robert. *A Catalogue of Many Natural Rarities*. London, 1664.

Imperato, Ferrante. *Historia Naturalae*. Venice, 1672.

James, Robert. *A Medicinal Dictionary*. Vol. 1. London, 1740.

Lemery, J. *New Curiosities in Art and Nature; Or, A Collection of the Most Valuable Secrets in All Arts and Sciences*. London, 1711.

Petiver, James. *Opera, Historiam Naturalem Spectantia or Gazophylacium*. Vol. 1. London, 1764.

———. *Musei Petiveriani Centuria Prima, Raroria Naturae*. London, 1764.

Ray, John. *The Correspondence of John Ray*. Ed. Edwin Lankester. London, 1848.

Ruysch, Frederick. *Thesaurus Anatomicus Primus*. Amsterdam: Joannem Wolters, 1701.

———. *Opera Omnia Anatomico-Medico-Chirurgica*. Amsterdam, 1737–43.

Sprat, Thomas. *History of the Royal Society*. London, 1667.

Tradescant, John. *Musaeum Tradescantinum; or, A Collection of Rarities Preserved at South Lambeth neer London*. London, 1656.

Wilkins, John. *Essay Towards a Real Character, and a Philosophical Language*. London, 1668.

Worm, Olaus. *Museum Wormianum Seu Historia Rerum Rarariorum*. Amsterdam, 1655.

Secondary Sources

d'Alembert, Jean Le Rond. "Preliminary Discourse." 1751. *Denis Diderot's The Encyclopedia: Selections*, trans. and ed. Steven J. Gendzier. New York: Harper Torchbooks, 1967. 1–41.

Ansell Pearson, Keith. *Viroid Life*. New York: Routledge, 1997.

———. *Germinal Life*. New York: Routledge, 1999.

Antin, David. "Video: The Distinctive Features of the Medium." In *Videoculture: A Critical Investigation*, ed. John G. Hanhardt. New York: Visual Studies Workshop Press, 1986. 141–66.

Appardurai, Arjun. *Modernity at Large*. Minneapolis: University of Minnesota Press, 1997.

Arnold, Ken R. "Cabinets for the Curious: Practicing Science in Early Modern English Museums." Dissertation, Princeton University, 1992.

Aronwitz, Stanley, Barbara Martinsons, and Michael Menser, eds. *Technoscience and Cyberculture*. New York: Routledge, 1996.

Ascott, Roy. "On Networking." *Leonardo* 21:3 (1988): 231–32.

Bailey, Cameron. "Virtual Skin: Articulating Race in Cyberspace." In *Immersed in Technology*, ed. Marianne A. Moser and David MacLeod. Cambridge, Mass.: MIT Press, 1996. 29–50.

Barnouw, Jeffrey. "The Beginnings of 'Aesthetics' and the Leibnizian Concept of Sensation." In *Eighteenth-Century Aesthetics and the Reconstruction of Art*, ed. Paul Mattick Jr. Cambridge: Cambridge University Press, 1993. 52–95.

Barrett, Edward, and Marie Redmond, eds. *Contextual Multimedia and Interpretation*. Cambridge, Mass.: MIT Press, 1995.

Baudrillard, Jean. "Xerox and Infinity." In *The Transparency of Evil*. London: Verso, 1993. 51–59.

———. "The System of Collecting." In *The Cultures of Collecting*, ed. John Elsner and Roger Cardinal. Melbourne: Melbourne University Press, 1994. 7–24.

Bennett, Jill. "The Aesthetics of Sense-Memory: Theorizing Trauma through the Visual Arts." In *Trauma and Memory: Cross-Cultural Perspectives*, ed. Franz Kaltenbeck and Peter Weibel. Graz: Passagen Verlag, 2000. 81–95.

Bentley, Peter. *Digital Biology: How Nature Is Transforming Our Technology*. London: Headline, 2001.

Biggs, Simon. "Introduction." *The Great Wall of China*, 1996. http://www .greatwall.org.uk.

Bijvoet, Marga. "How Intimate Can Art and Technology Really Be? A Survey of the Art and Technology Movement of the Sixties." In *Culture, Technology and Creativity in the Late Twentieth Century*, ed. Philip Hayward. London: J. Libbey, 1994. 15–37.

Bolz, N. "Navigation in Docuverse." *Mediamatic* 6:4 (summer 1992): 273–75.

Bolter, Jay David, and Richard Grusin. *Remediation: Understanding New Media*. Cambridge, Mass.: MIT Press, 2000.

Bostrom, Hans-Olaf. "Philipp Hainhofer and Gustavus Adolphus's Kunstschrank in Uppsala." In *The Origins of Museums: The Cabinet of Curiosities in Sixteenth- and Seventeenth-Century Europe*, ed. Oliver Impey and Arthur MacGregor. Oxford: Clarendon Press, 1985. 90–101.

Boundas, Constantin V. "Deleuze-Bergson: An Ontology of the Virtual." In *Deleuze: A Critical Reader*, ed. Paul Patton. London: Blackwell, 1996. 81–106.

Brook, James, and Ian A. Boal, eds. *Resisting the Virtual Life*. San Francisco: City Light Books, 1995.

Bukatman, Scott. *Terminal Identity*. Durham, N.C.: Duke University Press, 1993.

Bush, Vannevar. "As We May Think." http://www.theatlantic.com/unbound/ flashbks/computer/bushf.htm.

Buci-Glucksmann, Christine. *Baroque Reason: The Aesthetics of Modernity*. Tr. Patrick Camiller. London: Sage Publications, 1994.

Cache, Bernard. *Earth Moves: The Furnishing of Territories*. Ed. Michael Speaks, trans. Anne Boyman. Cambridge, Mass.: MIT Press, 1995.

Canguilhem, George. "Machine and Organism." In *Incorporations*, ed. Jonathan Crarey and Sanford Kwinter. New York: Zone Books, 1992. 44–69.

Cascone, Kim. "The Aesthetics of Failure: "Post-Digital" Tendencies in Contemporary Computer Music." *Computer Music Journal* 24:4 (winter 2000): 12–18.

Caslon Analytics. "Caslon Analytics Profile: Web Logs and Blogging." http://www .caslon.com.au/weblogprofile.htm.

Castells, Manuel. *The Rise of the Network Society*. Oxford: Blackwell Publishers, 2000.

Catts, Oron, and Ionat Zur. "Growing Semi-Living Sculptures: The Tissue Culture and Art Project." *Leonardo* 35:4 (2002): 365–70.

Certeau, Michel de. *The Writing of History*. New York: Columbia University Press, 1988.

Cloninger, Curt. *Fresh Styles for Web Designers: Eye Candy from the Underground.* Indianapolis: New Riders, 2001.

Cole, F. J. "The History of Anatomical Injections." In *Studies in the History and Method of Science*, vol. 2 ed. Charles Singer. London: Oxford University Press, 1921. 295–343.

Cook, R., ed. *Computer Graphics Proceedings*. SIGGRAPH '95 Conference Proceedings, August 6–11, 1995. New York: ACM SIGGRAPH Publication, 1995.

Cooper, Alan. *About Face: The Essentials of User Interface Design*. Foster City, Calif.: IDG Books, 1995.

Cotton, Bob, and Oliver R. Cotton. *Understanding Hypermedia*. London: Phaidon Press, 1993.

Cowling, Mary. *The Artist as Anthropologist: The Representation of Type and Character in Victorian Art*. Cambridge: Cambridge University Press, 1989.

Cubitt, Sean. "Orbus Tertius." *Third Text* 47 (summer 1999): 3–10.

———. *Digital Aesthetics*. London: Sage Publications, 1998.

Damasio, Antonio R. *The Feeling of What Happens*. London: Harcourt Brace & Company, 1999.

———. *Descartes' Error: Emotion, Reason and the Human Brain*. New York: G. P. Putnam's Sons, 1994.

Danton, Robert. *The Business of Enlightenment: A Publishing History of the Encyclopedie, 1755–1800*. Cambridge, Mass.: Belknap Press of Harvard University Press, 1979.

Daston, Lorraine, and Katherine Park. *Wonders and the Order of Nature*. New York: Zone Books, 1998.

Davidson, Hugh M. "The Problem of Scientific Order Versus Alphabetical Order in the Encyclopedie." In *Studies in Eighteenth Century Culture*, vol. 2, ed. Harold E. Pagliaro. Cleveland: Press of Case Western Reserve University, 1972. 33–49.

Davies, Char. "Changing Space: Virtuality as an Arena of Embodied Being." In *The Virtual Dimension: Architecture, Representation and Crash Culture*, ed. John Beckman. New York: Princeton Architectural Press, 1998. 144–51.

———. "Ephémère: Landscape, Earth, Body, and Time in Immersive Virtual Space." In *Reframing Consciousness*, ed. Roy Ascott. Exeter, England: Intellect Books, 1999. 196–201.

Deleuze, Gilles. *Francis Bacon: The Logic of Sensation*. Tr. Daniel W. Smith. London: Continuum, 2003.

———. *Essays Critical and Clinical*. Tr. Daniel W. Smith and Michael A. Greco. London: Verso, 1998.

———. *Cinema 1: The Movement Image*. Tr. Hugh Tomlinson and Barbara Habberjam. Minneapolis: University of Minnesota Press, 1997.

———. *Negotiations: 1972–1990*. Tr. Martin Joughin. New York: Columbia University Press, 1995.

———. *Difference and Repetition*. Tr. Paul Patton. New York: Columbia University Press, 1994.

————. *Cinema 2: The Time-Image.* Tr. Hugh Tomlinson and Robert Galeta. London: Athlone Press, 1989.

————. *The Fold.* Tr. Tom Conley. Minneapolis: University of Minnesota Press, 1993.

————. "Ethology: Spinoza and Us." In *Incorporations,* ed. Jonathan Crarey and Sanford Kwinter. New York: Zone Books, 1992. 628–33.

————. *Bergsonism.* Tr. Hugh Tomlinson and Barbara Habberjam. New York: Zone Books, 1991.

————. *Foucault.* Tr. and ed. Stephen Hand. Minneapolis: University of Minnesota Press, 1988.

————. *Nietzsche and Philosophy.* Tr. Hugh Tomlinson. New York: Columbia University Press, 1983).

Deleuze, Gilles, and Felix Guattari. *A Thousand Plateaus.* Tr. Brian Massumi. London: Athlone Press, 1988.

————. *What Is Philosophy?* Tr. Hugh Tomlinson and G. Burchell. New York: Columbia University Press, 1994.

Descartes, René. *The Passions of the Soul.* In *The Philosophical Writings of Descartes,* tr. John Cottingham, Robert Stroothoff, and Dugald Murdoch, vol. 1. Cambridge: Cambridge University Press, 1985. 328–404.

Dodge, Martin, and Rob Kitchin. *Mapping Cyberspace.* New York: Routledge, 2001.

Diderot, Denis. *A Pictorial Encyclopedia of Trades and Industry.* Ed. Charles Coulston Gillespie, vol. 1 New York: Dover, 1959.

Dix, Alan, Janet Finlay, Gregory Abowd, and Russel Beale. *Human-Computer Interaction.* London: Prentice Hall Europe, 1998.

Dunning, Alan, and Paul Woodrow. "Dérive." http://www.ucalgary.ca/~einbrain/derive.htm.

————. "Einstein's Brain Essay." http://www.ucalgary.ca/~einbrain/EBessay.htm.

Dyson, Frances. "'Space,' 'Being' and Other Fictions in the Domain of the Virtual." In *The Virtual Dimension: Architecture, Representation and Crash Culture,* ed. John Beckman. New York: Princeton Architectural Press, 1998. 26–45.

Edwards, Paul. *The Closed World: Computers and the Politics of Discourse in Cold War America.* Cambridge, Mass.: MIT Press, 1996.

Eco, Umberto. *The Search for the Perfect Language.* Tr. James Fentress. London: Fontana, 1997.

Ede, Sarah, ed. *Strange and Charmed: Science and the Contemporary Visual Arts.* London: Calouste Gulbenkian Foundation, 2000.

Emmeche, Claus. *The Garden in the Machine.* Princeton: Princeton University Press, 1994.

Erickson, Thomas D. "Working with Interface Metaphors." In *The Art of Human-Computer Interface Design,* ed. Brenda Laurel. Reading, Mass.: Addison-Wesley Publishing, 1990. 65–73.

Ernst, W. "Arsenals of Memory." *Mediamatic* 8:1 (summer 1994): 1913–20.

Fernandez, Maria. "Postcolonial Media Theory." *Third Text* 47 (summer 1999): 11–17.

Findlen, Paula. "The Museum: Its Classical Etymology and Renaissance Genealogy." *Journal of the History of Collections* 1, (1989): 59–78.

Fisher, Scott. "Virtual Environments: Personal Simulations and Telepresence." In *Virtual Reality: Theory, Practice and Promise,* ed. Sandra K. Hesel and Judith Paris Roth. London: Meckler, 1991. 101–10.

Foucault, Michel. *The Order of Things: An Archaeology of the Human Sciences*. New York: Vintage Books, 1970.

———. "Nietzsche, Genealogy, History." In *Language, Counter-Memory and Practice*, ed. Donald F. Bouchard. Ithaca: Cornell University Press, 1977. 139–64.

———. "The Subject and Power." In *Michel Foucault: Beyond Structuralism and Hermeneutics*, ed. Hubert L. Dreyfuss and Paul Rabinow. Chicago: University of Chicago Press, 1983. 208–26.

Fox Keller, Evelyn. "The Biological Gaze." In *FutureNatural*, ed. George Robertson, et al. New York: Routledge, 1996. 107–21.

———. *Making Sense of Life*. Cambridge, Mass.: Harvard University Press, 2002.

Fučiková, Eliška. "The Collection of Rudolph II at Prague: Cabinet of Curiosities or Scientific Museum?" In *The Origins of Museums*, ed. Oliver Impey and Arthur MacGregor. Oxford: Clarendon Press, 1985. 47–53.

Fuller, Matthew. "Breach the Pieces." http://www.tate.org.uk/webart/mat2.htm.

Gatens, Moira. *Imaginary Bodies: Ethics, Power and Corporeality*. New York: Routledge, 1996.

Gibson, Ross. "Ecologies of Meaning." *Media International Australia* 89 (November 1998): 11–20.

Gigliotti, Carol. "Aesthetics of a Virtual World." *Leonardo* 28:4 (1995): 289–95.

Goodman, Cynthia. *Digital Visions: Computers and Art*. New York: Harry N. Abrams, 1987.

Gould, Stephen Jay, and Rosamund Wolff Purcell. *Finders Keepers: Eight Collectors*. London: Hutchinson Radius, 1992.

Greenberg, Clement. "Modernist Painting." *Art and Literature* 4 (spring 1965): 193–201.

Greenblat, Stephen. "Resonance and Wonder." In *Exhibiting Cultures: The Poetics and Politics of Museum Display*, ed. Ivan Karp and Steven D. Lavine. Washington, D.C.: Smithsonian Institution Press, 1991. 42–56.

Griggers, Camilla. *Becoming Woman*. Minneapolis: University of Minnesota Press, 1997.

Grosz, Elizabeth. *Volatile Bodies: Toward a Corporeal Feminism*. Sydney: Allen and Unwin, 1994.

Guattari, Felix. *Chaosophy*. New York: Semiotexte, 1995.

———. *Chaosmosis: An Ethico-Aesthetic Paradigm*. Sydney: Power Publications, 1995.

———. "Regimes, Pathways, Subjects." In *Incorporations*, ed. Jonathan Crary and Sanford Kwinter. New York: Zone Books, 1992. 16–37.

———. "On Machines." *Journal of Philosophy and the Visual Arts* 6 (1995): 8–12.

———. "Part Two: Pragmatic/Machinic: Discussion with Felix Guattari and Charles J. Stivale." http://www.dc.peachnet.edu/~mnunes/guattari.htm/#p1.

Hanafi, Zara. *The Monster in the Machine*. Durham, N.C.: Duke University Press, 2000.

Haraway, Donna. *Symians, Cyborgs and Women: The Reinvention of Nature*. London: Free Association Books, 1991.

Hayles, N. Katherine. *How We Became Posthuman: Virtual Bodies in Cybernetics, Literature and Informatics*. Chicago: University of Chicago Press, 1999.

———. "Embodied Virtuality: Or How to Put Bodies Back into the Picture." In *Immersed in Technology*, ed. Marianne A. Moser and David MacLeod. Cambridge, Mass.: MIT Press, 1996. 1–28.

————. "Virtual Bodies and Flickering Signifiers." In *Electronic Culture: Technology and Visual Representation,* ed. Timothy Druckrey. New York: Aperture Foundation, 1996. 259–77.

Heidegger, Martin. *The Question Concerning Technology and Other Essays.* New York: Harper Torchbooks, 1977.

Heim, Michael. *The Metaphysics of Virtual Reality.* New York: Oxford University Press, 1993.

————. "The Design of Virtual Reality." In *Cyberspace, Cyberbodies, Cyberpunk: Cultures of Technological Embodiment,* ed. M. Featherstone and R. Burrows. London: Sage Publications, 1996. 65–77.

Hobbes, Thomas. *Leviathan.* 1651. Harmondsworth, Eng.: Penguin Books, 1968.

Holland, O. E., and C. R. Melhuish. "Getting the Most from the Least: Lessons for the Nanoscale from Mininimal Mobile Agents." In *Artificial Life V: Proceedings of the Fifth International Workshop on the Synthesis and Simulation of Living Systems,* ed. Christopher Langton and Katsunori Shimohara. Cambridge, Mass.: MIT Press, 1997. 59–66.

Holland, William Jacob. "Museums of Science." *Encyclopaedia Britannica,* 11th edition, vol. 19. Cambridge: Cambridge University Press, 1910–11. 64–69.

Holtzman, Steven. *Digital Mosaics: The Aesthetics of Cyberspace.* New York: Simon and Schuster, 1997.

————. *Digital Mantras: The Languages of Abstract and Virtual Worlds.* Cambridge, Mass.: MIT Press, 1994.

Huyssen, Andreas. *Twilight Memories: Marking Time in a Culture of Amnesia.* New York: Routledge, 1995.

James, Susan. *Passion and Action: The Emotions in Seventeenth-Century Philosophy.* Oxford: Clarendon Press, 1997.

Jardine, Lisa. *Ingenious Pursuits.* London: Little, Brown and Company, 1999.

Jeremijenko, Natalie. "A Response to the 'Paradise Now' Exhibition." Paper given in the panel "How to Understand Genetic Information—and Why?" in response to *Paradise Now: Picturing the Genetic Revolution* exhibition at Exit Art, New York, September 9–October 28, 2000.

Johnson, Steven. *Interface Culture: How New Technology Transforms the Way We Create and Communicate.* San Francisco: Harperedge, 1997.

Kahn, Douglas. "What Now the Promise?" In *Burning the Interface: International Artists' CD-ROM,* exhibition catalogue. Sydney: Museum of Contemporary Art, 1996. 21–30.

Kamthan, Pankaj. "Searching the Web." http://tech.irt.org/articles/js167/index.htm.

Kay, Alan. "User Interface: A Personal View." In *The Art of Human-Computer Interface Design,* ed. Brenda Laurel. Reading, Mass.: Addison-Wesley Publishing, 1990. 191–207.

Kay, Lily E. "Cybernetics, Information, Life: The Emergence of Scriptural Representations of Heredity." *Configurations* 5:1 (1997): 23–91.

Kelly, Kevin. *Out of Control: The New Biology of Machines.* London: Fourth Estate, 1994.

Kenseth, Joy. "A World of Wonders in One Closet Shut." In *The Age of the Marvelous* ed. Joy Kenseth, exhibition catalogue. Hanover, N.H.: Hood Museum of Art, Dartmouth College, 1991. 83–86.

Kenshur, Oscar. *Open Form and the Shape of Ideas*. London: Associated University Press, 1986.

Kernderdine, Sarah. "Inside the Meta-Center: A Wonder Cabinet." http://amol.org .au/about_amol/part3.asp#Metaphor.

Kluitenberg, Eric. "Human Art Is Dead: Long Live the Algorithmic Art of the Machine." http://www.metamute.com/issue9/machineart.htm.

Landa, Manuel de. *Intensive Science and Virtual Philosophy*. London: Continuum, 2002.

———. *A Thousand Years of Nonlinear History*. New York: Swerve Editions, 1997.

Landow, George P. *Hypertext: The Convergence of Contemporary Critical Theory and Technology*. Baltimore: John Hopkins University Press, 1992.

Lanier, Jaron. "A Vintage Virtual Reality Interview." http://www.well.com/user/ jaron/vrint.html.

Latour, Bruno. *We Have Never Been Modern*. Tr. Catherine Porter. Cambridge, Mass.: Harvard University Press, 1993.

Laurel, Brenda. *Computers as Theater*. Reading, Mass.: Addison-Wesley Publishing, 1992.

Laurel, Brenda, ed. *The Art of Human-Computer Interface Design*. Reading, Mass.: Addison-Wesley Publishing, 1990.

Leeuwenhoek, Anthony van. "The First Observations on 'Little Animals' (Protozoa and Bacteria) in Waters." In *Antony Van Leeuwenhoek and His "Little Animals,"* ed. and tr. Charles Dobell. New York: John Bale Sons and Danielson Ltd., 1932. 109–66.

Leibniz, Gottfried W. F. *Leibniz: Selections*. Ed. Philip Weiner. New York: Charles Scribner's Sons, 1951.

———. *Discourse on Metaphysics*. Tr. G. W. Montgomery. La Salle, Ill.: Open Court Publishing, 1962.

———. *The Monadology and Other Philosophical Writings*. Tr. Robert Latta. London: Oxford University Press, 1951.

———. *Theodicy: Essays on the Goodness of God, the Freedom of Man and the Origin of Evil*. London: Routledge and Kegan Paul, 1951.

Lessig, Laurence. "May the Source Be with You." 2001. http://www.wired.com/ wired/archive/9.12/lessig.html.

Levinson, Paul. *The Soft Edge*. New York: Routledge, 1997.

Lévy, Pierre. *Becoming Virtual: Reality in the Digital Age*. Tr. R. Bononno. New York: Plenum Trade, 1998.

———. "The Invention of the Computer." In *A History of Scientific Thought: Elements of a History of Science*, ed. Michel Serres. Oxford: Blackwell, 1995. 636–63.

Lorenzo-Hemmer, Rafael. "Re: Positioning Fear: Relational Architecture 3." http:// rhizome.org/artbase/2398/fear/.

Lough, John. *The Encyclopédie*. Geneva: Slatkine Reprints, 1989.

Lovink, Geert. *Dark Fiber*. Cambridge, Mass.: MIT Press, 2002.

Lueckenhausen, Helmet. "Wonder and Despite: Craft and Design in Museum History." In *Craft and Contemporary Theory*, ed. Sue Rowley. Sydney: Allen and Unwin, 1997. 29–42.

Lunenfeld, Peter. *Snap to Grid: A User's Guide to Digital Arts, Media, and Cultures*. Cambridge, Mass.: MIT Press, 2000.

Luyendijk-Elshoust, A. M. "Death Enlightened: A Study of Frederick Ruysch." *Jama* 212:1 (April 6, 1970): 121–26.

Lynn, Greg. *Bodies and Blobs: Collected Essays.* Brussells: La Lettre Volée, 1998.

Macgregor, Arthur, ed. *Tradescant's Rarities: Essays on the Foundation of the Ashmolean Museum, 1683, with a Catalogue of the Surviving Collections.* Oxford: Clarendon Press, 1983.

Magli, Patricia. "The Face and the Soul." In *Fragments for a History of the Human Body,* ed. M. Feher, R. Naddaff, and M. Tazi, vol. 2. New York: Zone Books, 1989. 81–127.

Mankeiwicz, Richard. *The Story of Mathematics.* London: Cassell, 2000.

Manovich, Lev. *The Language of New Media.* Cambridge, Mass.: MIT Press, 2001.

———. "Database as Symbolic Form." 1998. http://www.manovich.net.

———. "The Aesthetics of Virtual Worlds: Report from Los Angeles." 1995. http://www.ctheory.com/ga1.3-aesthetics.html.

———. "The Labor of Perception." 1995. http://www.manovich.net/TEXT/labor.html.

———. "The Paradoxes of Digital Photography." 1994. http://www.apparitions.ucsd.edu/~manovich/text/digital_photo.html.

Markley, Robert, ed. *Virtual Realities and Their Discontents.* Baltimore: John Hopkins University Press, 1996.

Maras, Steven, "The Bergsonian Model of Actualisation." *SubStance* 27 (1998): 48–71.

Maras, Steven, and David Sutton. "Medium Specificity Re-Visited." *Convergence: The Journal of Research into New Media Technologies* 6:2 (summer 2000): 99–113.

Maravall, José A. *The Culture of the Baroque: Analysis of a Historical Structure.* Tr. Terry Cochran. Minneapolis: University of Minnesota Press, 1986.

Massumi, Brian. "The Autonomy of Affect." In *Deleuze: A Critical Reader,* ed. Paul Patton. Oxford: Blackwell, 1996. 217–39.

———. "The Bleed: Where Body Meets Image." In *Rethinking Borders,* ed. John C. Welchman. London: MacMillan, 1996. 18–40.

———. "Stelarc: The Evolutionary Alchemy of Reason." In *The Virtual Dimension: Architecture Representation and Crash Culture,* ed. J. Beckman. New York: Princeton Architectural Press, 1998. 333–41.

———. "Line Parable for the Virtual (On the Superiority of the Analog)." In *The Virtual Dimension: Architecture, Representation and Crash Culture,* ed. J. Beckman. New York: Princeton Architectural Press, 1998. 304–21.

———. "Sensing the Virtual, Building the Insensible." *Architectural Design* 68 (May–June 1998): 16–25.

———. "Too-Blue: Colour-Patch for an Expanded Empiricism." *Cultural Studies* 14:2 (2000). 177–226.

———. *Parables for the Virtual: Movement, Affect and Sensation.* Durham, N.C.: Duke University Press, 2002.

McDonough, Thomas F. "Situationist Space." *October* 67 (winter 1994): 58–77.

McLuhan, Marshall. *Understanding Media.* New York: Signet, 1966.

Morse, Margaret. *Virtualities: Television, Media Art and Cyberculture.* Bloomington: Indiana University Press, 1998.

Mitchell, William J. T. *The Reconfigured Eye.* Cambridge, Mass.: MIT Press, 1994.

————. "Antitectonics: The Poetics of Virtuality." In *The Virtual Dimension: Architecture, Representation and Crash Culture,* ed. Jonathon Beckman. New York: Princeton Architectural Press, 1998. 204–17.

Moravec, Hans. *Mind Children.* Cambridge, Mass.: Harvard University Press, 1988.

Munster, Anna. "Compression and the Intensification of Information in Flash Animation." In *Long Paper Proceedings of the Fifth International Conference on Digital Arts and Culture.* Melbourne: RMIT Publications, 2003. 142–50.

————. "Low-Res Bleed: Congealed Affect and Digital Aesthetics." *Australian and New Zealand Journal of Art,* double issue, 2:2 (2001) and 3:1 (2002): 77–95.

Murphie, Andrew. "Electronicas: Differential Media and Proliferating, Transient Worlds." In *Long Paper Proceedings from the Fifth International Conference on Digital Arts and Culture.* Melbourne: RMIT Publications, 2003. 151–61.

Murray, Janet H. *Hamlet on the Holodeck: The Future of Narrative in Cyberspace.* Cambridge, Mass.: MIT Press, 1997.

Murray, Kevin. "Mouse, Where Is Thy Sting?" In *Burning the Interface: International Artists' CD-ROM,* exhibition catalogue. Sydney: Museum of Contemporary Art, 1996. 11–20.

Murray, Timothy. "Digital Incompossibility: Cruising the Aesthetic Haze of the New Media." *CTheory* (January 13, 2000). http://www.ctheory.net/text_file .asp?pick=121.

Nadin, Mihai. "Emergent Aesthetics—Aesthetic Issues in Computer Arts." *Leonardo,* supplemental issue: "Computer Art in Context" (1989): 43–48.

Negroponte, Nicholas. *Being Digital.* London: Hodder and Stoughton, 1995.

Neimanis, K., and E. Geber "'Come and Get It' to 'Seek and You Shall Find': Transition from a Central Resource to Information Meta Center." In *Museums and the Web Proceedings,* ed. D. Bearman and J. Trant. CD-ROM. Toronto: Archives and Museum Informatics, 1998.

Nelson, Robert. "The Semiotic History of the Fold: Deleuzians of Grandeur." *Agenda* 25 (1993): 27–30.

Nelson, Ted H. "The Right Way to Think about Software Design." In *The Art of Human-Computer Interface Design,* ed. Brenda Laurel. Reading, Mass.: Addison-Wesley Publishing, 1990. 235–43.

Neumann, John von. *Collected Works,* vol. 5. Ed. A. H. Taub. Oxford: Pergamon Press, 1963.

Neverov, Oleg. "'His Majesty's Cabinet' and Peter I's Kunstkammer." In *The Origins of Museums: The Cabinet of Curiosities in Sixteenth- and Seventeenth-Century Europe,* ed. Oliver Impey and Arthur MacGregor. Oxford: Clarendon Press, 1985. 54–61.

Neville, Ben. "An Interview with Kim Cascone." http://www.cycling74.com/ community/cascone.html.

Nielsen, Jakob. *Designing Web Useability: The Practice of Simplicity.* Indianapolis: New Riders, 2000.

————. "Why This Site Has Almost No Graphics." http://www.useit.com/about/ nographics.html.

Nietzsche, Friedrich. *On the Genealogy of Morals.* Tr. Walter Kaufman and R. J. Hollingdale. New York: Vintage Books, 1969.

Norman, Donald A. "Why Interfaces Don't Work." In *The Art of Human-Computer*

Interface Design, ed. Brenda Laurel. Reading, Mass.: Addison-Wesley Publishing, 1990. 209–19.

———. *The Psychology of Everyday Things.* New York: Basic Books, 1988.

Novak, Marcus. "Liquid Architecture in Cyberspace." In *Cyberspace: First Steps,* ed. Michael Benedikt. Cambridge, Mass: MIT Press, 1994. 225–54.

Oguibe, Olu. "An Interview with Olu Oguibe." Massimilano Gioni, interviewer. *Third Text* 47 (summer 1999): 51–57.

———. "Connectivity and the Fate of the Unconnected." *Social Identities* 5:3 (1999): 239–48.

Olmi, Guiseppe. "Science-Honour-Metaphor: Italian Cabinets of the Sixteenth and Seventeenth Centuries." In *The Origins of Museums: The Cabinet of Curiosities in Sixteenth- and Seventeenth-Century Europe,* ed. Oliver Impey and Arthur MacGregor. Oxford: Clarendon Press, 1985. 5–16.

Parker, Carol. *The Joy of Cybersex.* Kew, Vic., Aus.: Mandarin, 1997.

Parsegian, V. Lawrence. *This Cybernetic World.* New York: Anchor Books, 1973.

Penny, Simon. "Virtual Reality as the Completion of the Enlightenment Project." In *Culture on the Brink,* ed. Timothy Druckrey and Gretchen Bender. Seattle: Bay Press, 1994. 231–48.

Penny, Simon, ed. *Critical Issues in Electronic Media.* New York: State University of New York Press, 1995.

Penny, Simon, Jeffrey Smith, and Andre Bernhardt. "Traces: Wireless Full Body Tracking in the CAVE." 1999. http://www.ace.uci.edu/penny/texts/traces/.

Piper, Keith. "Tagging the Other." In *Iterations: The New Image,* ed. Timothy Druckrey. Cambridge, Mass.: International Centre of Photography and MIT Press, 1993. 120–25.

Plant, Sadie. *Zeros and Ones: Digital Women and the New Technoculture.* London: Fourth Estate, 1997.

———. "The Virtual Complexity of Culture." In *FutureNatural,* ed. George Robertson, et al. New York: Routledge, 1996. 203–17.

Pomian, Krzysztof. *Collectors and Curiosities.* Cambridge: Polity Press, 1990.

Popper, Frank. *The Art of the Electronic Age.* London: Thames and Hudson, 1997.

Punt, Michael. "CD-ROM: Radical Nostalgia? Cinema History, Cinema Theory and New Technology." *Leonardo* 28:5 (1995): 387–94.

Reiss, Timothy J. "Denying the Body? Memory and the Dilemmas of History in Descartes." *Journal of the History of Ideas* 57:4 (October 1996): 587–606.

Rheingold, Howard. *Virtual Reality.* New York: Summit Books, 1991.

Rifkin, Jeremy. *The Biotech Century.* London: Phoenix, 1998.

Rokeby, David. "Artist Statement for 'Very Nervous System.'" http://homepage.mac.com/davidrokeby/vns.html.

Rose, Steven. *Lifelines: Biology, Freedom, Determinism.* London: Allen Lane, 1997.

Rossi, Paolo. "Universal Languages, Classifications and Nomenclatures in the Seventeenth Century." *History and Philosophy of the Life Sciences* 6:2 (1984): 119–31.

Rousseau, Jean-Jacques. "A Discourse on the Moral Effects of the Arts and the Sciences." In *The Social Contract and Discourses.* 1750. London: Dent, 1973. 3–29.

Rutsky, R. L. *High Techne: Art and Technology from the Machine Aesthetic to the Posthuman.* Minneapolis: University of Minnesota Press, 1999.

Schulz, Elizabeth. "Notes on the History of Collecting and Museums in the Light of Selected Literature of the 16th and 17th centuries." *Journal of the History of Collections* 2:2 (1990): 205–18.

Schwarz, Hans-Peter. "Media-Art-History." In *Media Art History: Catalogue for Opening of the Media Museum ZKM*. Prestel: Center for Art and Culture, 1997. 11–88.

Seijdel, J. "Operation Re-Store the World." *Mediamatic* 8:1 (summer 1994): 1861–69.

Seltzer, Mark. "Wound Culture: Trauma in the Pathological Public Sphere." *October* 80 (1997): 3–27.

Shaviro, Steven. *Connected, or What It Means to Live in the Network Society.* Minnesota: University of Minnesota Press, 2003.

Shannon, Claude, and Warren Weaver. "The Mathematical Theory of Communication." In *The Bell Laboratory Technical Journal* 27 (July 1948): 379–423.

Silver, Lee M. *Remaking Eden: Cloning and Beyond in a Brave New World.* London: Weidenfield and Nicolson, 1998.

Smith, Daniel W. "Deleuze's Theory of Sensation: Overcoming the Kantian Duality." In *Deleuze: A Critical Reader,* ed. Paul Patton. Oxford: Blackwell, 1996. 29–56.

Snyder, Ilana. *Hypertext: The Electronic Labyrinth.* Melbourne: Melbourne University Press, 1996.

Sobchack, Vivian. "Beating the Meat/Surviving the Text, or How to Get Out of This Century Alive." In *The Visible Woman: Imaging Technologies, Gender and Science,* ed. Paula A. Treichler, Lisa Cartwright and Constance Penley. New York: New York University Press, 1998. 310–20.

Sofoulis, Zoe. "Interactivity, Intersubjectivity and the Artwork/Network." *Mesh* 10 (1996): 32–35.

Springer, Claudia. *Electronic Eros: Bodies and Desire in the Postindustrial Age.* Austin: University of Texas Press, 1996.

Stafford, Barbara Maria. *Good Looking: Essays on the Virtue of Images.* Cambridge, Mass.: MIT Press, 1996.

———. *Artful Science: Enlightenment Entertainment and the Eclipse of Visual Education.* Cambridge, Mass.: MIT Press, 1994.

———. *Body Criticism: Imaging the Unseen in Enlightenment Art and Medicine.* Cambridge, Mass.: MIT Press, 1993.

Stelarc. "Parasite Visions: Alternate, Intimate and Involuntary Experiences." 1997. http://www.aec.at/en/archiv_files/19971/E1997_148.pdf.

———. "From Psycho to Cyber Strategies: Prosthetics, Robotics and Remote Existence." *Canadian Theatre Review* 86 (spring 1996): 19–23.

Stewart, Susan. *On Longing: Narratives of the Miniature, the Gigantic, the Souvenir and the Collection.* Durham, N.C.: Duke University Press, 1993.

Stocker, Gerfried. "FleshFactor." 1997. http://kultur.aec.at/20Jahre/katalog .asp?jahr=1997&band=101.

Stone, Rosanne Alluquere. "Will the Real Body Please Stand Up? Boundary Stories about Virtual Cultures." In *Cyberspace: First Steps,* ed. Michale Benedikt. Cambridge, Mass.: MIT Press, 1994. 81–118.

———. "Virtual Systems." In *Incorporations,* ed. Jonathan Crarey and Sanford Kwinter. New York: Zone Books, 1992. 608–21.

Sundaram, Ravi. "Recycling Modernity: Pirate Electronic Cultures in India." *Third Text* 47 (summer, 1999): 59–67.

Sutton, John. *Philosophy and Memory Traces: Descartes to Connectionism*. Cambridge: Cambridge University Press, 1998.

Swatch. "Internet Time." 1998. http://www.swatch.com/fs_index .php?haupt=collections&unter=.

Thom, René. *Structural Stability and Morphogenesis: An Outline of a General Theory of Models*. Tr. Donald H. Fowler. Reading, Mass.: W. A. Benjamin, Inc., 1975.

Thompson, Adrian. "On the Automatic Design of Robust Electronics through Artificial Evolution." In *Proceedings of the Second International Conference on Evolvable Systems*. Vienna: Springer-Verlag, 1998. 13–24.

Tofts, Darren. *Memory Trade: A Prehistory of Cyberculture*. Sydney: 21C/Interface, 1998.

———. "Your Place or Mine? Locating Digital Art." *Mesh* 10 (spring 1996): 2–5.

Tribby, J. "Body/Building: Living the Museum Life in Early Modern Europe." *Rhetorica* 10:2 (spring 1992): 139–63.

Turkle, Sherry. *Life on the Screen: Identity in the Age of the Internet*. London: Phoenix, 1997.

Twenty-fifth Annual Policy Colloquium, American Association for the Advancement of Science. Washington, D.C. April 13, 2000. http://www.newt.org/speech.aaas .htm.

Ullman, Ellen. *Close to the Machine: Technophilia and Its Discontents*. San Francisco: City Lights Books, 1997.

Varela, Francesco J. *Principles of Biological Autonomy*. New York: North Holland Press, 1979.

Walking, Les. "The Desensitization of Photography." *Photofile* 60 (August 2000): 4–7.

Warwick, Kevin. *I, Cyborg*. London: Century, 2002.

Watson, James. Interview at the symposium Winding Your Way through DNA. University of California, San Francisco. 1992. http://www.accessexcellence.org/ RC/CC/watson.html.

Welchman, Alastair. "Machinic Thinking." In *Deleuze and Philosophy: The Difference Engineer,* ed. Keith Ansell Pearson. New York: Routledge, 1997. 211–19.

Whitaker, Kate. "The Culture of Curiosity." In *Cultures of Natural History,* ed. Nicholas Jardine, James A. Secord, and Emma C. Spary. Cambridge: Cambridge University Press, 1996. 75–90.

Whitelaw, Mitchell. "The End of New Media Art?" *Working the Screen 2000*, special issue, *Realtime* 38 (August–September 2000): 7.

Wiener, Norbert. *Cybernetics or Control and Communication in the Animal and the Machine*. Cambridge, Mass.: MIT Press, 1991.

Wigley, Mark. *The Architecture of Deconstruction: Derrida's Haunt*. Cambridge, Mass.: MIT Press, 1993.

Wilmut, Ian, Keith Campbell and Colin Tudge. *The Second Creation*. London: Headline, 2000.

Winston, Brian. *Media Technology and Society: A History from the Telegraph to the Internet*. New York: Routledge, 1998.

Wilden, Anthony. *System and Structure: Essays in Communication and Exchange*. London: Tavistock Publications, 1980.

Wolf, Gary. "The Curse of Xanadu." *Wired* 3:6 (June 1995): 138–200.

Wolfflin, Henry. *Renaissance and Baroque*. Tr. Kathrin Simon. Ithaca: Cornell University Press, 1992.

Woolley, Bernard. *Virtual Worlds: A Journey in Hype and Hyperreality*. Oxford: Blackwell, 1992.

Wright, Richard. "The Image in Art and 'Computer Art.'" Computer Art in Context supplemental issue, *Leonardo* (1989): 49–53.

Yates, Frances. *The Art of Memory*. New York: Routledge and Kegan Paul, 1996.

Zizek, Slavoj. "Of Cells and Selves." In *The Zizek Reader*, ed. Elizabeth Wright and Edmund Leo Wright. Oxford: Blackwell, 1999. 302–20.

New-Media Artworks and Audiovisual Resources.

010101. Exhibition. http://www.sfmoma.org/exhibitions/exhib detail.asp?id=2.

Amerika, Mark. *FILMTEXT 2.0*. 2002.

Ars Electronica. http://www.aec.at/en/index.asp.

Australian Museum. http://www.austmus.gov.au/.

Australian Museums Online, http://amol.org.au.

Bigelow, Katherine. *Strange Days*. 1996.

Biggs, Simon. *The Great Wall of China*. 1996. http://hosted.simonbiggs.easynet.co .uk/wall/thewall.htm.

Bitstreams. http://www.whitney.org/bitstreams.

Boombox. http://www.boombox.net/.

Brew, Kathy, and Roberto Guerra. *ID/entity: Portraits in the Twenty-first Century*. 2003.

Bunting, Heath. *BorderXing Guide*. 2000. http://irational.org/borderxing/home .html.

———. *Superweed*. 1997. http://www.irational.org/cta/superweed/.

Cameron, James, dir. *Terminator 2*. Carolco Pictures. 1991.

Cascone, Kim. *Dust Theories*. 2001. Cycling '74. C74004.

Cohen, Jonathon. *Artists in Cyberculture*. Third International Symposium of Electronic Arts. Sydney: Ronin Films, 1993.

Cooper, Justine. *Scynescape*. 2000. http://justinecooper.com/scyn_synopsis.html.

CounterStrike. http://www.counter-strike.net/.

Cunningham, Chris. *All Is Full of Love*. 1999. Music video.

Cyberlife. http://www.cyberlife.co.uk/.

Davies, Char. *Ephémère*. 1998.

———. *Osmose*. 1995.

Dement, Linda. *In My Gash*. CD-ROM produced in association with the Australian Film Commission. 1999.

Dunning, Alan, and Paul Woodrow. *Einstein's Brain Project*. 2000 onward. http:// www.ucalgary.ca/~einbrain/.

Eshkar, Shelley, and Paul Kaiser. *Loops*. 2001.

Everquest. http://eqlive.station.sony.com/.

Gabriel, Ulrike. *Breath*. 1992–93.

Gupta, Shilpa. *Sentiment-Express*. 2001.

Haines, Tim, and Jasper James. *Walking with Dinosaurs*. 1999.

Harwood, Graham. *Uncomfortable Proximity.* http://www.tate.org.uk/webart/mongrel/hom/default.htm.

Huge Harry. "On the Mechanism of Human Facial Expression as a Medium for Interactive Art." http://kultur.aec.at/20Jahre/katalog.asp?jahr=1997&band=101.

Jackson, Shelly. *My Body—A Wunderkammer.* 1997. http://www.altx.com/thebody/.

Jeremijenko, Natalie. *OneTree.* 1999 and ongoing.

Jevbratt, Lisa, and c5. *1:1.* 1999 and ongoing. http://www.c5corp.com/1to1/index.html.

Krueger, Myron. *VideoPlace.* 1974–86.

Legrady, George. *Making Visible the Invisible.* 2004–5.

———. *Pockets Full of Memories.* 2001.

Lorenzo-Hemmer, Rafael. *Re:Positioning Fear.* 1997.

Ludin, Diane. *Memory Flesh 2.0: A Micro Media Record.* 2004. http://www.turbulence.org/Works/ludin/index.htm.

Lynn, Greg. *Embyologic Housing.* 1996.

MAX/MSP. http://www.cycling74.com/products/maxmsp.html.

MapBlast! http://www.mapblast.com/(iqttpn45soucvl45fp4wjlbo)/Home.aspx.

.microsound. http://www.microsound.org/.

Mongrel. *Natural Selection.* 1998. http://www.mongrel.org.uk/index2.html.

Munster, Anna. *Wundernet.* http://wundernet.cofa.unsw.edu.au.

Net_Condition. 1999–2000. http://www.zkm.de/netCondition.root/netcondition/start/language/default.

Opus Creative Commons. http://www.opuscommons.net.

Parasites Remixes. http://www.microsound.org/parasites/.

Ramis, Harold, dir. *Multiplicity.* 1996.

raqs media collective. *location 'n'* 2002.

Richards, Catherine. *The Virtual Body.* 1993.

Rokeby, David. *Very Nervous System.* 1986–90.

Saul, Shiralee. *Wunderkammer: The Museum on the Digital Shoreline.* 1998. http://www.labyrinth.net.au/~saul/wunder/wunder2.html.

Segaller, Stephen. "Nerds 2.0.1: A Brief History of the Internet." *Wiring the World,* parts 5 and 6. 1998.

Smithsonian Institution. *Revealing Things.* Exhibition. 1998. http://www.si.edu/revealingthings/.

Stelarc. *Prosthetic Head.* 2003.

———. *Extra Ear 1/4 Scale.* In collaboration with the Tissue Culture and Art Project. 2003.

TGarden. 2001–3. http://www.gvu.gatech.edu/people/sha.xinwei/topologicalmedia/tgarden/index.html.

Tissue Culture and Art Project. http://www.tca.uwa.edu.au.

World Heritage Organization. http://www.unesco.org/whc/nwhc/pages/home/pages/index.htm.

Yugop. http://surface.yugop.com.

INDEX

Page numbers in *italics* represent illustrations.

absolutism, 46, 47

abstraction, 174, 179, 180, 185, 209n.57

actual, the, versus virtuality, 16, 90–91, 96, 114

aesthetics: baroque, 42–47; of failure, 37; of information oversaturation, 162; Kantian, 151. *See also* information aesthetics

affect: affective mappings of dynamic body-code interfaces, 138–43; in baroque space, 6; in immersion in virtual environment, 89; informatic, 140; in *Loops*, 180; as not substance, 139; in TGarden environment, 181; in *Wunderkammer*, 11. *See also* passions

Alembert, Jean Le Rond d', 77–78

All Is Full of Love (Björk), 65–66, 196n.26

alternative IT economy, 168

American Computer Machinery Conference on Computer Graphics and Interactive Technologies (SIGGRAPH), 1–2, 10, 14–15

Amerika, Mark, 23, 176–77

analog, the, and the digital, 13, 19–20, 114

Anatomy Museum, 76–77, 198n.61

animation: architects using software from, 51; in Dement's *In My Gash*, 160; in Lynn's *Embryologic Housing* project, 52; in Stelarc's *Prosthetic Head*, 130; in *Walking with Dinosaurs* television series, 17, 95

Ansell Pearson, Keith, 13, 15

anthropomorphism, 20, 131, 132, 135

Antwerp '93 Festival, 87

Appardurai, Arjun, 166

Apple Computer, 123, 124

Apple iPod, 19

approximation, 68, 159–60

arcade games, 89, 91

Archer, Mike, 26

architecture: deconstructivist, 50; folding in, 50; in Lorenzo-Hemmer's *Re: Positioning Fear*, 147, 148; Lynn's *Embryologic Housing* project, 52; rococo, 127; topological, 9, 50–54; Yokohama Port Authority, 51–52

Architecture Machine Group (MIT), 101

Ars Electronica, 133, 150, 205n.42, 210nn. 6, 10

Art and Technology Movement, 154, 207n.15

artifice, 126–27, 183

artificial life, 30, 34, 191n.19, 195n.21

art-science collaboration, 182

Ascott, Roy, 154

Aspen Movie Map, 101

assemblage, 35–36, 53, 56

Assumption of the Virgin, The (Valdés Leal), 45, 46

Asymptote, 9, 50

audio. *See* sound

Australian Museum, 25–26

Australian Museums Online, 80, 187n.8

automata, 26–27

Barnouw, Jeffrey, 42

baroque, the: aesthetics of, 42–47; automata, 26–27; classicism distinguished from, 5, 7, 43–44; clusters of objects in, 6; continuity of perceptual experience in, 119; decorative excess of late, 126–27; defined, 5; differential logic in, 5, 6–7, 9, 32, 185; the digital as part of baroque event, 5–7, 25–54; folding in, 7–8, 38–42; inflection points evoking, 54; on knowledge and passion, 11, 32; modes of visual display of, 5; natural and artificial balanced in, 6; ornamentation and postmodern simulation, 40–41; passion and knowledge in thought of, 11–12, 67–68, 116,

baroque, the (*continued*)
185; as plateau of folding, 41; tricks
and astonishment in, 73, 198n.52;
as unfolding ongoing event, 41; and
virtuality, 88–89
Baudelaire, Charles, 103
Baumgarten, Alexander, 42
Beckman, John, 88
"being in the world," 111
Benjamin, Walter, 103
Bergson, Henri, 99
Berkel, Ben van, 50
Bernhardt, Andre, 210n.6
Bernini, Gian Lorenzo, 45
Bigelow, Katherine, 97
Biggs, Simon, 23, 175–76
binary code. *See* digital code
binary notation, 190n.8
bioart, 182–83
biology: as code, 61; folding in, 8;
as materialization of information,
185; post-biological life forms, 132,
133, 134. *See also* biotechnology;
genetics
biotechnology: bioart, 182–83; increasing fascination for, 25; new media
art opening into, 124; as parasitic,
134; sameness as mark of, 27. *See
also* cloning; flesh-machine fusion
bitmapped graphics, 23, 173, 176
Bitstreams, 150, 206n.3
Björk, 65–66, 196n.26
"blob" forms, 53, 193n.64
blogging, 172, 209n.52
Boal, Ian A., 188n.16
body, the: aesthetics of informatic,
143–49; anthropomorphism, 20, 131,
132, 135; computers as biased against,
1, 3–4; computers as multiplications
and extensions of, 33; digital embodiment, 16–20, 22, 62–66, 184; embodiment distinguished from,
62–63; emerging tendencies in
embodied information aesthetics,
178–86; hybridizing of technology
and, 18; informatic renderings of,
138–43; knowledge and passion in

baroque thought, 11–12, 67–68;
Leibniz on bodies in relation to each
other, 44–45; media as extensions of,
18; new media seen as privileging
consciousness over embodiment,
9–11; as not antinomy of digital
code, 184–85; in Richards's *The
Virtual Body*, 86–88, 90; speed of
embodied interactions, 160; in
virtual reality environments, 89–91,
100–101, 108–16. *See also* brain;
faciality; flesh-machine fusion;
mind/body dualism; perception;
sensation
BorderXing Guide (Bunting), 104, 105,
105–6
Borromini, Francesco, 45
Bos, Caroline, 50
Bostrom, Hans-Olaf, 198n.52
brain: as computer, 195n.21; Descartes
on folding structure of, 72, 188n.12;
as information system, 128
Breath (Gabriel), 3–4
Buci-Glucksmann, Christine, 43,
192n.44
Bukatman, Scott, 3, 187n.5
Bunting, Heath, 104–6, 183, 210n.10

cabinet making, 77
Cache, Bernard, 9, 50, 53–54
calculus, differential, 31–32, 39, 69
call centers, 164, 167, 170
Campbell, Keith, 27
Cartesian coordinate system, 1–3, 14–15,
51, 91, 109, 173
cartography, virtual space and, 101–3
Cascone, Kim, 37, 48–50
Castells, Manuel, 18, 191n.24
CAVE project, 110–11, 181, 201n.38,
210n.6
Centre for Computational Neuroscience
and Robotics (University of Sussex),
204n.32
Centrum Voor Beeldcultuur (Belgium),
87
cheap labor, 169–70
chromosomes, 8

cinema: Deleuze on shift from movement-image to time-image in, 172; digital, 24; the digital's relationship to, 162; faciality in, 129–30; lines of expression in, 139; logic of excess in, 139, 140

class: in British art canon, 156; digital "haves" and "have nots," 152; as marker of embodiment, 22

classicism: baroque contrasted with, 5, 7, 43–44; the digital's classical inheritance, 47–48, 54; science and, 68

cloning, 25–31; clones as protosubjectivities, 66; Dolly the sheep, 27; Jeremijenko's *OneTree* project, 29–31, 32; mutations in, 28; sameness as mark of, 27; Thylacine project, 25–26, 32

code. *See* digital code

collecting: in early modern period, 69; wonder and passion for, 73–77. See also *Wunderkammer*

combinatorics, nonlinear, 1

composition, 157–58, 208n.24

computational space, 52–53, 92–93, 119

computer-aided design (CAD), 51, 53, 77

computer gaming: Amerika's *FILM-TEXT 2.0* and, 177; arcade games, 89, 91; doubling in, 63–64; nonlinear time in, 17, 94, 171; semi-immersive environments in, 98; virtual reality compared with, 100

computers: abstraction in computational space, 92–93; as biased against the body, 1, 3–4; brain likened to, 195n.21; evolutionary hardware, 204n.32; facialization in, 123; globalization of computing technologies, 151, 152; history of the digital and, 55–56; as multiplications and extensions of the body, 33; outsourcing of software skills, 167; personal computer revolution, 56; realist aesthetics associated with, 93; "terminal identity," 3. *See also* computer gaming; human-computer interaction; networking

connectivity: access and control afforded by, 36; access to technology and, 152–53, 164; baroque concepts of differentiation and, 54, 185; gaps and, 6–7; as promise of "Internet time," 170; theorizing about, 39–40

convergence: in the baroque, 46, 68; of binary pairs in understanding digital culture, 5; in differential calculus, 32; of differential unfolding of new media, 99; in digital fold, 50; enfolding of virtual spaces, 102; between information and material world, 29; of information spheres, 36; of machine-body events, 31; as shaping outcomes of new media technologies, 185

Cooper, Justine, 21, 143–45, 147, 206n.65

CounterStrike, 177

crawlers, 82

cross-referencing, 78

Crouch, Nathaniel, 76

Crucible, The (Dunning and Woodrow), 143

Cubitt, Sean, 151, 163, 164

Cunningham, Chris, 65–66, 196n.26

Cunningham, Merce, 178–79, 180

curiosity, 11, 69–70, 73, 76, 197n.42

curiosity cabinet. See *Wunderkammer*

Cyberlife, 125, 126, 203n.20

cybernetics: information separated from matter in, 60, 195n.15; posthumanism and, 133; video for Björk's *All Is Full of Love* and, 65, 66; Warwick and, 10

cyberpunk, 189n.5

cyberspace: bodily markers lacking in, 163; Cartesian dualism in conceptions of, 50; connectivity of, 170; gap between physical space and, 89–90; global reaches of, 163; as navigable, 103; omnidirectionality of, 173; ontology of, 116; as space in the making, 101. *See also* virtual space

cyborgs: body and code treated as predefined unities, 31; clones contrasted
with, 27; and early modern monsters,
40; as graft of machine and body, 25,
28, 189n.5; as protosubjectivities,
66; in video for Björk's *All Is Full of
Love*, 65–66; Warwick as, 10

Damasio, Antonio, 141–42, 205n.56
dance, 178–79
databanks, 36
database approach in new media art,
78–85
Davidson, Hugh, 78
Davies, Char, 17, 111, 114, 115, 202n.50
Debord, Guy, 104
decompositions of other media, 158
deconstructivist architecture, 50
decorative, the, 126–27
Deleuze, Gilles: ambivalence about
digital coding, 34, 190n.16; on
Bergsonian duration, 99; on blocks
of sensation, 208n.27; on codification, 158; on composition, 208n.24;
on ethological dimension, 152; on
faciality, 21, 123, 127, 137–38; on the
fold, 38; on Leibniz and the fold, 7,
187n.10; on the machinic, 13, 14, 35;
on plateau, 192n.36; on shift from
movement-image to time-image in
cinema, 172; on superfold, 33–34;
Thom's influence on, 188n.24; on
"war machines," 43
dematerialization: digitization seen as
leading to, 11, 29, 153, 159; in
Human Genome Project, 120; in
information interfaces, 19; new
media artists responding to, 120;
in virtual reality, 17, 91, 116;
Wunderkammer and, 77
Dement, Linda, 160–62
"demo-or-die" aesthetic, 154
dérive (drift): Bunting inspired by, 104,
105; in Cooper's *Scynescape*, 145;
in Debord's *Naked City*, 104; in Dunning and Woodrow's *Einstein's Brain*,

106, 107, 108; for engaging with
urban space, 103, 104
Descartes, René: Cartesian coordinate
system, 1–3, 14–15, 51, 91, 109, 173;
on clear and distinct ideas, 42; on
folding structure of brain, 72, 188n.12;
on intellectual emotions, 71–72;
mind/body dualism of, 2, 15, 39, 50,
70, 72; on passions, 11, 70–73, 185;
on physiology of memory, 72; polarized responses to, 2; rationalist
legacy of, 44; on wonder, 70–73
desktop metaphor, 121, 124–25
Dewey decimal system, 79
diagrams, 35–36, 113
Diderot, Denis, 78
differential calculus, 31–32, 39, 69
differentials: baroque's differential
logic, 5, 6–7, 9, 32, 185; and body-
computer interface in new media
art, 118; computational space accom-
modating, 53; in differential calculus, 31–32; differentiality, 29; the digital as differential, 6–7, 8, 152; digital
embodiment and, 64; distribution of
media affected by, 171–72; elimina-
tion of interface as space of differentiation, 127–29; interfacializations
for overcoming, 123; lag as mode
of differentiation, 164; in Lorenzo-
Hemmer's *Re: Positioning Fear*, 148;
in Lynn's *Embryologic Housing* project, 52; and machinic superfolding,
50; naturalizations as differential
productions, 61–62; proximity resulting from, 68; speeds, 169,
175; and Stelarc's posthuman experiments, 135; in unfolding of new
media, 99; in video for Björk's *All
Is Full of Love*, 65; virtualization as
expanding and contracting field of
differentiation, 114
digital, the: and the analog, 13, 19–20,
114; binary logic in culture of, 3;
Cartesian coordinate system in, 1–3,
14–15, 91; classical inheritance of,

47–48, 54; clusters of objects in, 6; continua translated into discontinuous code in, 139, 148; dematerialization associated with, 11, 29, 153, 159; differential logic in, 6–7, 8, 152; digital culture as series of diagrammatic lines, 24; digital embodiment, 16–20, 22, 62–66, 184; digital technology versus digitality, 55; and ethico-aesthetic paradigm for information, 150–77; folded sense of, 47–54; folding and new genealogy for, 8–9; "haves" and "have nots," 152; history and digital media, 17, 55–56; locating a digital aesthetic, 150–55; as machinic, 13–16, 204n.32; mutability as immanent to, 151; naturalizing, 55–62; nondifferentiation of cultural and aesthetic spaces in, 50; old epistemologies and ontologies in, 15; and other media forms, 162; as part of baroque event, 5–7, 25–54; sets of unfolding differential relays in, 6; shift from spatialization to temporalization in, 171–77; as virtual ecology, 155; virtuality associated with, 86, 90, 92; virtual limit pole of, 16. *See also* digital audio; digital code; digital images; new media; virtuality

digital audio: in Cascone's *Dust Theories*, 48–50; microsound, 37–38, 50; sampling, 29, 38; versus "target-message-impact" technologies, 153

digital code: as adding something to the mix, 37–38; aesthetics of informatic bodies, 143–49; the body as not antinomy of, 184–85; as control mechanism, 36; encoding process, 28–29; folding of biology and, 56; as infinitely reconfigurable, 93; informatic renderings of the body, 138–43; multiples of same file, 34, 190n.15; noise reduced by, 37; replication of, 27, 29; the superfold, 33–38

digital images: aesthetics of informatic bodies, 143–49; bitmapped graphics, 23, 173, 176; Flash software for, 173–75; in Harwood's *Uncomfortable Proximity*, 156, 157; informatic renderings of the body, 138–43; replication of, 29; in *Revealing Things* exhibition, 57–58; vector graphics, 173–74

"digital revolution," 9–10

Disclosure (film), 89

Disney World, 89, 92

Dissertatio de arte combinatoria (Leibniz), 68–69

distribution: as characterizing new media, 22–23; distributed aesthetics, 171–77

divergence: in the baroque, 68; of binary pairs in understanding digital culture, 5; in differential calculus, 32; of differential unfolding of new media, 99; in digital fold, 50; between information and material world, 29; of machine-body events, 31; as shaping outcomes of new media technologies, 185; unfolding of virtual spaces, 102

"dividuals," 36

Dix, Alan, 128

DJ4'33", 49

DNA, 26, 60

Documenta 11 exhibition, 168

Dodge, Martin, 101

Dolly the sheep, 27

"dot.com" economy, 170

doubling, 64, 92, 145, 146, 148, 179

Downie, Marc, 178, 180

drift. See *dérive*

dualism. *See* mind/body dualism

Dunning, Alan, 106–8, 143, 147

duration, 24, 96, 99, 100–101, 160

Dust Theories (Cascone), 48–50

Dyson, Frances, 116

Ear on Arm (Stelarc), 19, 20

Eckenberg, Jan, 82

écouteur, 18–19

EDSAC (Electronic Delay Storage Automatic Computer), 60, 194n.4
Einstein's Brain (Dunning and Woodrow), 106–8, *107*, 143
Elsenaar, Arthur, 136–37
embodiment. *See* body, the
Embryologic Housing project (Lynn), 52
embryology, 8
empiricism, 43
encyclopaedism: memory and, 69; museums as encyclopaedic, 81; order in, 77–78
Encyclopédie, 77–78
engagement, 152
Englebart, Douglas, 121
entropy, 66
Ephémère (Davies), 111, 115
equilibrium, 66
Eshkar, Shelley, 178–79, *180*
ethics: embodied relations to others and, 163; ethico-aesthetic paradigm for information, 152–77; new media artists turning attention to, 182
Ethics (Spinoza), 69
European Union, 163
Evelyn, John, 55
Everquest, 177
Exstasis (Metraform), 210n.6
Extra Ear 1/4 Scale (Stelarc), 183

faciality, 21; in computers, 123; in Huge Harry, 137–38; interface and problem of facialization, 117–24; portraiture, 179; soul and thought expressed in face, 125–26; in Stelarc's *Prosthetic Head*, 130–32; and subjectivation, 122–23; in television, 129–30. *See also* interfaciality
Fernandez, Maria, 163–64
FILMTEXT 2.0 (Amerika), 176–77
Fisher, Scott, 101, 109, 112, 113, 115, 203n.9
flâneur, the, 18, 103
Flash software, 173–75, 176, 177
FleshFactor festival, 133
flesh-machine fusion: and the biotechnological, 25; clones contrasted with,

28; as reductive cyberfantasy, 9, 20; in Western cultural imagination, 27. *See also* cyborgs
FoAM, 210n.4
folding, 31–33; in the baroque, 7–8, 38–42; and body-computer interface in new media art, 118; as bringing informatic selves and organic bodies into proximity, 116; in culinary context, 32–33; Descartes on folding structure of brain, 72, 188n.12; of digital code and biology, 56; folded sense of the digital, 47–54; folds as both confluent and dissonant, 31; in information aesthetics, 8, 32; interfolding, 139, 148; in Leibnizian system, 45; in life sciences, 8; and new genealogy for digital culture, 8–9; proximity and, 68; and Stelarc's posthuman experiments, 135; as strategy for dealing with history, 41; superfold, 33–38, 50, 62; terminology of, 50; as transversal and specific, 41
Foreign Office (architectural firm), 9, 50, 51–52
Forrest Gump (film), 94
Foucault, Michel, 2, 62, 196n.32
Frankenstein's monster, 27
free software initiatives, 168, 169
Fuller, Mathew, 150, 156

Gabriel, Ulrike, 3–4
games. *See* computer gaming
gaps (intervals), 6, 7, 53, 139, 146
genealogy, 3, 5, 8–9, 61, 67
genetics: code in, 27; the fold as organizing principle in, 8; Human Genome Project, 26, 35, 36, 120, 139
Gingrich, Newt, 194n.3
globalization: in Bunting's *BorderXing Guide*, 105, 106; corporate and military surveillance in, 163; of digital culture, 185; "global village," 39, 164; lag in, 164–67; social relations and, 151, 152
Goodman, Cynthia, 154

GPS (Global Positioning System) satellites, 102
Great Wall of China (Biggs), 175–76
Greenberg, Clement, 154
Greenblat, Stephen, 198n.60
Griggers, Camilla, 129–30, 134
Guattari, Felix: on blocks of sensation, 208n.27; on composition, 208n.24; on faciality, 21, 123, 127, 138; on lines of expression, 139; on lines of virtuality, 115; on the machinic, 13, 14, 35; on obsessive-compulsive behavior, 142; on plateau, 192n.36; Thom's influence on, 188n.24; on universes of reference, 56; on virtual ecology, 86; on virtual reality technologies, 113; on "war machines," 43
Gupta, Shilpa, 22, 105, 168, 169–70

habit, 146–47
hacking, 155, 207n.19
Haraway, Donna, 27, 189n.5
Harwood, Graham, 22, 155–59
Hayles, Katherine, 19, 62–63, 132, 138, 160
head-mounted display, 96, 109, 110, *110*
Heidegger, Martin, 111, 202n.42
Heim, Michael, 111, 114
Historiam Naturalem (Petiver), 75, *75*
Historia Naturalae (Imperato), *12, 74*
history: and digital media, 17, 55–56; folding as strategy for dealing with, 41; museums making, 56; virtual recreation of, 94. *See also* natural history
Hobbes, Thomas, 69, 197n.42
"Hogarth, My Mum 1700–2000" (Harwood), *158*
Hooke, Robert, 39, 191n.31
Huge Harry (voice synthesis program), 21, 133, 136–38
human-computer interaction (HCI): consolidation from 1980s, 121–22; faciality in, 20–21; posthumanism and, 133. *See also* interfaciality
Human-Computer Interaction (Dix), 128

Human Genome Project (HGP), 26, 35, 36, 120, 139
hybrids, 18, 25, 77, 133
hyperarchitecture, 50
hyperreality, 5, 17
hypertext, 203n.9

icons, 121, 124, 230n.9
images. *See* digital images
Imperato, Ferrante, *12, 74*
incorporeal universes of reference, 112–13
India, 164–70
inflection points, 54
infomanic, the, 16
information: biology as materialization of, 185; building organisms from, 26, 29; digital code as controlling flow of, 36; human treated as system of, 128; information science, 77; information society, 14, 16, 99, 183; materiality as carrier of, 114; materiality contrasted with, 63; networked, 36, 80, 152; and noise, 196n.24; nonstandardized flows of, 22; separation of matter from, 60, 195n.15. *See also* information aesthetics
information aesthetics: as approximation, 159–60; broadening and complicating generative base of, 4–5; as critical commentary and new kind of aesthetics, 38; differential logic in, 6–7, 9, 32; distributed aesthetics, 171–77; embodied sense of, 63; embodiment as means for crossing gaps in, 139; emerging tendencies in embodied, 178–86; and ethico-aesthetic paradigm for information, 150–77; folding in, 8, 32; locating a digital aesthetic, 150–55; logic of expressive dearth in, 140; on materializing new media culture, 184; medium specificity for, 22; nonlinear time in, 98–99; return of *Wunderkammer* in, 77–85; virtuality and interactivity as dominating tendencies in, 86. *See also* new media

"information age," 9–10, 36, 163, 188n.16
information technology (IT) economy, 165, 166, 167–68, 170
In My Gash (Dement), 160–62, *161*
interfaces: classicism and, 47; desktop metaphor, 121, 124–25; embodied, 21; erasure of, 127–29; faciality in, 20–21, 117–24; mind/body dualism in, 50; in new media art, 81–85, 184; old kinaesthetic and proprioceptive arrangements in, 3, 19; temporal dimension in, 175; user-friendliness of, 122, 123, 124, 132, 203n.9. *See also* interfaciality
interfaciality, 117–49; affective mappings of dynamic body-code interfaces, 138–43; at Ars Electronica 1997 festival, 133; as being caught between faces, 130; of database portraiture, 179; defined, 21; *FleshFactor* festival and, 133; human-computer interface premises organized by, 122; interfacing with posthuman subjectivities, 132–36; interfacing with programmatic subjectivities, 136–38; as multiplying the face, 138; two poles of, 124–25; undervaluation of body as consequence of, 148. *See also* interfaces
interfolding, 139, 148
Internet: Biggs's *Great Wall of China*, 175–76; Bunting's *BorderXing Guide*, 106; corporate attempts to standardize, 166–67; Gupta's *sentiment-express*, 169–70; Harwood's *Uncomfortable Proximity*, 155–59; "Internet time," 167, 170; Jevbratt's *1:1* project, 82–85; lag as device in Internet art, 169; Lorenzo-Hemmer's *Re: Positioning Fear*, 147; Ludin's *Memory Flesh 2.0*, 120; open source movement, 168
intervals (gaps), 6, 7, 53, 139, 146
intimacy, 1, 135
iPod, 19
ISEA (International Society for the Electronic Arts), 150

Jackson, Shelly, 199n.79
James, Robert, 76
James, Susan, 71
Jeremijenko, Natalie, 29–31, 32
Jevbratt, Lisa, 82–85
joystick-controlled videogames, 91
Jurassic Park (film), 94

Kaiser, Paul, 178–79, *180*
Kantian aesthetics, 151
Kay, Alan, 203n.9
Kay, Lily, 195n.15
Keaton, Michael, 28
Kelly, Kevin, 10, 193n.53
Kernderdine, Sarah, 80
keyboards, 122
Kipnis, Jeffrey, 50
Kitchin, Rob, 101
Kluver, Billy, 154
Knox, Alec, 95
Krueger, Myron, 21, 145–46

lag, 162–71; as characterizing new media, 22, 169; between data and delivery times, 170; in Gupta's *sentiment-express*, 169–70; of information and globalization, 155; in temporality of digital embodiment, 64; theorizing new media art lagging behind the work, 159; time difference between India and America, 167
Landa, Manuel de, 1, 12–13, 41, 192n.37, 196n.29
Lang, Fritz, 27
Latour, Bruno, 55
Laurel, Brenda, 117, 121, 122, 127, 128–29, 202n.3, 204n.35
Lawnmower Man (film), 89
Leeuwenhoek, Anthony van, 38–39
LeFebvre, Henri, 103
Legrady, George: *Making Visible the Invisible*, 78–79; *Pockets Full of Memories*, 58–60, 62, 78
Leibniz, Gottfried Wilhelm: on bodies as in flux, 25; on bodies in relation to each other, 44–45; differential calculus of, 31–32, 39; and folding, 7–8;

on knowledge and passion, 11; on mind and matter, 39; on mnemonics, 68–69; on monads, 45, 60, 84; on sensory perception, 42
Lessig, Laurence, 168
Leviathan (Hobbes), 69
Levinson, Paul, 60–61, 195n.18
Lévy, Pierre, 90, 92, 194n.4
liberal subjectivity, 132, 136, 138
Licklider, J. C. R., 121
lines of expression, 139
Linux, 168
location n (raqs media collective), 164–66, *165*
Loops (Kaiser, Eskhar, Cunningham, and Downie), 178–80
Lorenzo-Hemmer, Rafael, 21, 147–48
Lovink, Geert, 166–67
Ludin, Diane, 120–21, 122, 140, 202n.6
Lueckenhausen, Helmet, 77
Lunenfeld, Peter, 95, 154
Lynn, Greg, 9, 50, 52, 193n.64

machines: the machinic, 13–16, 35–36, 204n.32. *See also* computers; flesh-machine fusion
Macintosh computer, 123, 124
Magli, Patricia, 126
Making Visible the Invisible (Legrady), 78–79
Manovich, Lev, 24, 97, 210n.3
MapBlast!, 102
maps, virtual space and, 101–3
Maravall, José, 47
"mashed-up pop," 172, 209n.52
Massumi, Brian: on actualization of architecture, 53; on affective embodiment and the analog, 114; on computational and modernist space, 209n.57; on diagrams, 113; on felt thought, 94; on Lorenzo-Hemmer's work, 148; on missing period in affect, 140; on topological shift in architecture, 50–51; on the virtual as lived paradox, 115
materiality: biology as materialization of information, 185; as carrier of

information, 114; information contrasted with, 63; information seen as separated from matter, 60, 195n.15; materializing new media culture, 184; of silicon, 204n.32; in *Wunderkammer*, 11, 77. *See also* body, the; dematerialization
MAX/MSP, 48–49, 203n.7
McLuhan, Marshall, 18, 39
media: as extensions of the body, 18. *See also* cinema; new media; television
Medicinal Dictionary, A (James), 76
memory: in the brain, 128; in Dement's *In My Gash*, 160–61; Descartes on physiology of, 72; encyclopaedism and, 69; as multimodal, 99–100; science and, 68–69; virtual, 97, 99
Memory Flesh 2.0 (Ludin), 120–21, *121*, 202n.6
meta-centers, 80–81
metadata tags, 81
Metraform, 181–82, 210n.6
Micrographia (Hooke), 39
microscopy, 38–39, 44
microsound, 37–38, 50, 191n.25
migrant labor, 106
military surveillance, 102, 163
mind/body dualism: in context of baroque culture, 15, 54, 72; in debate on contemporary machines, 2–3, 50, 70; Heidegger's "being in the world" as bridging, 111; Leibniz and, 39
mirroring sites, 155
Mitchell, William J. T., 29, 199n.68
mnemonics, 68–69
mobile phones, 36
mobility, 18
modernism, 154, 174, 179, 209n.57
"Modernist Painting" (Greenberg), 154
monads, 45, 60, 84
Mondo 2000 (magazine), 189n.5
Mongrel (collective), 22, 105, 155, 207n.19
motion sensors, 178, 180
MP3 players, 18–19
MRI scans, 143, 144

Multiplicity (film), 28
multi-user online role-playing games (MORPGs), 177
Murphie, Andrew, 153
Murray, Janet, 91, 92, 101
museums: Australian Museums Online, 80, 187n.8; digitizing Great Masters, 94; as encyclopaedic, 81; new media in, 56–60; as not monolithic, 156; online, 187n.8; *Smithsonian Without Walls*, 57–58, 187n.8; Tate Gallery, London, 155–59, 169; *Wunderkammer* as foundation of, 11, 12, 67, 81
Museum Wormianum (Worm), 74, *74*

Naked City (Debord), 104
NASA-Ames workstation, 17, 101, 109, *110*, 112, 113
natural history: extending to the digital, 66–69; Foucault on, 196n.32; naturalizing the digital, 55–62; new digital biology and, 11; tracing differential histories of, 85; *Walking with Dinosaurs* television series as reimagining, 95; in *Wunderkammer*, 11–12, 73–77
Natural History (Pliny), 56
Natural Selection project, 207n.19
Negativland, 38
Negroponte, Nicholas, 125, 167, 203n.9
Nelson, Ted, 203n.9
neoliberalism, 133
Net_Condition, 150, 206n.3
networking: networked information, 36, 80, 152, 172; networked society, 36, 167, 172, 174–75, 191n.24. *See also* Internet
Neumann, John von, 25, 37, 190n.8
Neville, Ben, 49
new media: affectivity emerging through, 143; in biotechnology, 124; and blocks of sensation, 160; bodies enticed to incorporeal flows by, 18; continuity of perceptual experience in, 119; database approach in, 78–85; defining characteristics of, 22; defining via the medium, 153–54; digital

embodiment in, 64–66; dynamic participation as characteristic of, 58; embodied experience in artworks, 3–4, 21; expectations for, 160; fluid subjectivities in rhetoric about, 163–64; folding and engagement with technologies, 8; impossible bodily transformations in, 19–20; in India, 164–66; informatic visualizations of bodies in, 140; interface design experiments in, 118; interfacialization modes in, 123; lag as characterizing, 22; lag as device in, 169; lag between "cutting edge" and outmoded art, 164; materializing new media culture, 184; and modernist tradition, 154; moving beyond disembodiment and extension in space, 179–80; in museum environments, 56–60; nonlinear time in, 98–99; older media's relationship to, 23–24; postcolonial art, 166; as privileging consciousness over embodiment, 9–11; sensory and effective elements engaged in, 181; speed associated with, 159, 160; on synaesthetic disruptions and reconfigurations, 19; theorizing lagging behind the work, 159; three vectors that characterize, 22–23; topological architecture, 9, 50–54; and uneven access to technology, 164. *See also* animation; digital audio; digital images; information aesthetics; virtual reality (VR)
Nielsen, Jakob, 122, 126
Nietzsche, Friedrich, 61
noise, 37, 196n.24
non-copyrighted software, 168
nonlinear time, 17, 98–100, 171, 173
Norman, Donald, 117, 118, 121, 122
"norns," 125, 126, 203n.20
Novak, Marcus, 51

Oguibe, Olu, 150, 152
omnidirectionality, 173
1:1 project (Jevbratt), 82–85, *83*, *84*

One Tree project (Jeremijenko), 29–31, 32
open source movement, 168–69
"Opus" (Open Platform for Unlimited Signification), 168, 169
order: in encyclopedias, 77–78; in *Wunderkammer*, 5, 73–77, 198n.54
Osmose (Davies), 111, 115
other, the: baroque, 44–45; the baroque as, 43; homogenizing forces in othering, 164; in Piper's *Tagging the Other*, 163
Out of Control: The New Biology of Machines (Kelly), 10
outsourcing, 167

Pacman, 101
panopticon, 2
Parasite (Stelarc), 135
Parasites CD, 37, 191n.28
Parker, Carol, 204n.35
passions: Descartes on, 11, 70–73, 185; and knowledge in baroque thought, 11–12, 67–68, 115, 185
Passions of the Soul, The (Descartes), 69, 70
"patches," 48, 49, 49, 203n.7
pathognomics, 192n.43
Penny, Simon, 181, 210n.6
perception: Leibniz on continuity of, 42, 119. *See also* proprioception; sensation
periodization, 41
Perrella, Stephen, 53
Petiver, James, 75, 75
pets, virtual, 125–26
PET scans, 139, 141
photography, 158, 161, 162
physiognomics, 192n.43
Piper, Keith, 105, 163, 164
pirating, 168
Pliny, 56
Pockets Full of Memories (Legrady), 58–60, 59, 62, 78
Popper, Frank, 154
portraiture, 179
postcolonialism, 164, 166
posthumanism: and the biotechnological, 25; body and code treated as predefined unities, 31; implications of, 184; interfacing with posthuman subjectivities, 132–36; posthuman subjectivity as mode of facialization, 123, 132; as subordinating body to technology, 21; Warwick's cyborg and, 10–11
postmodernism, 40–41, 43
power relations, subjectivation and, 122
programmatic subjectivity, 123, 136–38
proprioception: in Cooper's *Scynescape*, 145; in digital space, 6; in information interfaces, 3, 19; in Krueger's *VideoPlace*, 145, 146; as sixth sense, 146; in virtual environments, 89, 90, 95–96, 115
Prosthetic Head (Stelarc), 130–32, *131*, 136, 205n.38
proximity, 155–62; approximation, 159–60; as characterizing new media, 22; in Dement's *In My Gash*, 160–62; as folding, 68; folding as bringing informatic selves and organic bodies into, 116; in Harwood's *Uncomfortable Proximity*, 155–59
Public Communication Offices, 168
public domain, 166–67, 168, 169, 171
public space, 106

RAPT I (Cooper), 143, 206n.65
RAPT II (Cooper), 143, *144*, 206n.65
raqs media collective, 22, 164–66, 168, 169
rationalism, 2–3, 43–44
Rauschenberg, Robert, 154
real, the: computational aesthetics as realist, 93; digital reconstructions of, 94; hyperreality, 5, 17; versus virtuality, 89–91; virtual space and, 102
recycling, 166, 168–69
Reiss, Timothy, 72
relational architecture, 147, 148
relations: globalization and social, 151, 152; information aesthetics and social, 182; in *Revealing Things* exhibition, 57–58; in *Wunderkammer*, 81

Remaking Eden: Cloning and Beyond in a Brave New World (Silver), 10

Re: Positioning Fear (Lorenzo-Hemmer), 147–48

Revealing Things exhibition (Smithsonian Institution), 57–58, 187n.8

Rheingold, Howard, 86, 89, 91, 200n.7

Richards, Catherine, 17, 86–88, 90

robots: computers seen as, 125; as proto-subjectivities, 66

rococo architecture, 43, 127

Rokeby, David: on computers as biased against the body, 1; informatic visualizations of bodies in work of, 140; interfaces in work of, 118. See also *Very Nervous System*

Rose, Steven, 99–100, 195n.16

Rosicrucianism, 69

Rossi, Paolo, 196n.33

Rousseau, Jean-Jacques, 126

Rutsky, R. L., 207n.12

Ruysch, Frederick, 76–77, 198n.61

sampling, 27, 28, 29, 38

San Francisco Museum of Modern Art, 206n.3

Sarai New Media Initiative, 22, 166, 168, 169

Saul, Shiralee, 199n.79

science: art-science collaboration, 182; information science, 77; instrumentalist, 69, 197n.36; knowledge and passion in baroque thought, 11–12, 67–68, 116, 185; memory and, 68–69, 196n.33; scientific revolution, 68; wonder and, 69, 70; *Wunderkammer* and development of, 11–12, 67–68. See also biology

Scynescape (Cooper), 144–45

Seattle Public Library, 78–79

self, the. See subjectivity

self-composition, 162–64, 166

sensation: and concept, 5; in *écouteur*, 19; Leibniz on, 42; in *Loops*, 180; new media for engaging affect and, 181; in tandem with information, 29. See also perception; proprioception

sentiment-express (Gupta), 169–70, 171, 208n.49

Shaviro, Steven, 152

SIGGRAPH (American Computer Machinery Conference on Computer Graphics and Interactive Technologies), 1–2, 10, 14–15

silhouettes, 145, 146–47

silicon, 19, 190n.16, 204n.32

Silicon Valley, 167

Silver, Lee, 10, 190n.10

Situationists, 103–4, 105, 106

Smith, Daniel, 34

Smith, Jeffrey, 210n.6

Smithsonian Without Walls, 57–58, 187n.8

Soft Edge, The (Levinson), 60–61

sound: in Amerika's *FILMTEXT 2.0*, 176–77; in Cooper's *Scynescape*, 144–45; the *écouteur*, 18–19; in Rokeby's *Very Nervous System*, 118–20; as temporal medium, 175. See also digital audio

space: Cartesian coordinate system, 1–3, 14–15, 51, 91, 109, 173; computational, 52–53, 92–93, 119; public, 106; shift from spatialization to temporalization, 171–77; urban, 18–19, 103–4; visually flattened, 174. See also cyberspace; virtual space

speed, 16, 64, 159, 160, 169, 175

Spinoza, Benedict, 69

splitting, 64, 89, 91, 92, 115

sponge, 210n.4

Stafford, Barbara Maria, 5, 74, 192n.43

standardization, 22, 164, 165–67, 171

Star Trek/Voyager (television series), 27

"state of the art" technology, 153–54, 207n.12

Stavely, Joan, 1–2

Stelarc: *Ear on Arm*, 19, 20, 189n.27; *Extra Ear 1/4 Scale*, 183; *Parasite*, 135; and posthuman-computer interaction, 21, 130, 133–36; *Prosthetic Head*, 130–32, 136, 205n.38

stereoscopy, 96, 109

Stocker, Gerfried, 133

Stone, Alluquere Rosanne, 2, 89–90
Strange Days (film), 97, 99
subjectivity: affectivity, 141; Cartesian, 7; dematerialization and breakup of, 91; facialization and, 122–23; fluid, 163–64; liberal, 132, 136, 138; posthumanist, 123, 132–36; programmatic, 123, 136–38; protosubjectivities, 66; in virtual reality, 113, 114
Sundaram, Ravi, 166, 167–68, 168–69
superfold, 33–38, 50, 62
Superweed (Bunting), 183, 210n.10
surveillance, 102, 163
Sutherland, Ivan, 121
Sutton, John, 68
Swatch, 167
Symbiosis (Metraform), 210n.6

Tagging the Other (Piper), 163
Tate Gallery (London), 155–59, 169
taxonomic ordering, 74
TDK, 19
technē, 111, 202n.42
technology: Art and Technology Movement, 154, 207n.15; Heidegger's critique of, 111, 202n.42; hybridizing of body and, 18; information technology economy, 165, 166, 167–68, 170; seen as reaching its apotheosis in the digital, 9–10; "state of the art," 153–54, 207n.12; uneven access to, 164. *See also* biotechnology; computers; machines
tele-absence, 147
telepresent artworks, 19, 22
television: faciality in, 129–30; interactive, 24
Terminator 2 (film), 189n.5
text messaging, 172
TGarden Sensor Lab, 180–81, 210n.4
Theodicy (Leibniz), 46
Thinkmap program, 58
Thom, René, 188n.24
three-dimensional modeling software, 51
Thylacine project, 25–26
time: commodification into instances, 97; difference between India and

America, 167; duration, 24, 96, 99, 100–101, 160; electronic art and different kinds of, 5; folding as strategy for dealing with, 41; "Internet time," 167, 170; nonlinear, 17, 98–100, 171, 173; shift from spatialization to temporalization, 171–77; sound as medium of, 175; standardized, 165–67; temporality of digital embodiment, 64. *See also* lag
time multiplexing, 96
Tissue Culture and Art(ificial) Womb 2000, 210n.10
Tissue Culture and Art Project, 19, 183, 210n.10
Tomb Raider (game), 100
Topological Media Laboratory (Georgia Institute of Technology), 210n.4
topology: Flash software and, 174; in information visualization, 179; as providing contours of the virtual, 113; in TGarden environment, 181; topological architecture, 9, 50–54
Traces (Penny), 181, 210n.6
trompe l'oeil, 5, 40
Turkle, Sherry, 163
twenty-four hour working day, 166, 167
Twine, 176

Uncomfortable Proximity (Harwood), 155–59, *158*
Underground Movement (Bunting), 104
Unitary Urbanism, 103
UN Studio architects, 50
urban space, negotiating, 18–19, 103–4
useability discourse, 122, 126–27
user-friendliness, 122, 123, 124, 132, 203n.9

Valdés Leal, Juan de, 45, *46*
vector graphics, 173–74
Vega, Mark, 176
Very Nervous System (Rokeby), 118–21, *119*; as ahead of its time, 4; embodied experience in, 3–4; interface of, 119; origins of, 202n.4; user movement restricted in, 122

VideoPlace (Krueger), 145–46
Virtual Body, The (Richards), 86–88, 87, 90
virtuality: versus the actual, 16, 90–91, 96, 114; in the baroque, 47; the digital associated with, 86, 90, 92; as expanding and contracting field of differentiation, 114; de Landa on, 41, 192n.37; as pole of machinic movement, 13–14; versus the real, 89–91; reexamining notions of, 17; the virtual dimension, 88, 92, 93, 115. *See also* virtual reality (VR); virtual space
virtual pets, 125–26
virtual reality (VR), 86–116; aesthetic of informatic bodies contrasted with, 143; Aspen Movie Map, 101; in Bigelow's *Strange Days*, 97; the body in, 89–91, 100–101, 108–16; Cartesian dualism in conceptions of, 50; CAVE project, 110–11, 181, 201n.38, 210n.6; commodification of, 97–98; Davies's works, 111, 115; dematerialization associated with, 17, 19; disorientation in, 103; Dunning and Woodrow's *Einstein's Brain*, 106–8; as entertainment, 89, 91–92; experiential loss of duration in, 96, 98, 100–101; head-mounted display, 96, 109, 110, 110; incorporeal universes of reference for, 112–13; NASA-Ames workstation, 17, 101, 109, 110, 112, 113; nonlinear time in, 17, 98–100, 171; as only one possible organization of virtuality, 116; as parasitic, 134; Richards's *The Virtual Body*, 86–88, 87, 90; semi- and fully-immersive environments, 6, 98, 101, 182; TGarden environment compared with, 181; virtual space production in, 101–8; virtual time production in, 94–101
Virtual Reality Markup Language (VRML), 98
virtual space, 101–8; military heritage of, 102; as moebius-like, 96; seen as disembodied, 17; user's experience of, 96; in virtual time production, 95–96. *See also* cyberspace
virtual time, 94–101
Visible Human Project, 141
Visitor's Guide to London (Bunting), 104
voice-activated commands, 125

Walking with Dinosaurs (television series), 17, 94–95
"walk-man," 18
Warwick, Kevin, 10
Watson, James, 36
Web, the. *See* Internet
Welchman, Alastair, 195n.21
Whitaker, Kate, 73
Whitelaw, Mitchell, 151, 208n.26
Whitney Museum of Art, 150, 206n.3
Wiener, Norbert, 195n.15
Wilkes, Maurice, 194n.4
Wilmut, Ian, 27
wireless technology, 36
Wolfflin, Henry, 44
wonder: Descartes on, 70–73; in early modern thought, 69–73; in *Wunderkammer*, 11–12, 76
Woodrow, Paul, 106–8, 143, 147
Workhorse Zoo (Zaretsky), 210n.10
Worm, Olaus, 74, 74
Wunderkammer (curiosity cabinet): in baroque visual display, 5; classicism contrasted with, 5, 7; excess in, 127; in Imperato's *Historia Naturalae*, 12; as meta-centers, 80–81; online spaces compared with, 5, 187n.8; order in, 5, 73–77, 198n.54; return in information aesthetics, 77–85; thought and passion activated by, 11–12, 67–68

Yates, Frances, 68, 69
Yokohama Port Authority, 51–52
Yugop, 174

Zaretsky, Adam, 183, 210n.10
010101, 150, 206n.3
Zizek, Slavoj, 140